APPEASEMENT OF THE DICTATORS

APPEASEMENT OF THE DICTATORS

Crisis Diplomacy?

Edited by W. LAIRD KLEINE-AHLBRANDT
Purdue University

HOLT, RINEHART AND WINSTON
New York · Chicago · San Francisco · Atlanta
Dallas · Montreal · Toronto · London · Sydney

Cover illustration: Hitler greets Neville Chamberlain at the Hotel Breesen, Godesberg, September 23, 1938. *(Black Star)*

CONTENTS

Introduction   1

DEFINITION AND FORMATION

MARTIN GILBERT—The Roots of Appeasement   7

JOHN WHEELER-BENNETT—The Road to Appeasement   17

OMISSION AND COMMISSION: MUSSOLINI AND THE CRISIS IN THE MEDITERRANEAN

GEORGE W. BAER—Ineffective Appeasement   27

HENDERSON B. BRADDICK—The Hoare-Laval Plan   33

HERBERT FEIS—The American Circuit of Indecision   45

ALAN BULLOCH—The Crisis and Hitler   52

OMISSION AND COMMISSION: HITLER AND THE CRISIS IN CENTRAL EUROPE

WILLIAM L. SHIRER—The Surrender at Munich   62

CHARLES LOCH MOWAT—The Popularity of Munich   71

A. J. P. TAYLOR—Hitler's Opportunism   82

CHRISTOPHER THORNE—Continuing Appeasement   91

ROLAND N. STROMBERG—The United States and Collective Security   98

GEORGE F. KENNAN—Russia and the Czech Crisis   105

DECISIONS AND REVISIONS

MAURICE BAUMONT—French Critics and Apologists Debate Munich   115

D. C. WATT—The Rise of a Revisionist School   122

Suggestions for Additional Reading   135

Chamberlain, with Joachim von Ribbentrop, reviews German guards at Cologne airport, September 24, 1938. *(Wide World Photos)*

INTRODUCTION

Appeasement is a technique of diplomacy. With either a balance of power or a preponderance of power, conciliation can adjust ambitions and rivalries, compensate change, and maintain international equilibrium and harmony among states. The value of appeasement has been seriously questioned, however, as a result of European politics before World War II. Associated with diplomatic failure, surrender to political blackmail, betrayal of fundamental principle, and sacrifice of vital interest, the policy of appeasing the dictators produced strongly hostile camps of enemies and partisans. The controversy continues. Few subjects in the history of contemporary international relations have been exposed to such extensive scrutiny. The road to objectivity is rutted with old apologies and polemics, and with controversial personalities and complicated circumstances.

The study of appeasement has usually been confined to the British and French attempts to pacify Hitler and Mussolini. But in fact the idea and technique of appeasement are very old. Wherever the leaders of nations do not regard warfare as the inevitable way of resolving disputes, the door has been open for appeasement. Appeasement of the dictators lasted a short time, from 1933 to 1939, but its antecedents can be traced to World War I. According to Martin Gilbert, "Appeasement was born in the minds of those who said that the war need never have come, that it was accidental, and that neither Britain nor Germany was more responsible than the other for its onset."

Appeasement was born with the determination that nothing like the past holocaust should be allowed to reoccur. The Great War was the greatest concentrated cataclysm the world had ever seen. It destroyed all the governments of the defeated powers and four empires; it smashed the economic stability of an entire continent; it crippled or killed thirty million people and cost 332 billion dollars. After the war a power vacuum existed in the Balkans and a precarious French hegemony in the West. Germany, although defeated, was neither crushed nor conciliated. Even before they were signed, the Paris treaties germinated revisionism. Gilbert believes the first appeaser to have been the British prime minister David Lloyd George, who sought a lenient peace with Germany. Lloyd George hoped the peace would endure long after the memories of the war had faded, and he therefore warned against a treaty of humiliation which separated two million

Germans from their nation and left them under alien rule. He opposed a peace in which reparations would last beyond the generation that made the war. Although this advice in his Fontainebleau Memorandum was not incorporated in the text of the Treaty of Versailles, Lloyd George nonetheless hoped to carry its spirit into the postwar diplomatic conferences. The results of attempts to do so are examined by Gilbert in a chapter entitled "The First Appeasement."

Britain tried to reconcile Franco-German differences in a permanent European equilibrium. France, though, was too concerned with keeping intact the terms of the Treaty of Versailles, while Germany was too occupied with vindicating her national honor. An escape from the impasse was believed found at Locarno. In that Swiss resort town, Germany, France, Britain, Belgium, and Italy agreed that all their disputes would henceforth be settled through arbitration. The German-Belgian and the German-French frontiers were guaranteed inviolable, and although the eastern boundaries were not similarly recognized, Germany agreed that they would not be changed through force. A willing partner to the Locarno Agreements Germany recognized the demilitarization of the Rhineland and agreed to continue to pay reparations. The Locarno settlement created a spirit of security and friendship which, as Austen Chamberlain believed, might have marked the dividing line between the years of war and the years of peace.

But Locarno was a great illusion. The most controversial section of the Treaty of Versailles was not settled. In not affirming the eastern boundary clauses, Locarno acknowledged the right of revision. It was a victory for Germany. Great Britain and France plainly could not agree on how much power should be permitted Germany before she threatened their vital interests. France held a strict interpretation of the Treaty of Versailles. Britain showed willingness to disregard eastern Europe as a sphere of interest. Locarno was considered a victory for the British policy of appeasement, an effort in constructive peacemaking, and a hope that the reconciliation of former enemies was the key to a tranquil future. Unlike later appeasement of the dictators, there was no talk of threats, of blackmail, of surrender. Appeasement in 1925 was not a policy of weakness determined by the demands of aggressors, but a policy of strength directed by the victors.

The appeasement of Germany continued after Locarno, notably in the early ending of the occupation of the Rhineland and the virtual scrapping of reparations. Thus when Adolf Hitler came to power in 1933, the path had been cleared for future appeasement. But Hitler brought a new set of rules into the game. Was the continuance of appeasement in this new period valid? The tenacity with which Britain maintained the policy demonstrates the hold it had on the minds of her statesmen, who like military commanders fought the wars of the future along the lines of those of the past. John Wheeler-Bennett finds reaction of the British to the tactics of Hitler confused and bewildered; he writes that their attempts to appease were plagued by a naïve failure "to comprehend the lengths of evil, dishonesty and deception to which the Nazi mentality could extend."

Britain and France were sufficiently alarmed at Hitler, however, to solicit the friendship of the Italian dictator Benito Mussolini. The French favored such diplomacy. They never abandoned the practice of insuring their security with a powerful alliance system. The French premier and foreign minister Pierre Laval prided himself particularly on his ability to negotiate with the Italians. At Stresa in April 1935 France, Britain, and Italy signed an agreement whereby they promised to oppose "by all practical means any unilateral repudiation of treaties which may endanger the peace of Europe."

Not interested in a European *status quo* for its own sake, Mussolini favored this common front against revision of the peace treaties only in so far as it permitted him to operate with a free hand in Ethiopia. The Stresa agreement contained no clause opposing such maneuvers. Laval had no objection to Mussolini's drawing the obvious conclusions, but the British leaders could not afford such sanguinity.

A nation with world-wide interests, Britain was highly sensitive to any changes in the Mediterranean. She might be sympathetic to Mussolini's acquiring a colony or two if such appeasement were important for guaranteeing the stability of the Mediterranean area. But how could Britain peacefully help satisfy Mussolini's colonial ambitions? And at what price? George W. Baer argues that it would have been more to Britain's interest and more to the interest of European peace and security if she had effectively asserted her strength before Mussolini began his invasion of Ethiopia. A reasonable diplomatic settlement could have been reached, and Britain would have averted the crisis that destroyed the League of Nations.

Mussolini's determination to turn Ethiopia into an Italian colony did not mean that his friendship was undesirable. In spite of their official support of the League of Nations, the British and French governments tried to re-establish the unity of the Stresa front. To appease Mussolini and return peace to the Middle East, the British foreign secretary Sir Samuel Hoare and Pierre Laval formulated a compromise proposal whereby two thirds of Ethiopia would be ceded to Italy. The British public reacted violently. The Hoare-Laval Plan was regarded as a cynical sacrifice of weak nations, a reward for aggression, and a flagrant betrayal of national honor. There were constant appeals to the hallowed principles of collective security. Three weeks before the invasion of Ethiopia, Hoare had addressed the League Assembly: "The League stands and my country stands with it, for the collective maintenance of the Covenant in its entirety and particularly for the steadfast and collective resistance to all acts of unprovoked aggression." But the risks of such a policy were little considered by those who now denounced their government. In all of Europe there was no desire to actually go to war to defend Ethiopia. Devotion to the principles of collective security meant worshiping the word more than the deed.

As seen by Henderson B. Braddick, the Hoare-Laval Plan was a compromise for want of a policy. The British government had been elected to give the League of Nations a support it had no intention of giving by an electorate demanding an action it had no intention of supporting. Stanley Baldwin accepted the resignation of Hoare, who wrote that the failure of his plan contributed to the eventual formation of the Italian rapprochement with Germany; he criticized the confused unrealistic British electorate. Six months later Hoare was back in the Cabinet.

Ethiopia's fate, however, was sealed. The Italian army occupied Addis Ababa on May 5, 1936, and four days later the country was officially annexed to the Kingdom of Italy. As an instrument for solving international disputes, the League of Nations was dead, and the war increased Mussolini's contempt for the democracies.

The United States shared the reluctance of Britain and France to risk a confrontation with Mussolini. Bound by rigid rules of isolation, this country had no desire to intervene in the faraway crisis. Herbert Feis strongly criticizes this shortsightedness; he believes that the United States was the "one country strong enough and free enough to turn the balance of events" against Mussolini.

The Spanish Civil War, which began shortly after the end of the Ethiopian crisis, gave the dictators further opportunity to flaunt their power. Mussolini and Hitler, supplying the insurgents with military aid, posed a new threat in the Mediterranean and created a serious preclusion to British appeasement. Nonetheless Britain still hoped for rapprochement. Her offers of friendship, however, only convinced Mussolini of her weakness, pacifism, and decadence.

Unlike Mussolini who used the Spanish war to extend his power in the Mediterranean, Adolf Hitler intervened to mask his ambitions in Central Europe. Alan Bullock writes that Hitler had already reaped immense profit from the weakness of Britain and France toward Mussolini's invasion of Ethiopia. If the British failed to make a stand in the Mediterranean where they had vital interests, how could they be expected to do anything in Central Europe where, since Locarno, there was every reason to believe they felt no commitment whatsoever? The Spanish conflict brought the dictators into close cooperation. It demonstrated once again the Anglo-French desire to avoid war. Hitler's policy, as revealed by Bullock, was conditioned by no parallel scruple.

When Neville Chamberlain became prime minister in 1937, like his predecessors Lloyd George, MacDonald, and Baldwin, he was already disposed toward a policy of appeasement. Circumstances strengthened this inclination. The League of Nations was ineffective; France was defeatist; rearmament had just begun. What other policy than to seek out the dictators, find out their demands, and within reason satisfy them? Although Chamberlain's determination for appeasement reflected his own personal set of values, the policy was also the conviction of the great mass of the British citizenry. But how valid was appeasement during the 'thirties? And how effective was Chamberlain's direction of that policy?

William L. Shirer is vehement in condemning both appeasement and Chamberlain's leadership: the policy was unnecessary, its implementation a disaster.

Shirer believes that if war had erupted in 1938, Britain would have had the advantage of being better prepared to fight than she was two years later. Much of the controversy that surrounds the Czechoslovak crisis involves this question of military preparation. Not all agree with Shirer. Charles Loch Mowat, for example, feels that Britain bought valuable time with the two-year delay. Mowat considers some of the alternatives to appeasement. He finds much to criticize about Chamberlain, especially his quality of leadership, but he sees appeasement's general popularity as an attenuating circumstance.

The orthodox school on appeasement research has produced a predictable tableau of historical colors. Hitler naturally is painted in the darkest of blacks; Chamberlain, although still somber, several shades lighter; Winston Churchill, almost white; the Czech president Eduard Beneš, brightest of all. Such impressions held sway among historians' research until the beginning of the 1960s. The most famous exponent of the revisionist school is perhaps A. J. P. Taylor. Under his brush all colors appear shades of gray. Hitler is no longer the aggression-hungry *fauve,* but more a traditional German politician. Beneš has changed markedly. No longer the innocent martyrized leader, he becomes a man who is compromised by his own crafty game of politics. Taylor believes that Beneš deliberately heightened tension with the Sudeten Germans in order to provoke a crisis that would assure him Anglo-French support. In trying for a solution, Britain created the crisis of which Hitler took advantage.

Undisputed master of Central Europe after the Munich Conference, Hitler proceeded to dismember the rest of the Czecho-Slovak state. He assured support to separatist movements in Slovakia and Ruthenia, and in March 1939 he forced the Czech president Emil Hácha to place his country under German protection. German troops marched into Prague and assumed full control. Three days later, on March 17, Chamberlain made a speech in the Commons in which he denounced Hitler's violation of the Munich agreement. "Is this the last attack upon a small state or is it to be followed by another? Is this in fact a step in the direction of an attempt to dominate the world by force?"

Appeasement was abandoned. "Right about turn," intoned Winston Churchill. Was this really the case? Certainly there were changes, but according to Christopher Thorne they were more apparent than real. Chamberlain, even though angry over Hitler's broken word, still retained a hope that the German dictator could be brought into successful negotiations.

Munich was the last great settlement in which the fate of Europeans was decided without the participation of either the Soviet Union or the United States. In 1938 the United States could hardly have cared less. Roland N. Stromberg sees this country with little desire to become involved in the affairs of Europe. The United States had world interests, and events in the Far East seemed every bit as important as those in Europe, although neither seemed important enough to induce her to change her neutrality. The security of the country, geographically removed from both areas, hardly seemed threatened. Such was not the case with the Soviet Union.

According to the still accepted Stalinist version of history, the British and French not only wanted to isolate Russia from the rest of Europe but at Munich they actively plotted with Adolph Hitler—acquiesced in his destruction of Czechoslovakia—in order to turn him against the Soviet Union. Chamberlain's statements pandered to the Russian dictator's xenophobia, "How horrible, fantastic, incredible it is, that we should be digging trenches and trying on gas masks here because of a quarrel in a far away country between people of whom we know nothing." There were those in Moscow like the foreign minister Maxim Litvinov who desired to create an anti-Hitler coalition and found the weakened disinterest of the democracies a bitter disappointment. After the extinction of Czechoslovakia, the British opened negotiations with the USSR, but Stalin found a nonaggression pact with Nazi Germany more to his liking, especially since it promised acquisition of Polish territory. There has been much speculation on the failure of the West to negotiate an alliance with the Soviet Union. George F. Kennan seriously questions whether Russia would have been a fit partner for the West. Stalin feared the effect such an association might have on his reign, and his purges of the Communist leadership gravely affected his ability to assume a strong role in any coalition.

The historian can best explain a policy of victory. Failure is more difficult to assess. The policy of appeasement in the 'thirties is associated with British weakness. Even Chamberlain realized that an effective policy must follow from a position of strength. Any historical problem involves an understanding of resources as much as it involves an understanding of men. To hold men to be sincere or insincere, to have good intentions or bad intentions, to fulfill or betray confidence has little bearing on success or failure. This study has considered the many-faceted circumstances of the policy of appeasement. Appeasement is seen in principle and practice, and the concluding selections discuss its characteristics, its intentions, its limitations, and results. The evident disagreement continues, vitally affirmed by Maurice Baumont and D. C. Watt. A study of appeasement, however, is important not only because it is a good subject for the classroom; much more is involved. The implications of appeasement lie at the foundation of international relations, and its practice will stay controversial as long as sovereign states exist.

In the reprinted selections footnotes appearing in the original sources have in general been omitted unless they contribute to the argument or better understanding of the selection.

A fellow of Merton College, Oxford, MARTIN
GILBERT (b. 1936) believes the first manifestation of
appeasement to have been the Fontainebleau
Memorandum of Lloyd George, who wrote, "Our terms
may be severe, they may be stern and even ruthless but at
the same time they can be so just that the country on
which they are imposed will feel in its heart that it has no
right to complain." The British prime minister's pursuit of
a just settlement is discussed by Gilbert in the following
selection.*

Martin Gilbert

The Roots of Appeasement

Lloyd George did not allow the disappointments of the Versailles Treaty to depress him unduly. Although he was somewhat deflated by his difficulties in obtaining all the modifications which he had wished, he was determined to exert a moderating influence upon those carrying out the Treaty. Between January 1920 and December 1922 there were twenty-three international conferences, most of which he attended, and where his voice was raised continually in favour of appeasement. The French resented his attitude and made every possible effort to challenge it. Two years of intensive and acrimonious debate created strong anti-French feeling in British official circles, and also made it quite easy for the Ger-

man Government to appeal effectively to Britain for protection against the "ferocity" of French policy.

Although the Peace Treaty with Germany was signed in June 1919, its final form needed much further negotiation. The precise amount of reparations had still to be fixed, and the German "war criminals" had yet to be brought to trial. Both these tasks required the help of American arbitration to prevent them from becoming the cause of violent and prolonged Anglo-French friction. But in November 1919 the United States' Senate refused to ratify the Treaty. America rejected responsibility in the finalization and execution of a settlement which President Wilson had done so much to shape. His policy of supervising

*Reprinted by permission of The World Publishing Company and George Weidenfeld & Nicholson Ltd. from *The Roots of Appeasement* by Martin Gilbert. An NAL book. Copyright © 1966 by Martin Gilbert. Pp. 68–80.

European developments and soothing European tempers was, literally overnight, abandoned in favour of isolation. The shock of America's withdrawal was a severe one, and threw an immense burden upon Britain and France, both of whom had built up hopes, often conflicting and at times somewhat naïve, of winning Wilson to their particular point of view, and of using his support to turn the balance of opinion decisively in their favour.

Harold Nicolson wrote shrewdly on this problem in retrospect:

> The whole Treaty has been constructed on the assumption that the United States would be not merely a contracting but an actively executant party. France has been persuaded to abandon her claim to a buffer state between herself and Germany in return for a guarantee of armed support from the United States. The whole Reparation settlement was dependent for its execution on the presence on the Reparation Commission of a representative of the main creditor of Europe. The whole Treaty had been deliberately, and ingenuously, framed by Mr Wilson himself to render American co-operation essential.[1]

With this co-operation lost, Lloyd George became, unwittingly, the sole non-German spokesman for the German view. Partly because of continual examples of French extremism and partly by reason of his own lack of vindictiveness, he emerged as the only European statesman willing to examine each allied proposal in the light of pragmatism rather than of passion.

Within a week of the ratification of the Versailles Treaty on 10 January 1920, the first inter-allied conference, at Paris, came to an inconclusive end. It had as one of its purposes the drawing up of a list of German "war criminals" whom the allied powers would ask Germany to make available for trial, presumably by arresting

them. It was agreed that Britain, France, Belgium, and Italy would draw up lists of those whom they considered culpable. But no standards of culpability were laid down. No difference was specified between necessary actions as a result of obeying orders, and actions flagrantly violating the rules of war. When the French list was shown to Lloyd George he was furious to find on it the names of Bethmann-Hollweg, the Imperial Chancellor from 1909–17, and of Hindenburg and Ludendorff, Germany's two national heroes, probably the only two leaders who had emerged from the war with credit in German eyes. Lloyd George felt that the trial of these three would so antagonize the German public as to drive them into total refusal to carry out any further Treaty demands, including reparations payments. The Cabinet agreed with Lloyd George, and sent the Lord Chancellor, Lord Birkenhead, to Paris on 6 February 1920 to put their views as forcibly as possible. Birkenhead spoke to [French President] Millerand in no uncertain terms:

> ...in the history of war, so far as I am aware, no such demand has ever been made.... We know full well that the Germans have signed an undertaking which they seem to be attempting to evade. But although from the legal point of view the Germans are bound by their signature, we have to consider the situation that exists in Germany today and the actual power of the German Government to control the situation.... Time has now passed—considerable time—since the Treaty of Peace, or those articles of it—were considered. The passage of time has itself produced, both in our country and in Germany, changes of which we feel bound to take cognizance, and which urge that these matters be reconsidered.[2]

The French did not take kindly to the concept of reconsideration, which, in their

---

[1] Harold Nicolson, *Peacemaking 1919*, p. 207.

[2] *British Documents on British Foreign Policy*, series 1, vol. 9, No. 601. Record of a Meeting held at the Quai D'Orsay on Friday, 6 February 1920.

view, could only result in changes favourable to Germany, and in a greater leniency than they were willing to countenance. Millerand pressed for a literal and exact fulfilment of the terms of the Treaty. When the French list was finally published, against Lloyd George's wish, it roused much anger in Germany, and some scorn in Britain. A week later Millerand was in London for the second of the myriad conferences upon which the European statesmen were now, at great personal inconvenience, embarked. Within ten minutes of the opening of discussions, Lloyd George raised the question of the list of criminals. He was convinced, he said, that

... to demand the surrender and prosecution of Hindenburg before a tribunal of his enemies was to ask something which no nation could agree to, however crushed and defeated it might be.... To demand Hindenburg was a political mistake of the first magnitude.... If the Germans said they would not give up Hindenburg, what would be the position? Would any country go to war for that reason? Would Italy, Great Britain, or France go to war in order to force the surrender of Hindenburg? It was incredible....

He hoped therefore that his colleagues would not press for the handing over of men in these categories [who were merely carrying out the war]. It meant a new war, in which the British Government would not engage, and against which the common sense of the world would protest, and the Allies would be humiliated.[3]

Millerand replied that once the Allies began to compromise, the Germans would assume that they could by vigorous protest obtain modifications in every aspect of the Treaty. The Belgian Prime Minister, Delacroix, insisted that allied unity was essential, and that it would be dangerous to give the Germans any hint of allied disagreement. He was willing to see the lists modified, provided this could appear as a unanimous inter-allied decision. Lloyd George gladly accepted modification, but went on to point out that the decision did not rest entirely upon the personal wishes of those at the Conference, but rather that:

Everything depended upon the Allied Governments having public opinion behind them. It was no use their trying to enforce anything if they were not fortified by this public opinion. He was sure public opinion generally would not stand Marshal Hindenburg and General Ludendorff being surrendered for trial, as this would be repugnant to the ordinary citizen.[3]

Lloyd George was successful. The trials were abandoned. Appeasement won its first triumph. But his arguments were misleading. Public opinion in Britain was indeed turning away from its initial support of a punitive peace, but hardly to the extent of finding judicial trials "repugnant." Lloyd George posed as the man responding to a public mood; in reality he sought to control and modify that mood. He saw clearly what he hoped would happen in Europe in the coming decade. The public could not be expected to have such a clear vision. In using the argument of a non-vindictive public, Lloyd George was casting his own hopes for the future of Europe into the mould of a non-existent situation. The desire for appeasement did not yet command a majority of English opinion. It was not as a reaction to Versailles that appeasement gained its main adherents. The harsh peace had created the mood, but it had not ensured its universal acceptance. The public mind in 1920 was still clouded by doubts and hesitations. The idea of a working partnership with Germany had not yet found a wide or enthusiastic audience. It was a fear of French recalcitrance, fear of France forcing Germany to arms again, that confirmed the

[3]*Documents on British Foreign Policy,* series 1, vol. 7, No. 1. Notes of an Allied Conference held at 10 Downing Street on Thursday, 12 February 1920.

public in its views, and strengthened them. French "folly" was the fertilizer which turned appeasement from a feeble offshoot into a frantic bloom.

In March 1920 a Communist revolution broke out in the Ruhr. The German Government asked the Allies if it could move troops into the Ruhr to suppress the uprising. Fear of German communism was a consistent theme in British foreign policy. The Cabinet were well aware of the dangers of bolshevism on the Rhine. Not only were the doctrines of communism abhorrent to the rulers of the non-Bolshevik world, they were also doctrines which denied the validity of former war debts and treaty obligations. Bolshevik Germany would repudiate Versailles and not pay reparations, just as Bolshevik Russia had repudiated Tsarist debts and denounced all Tsarist treaties. It was therefore necessary, in Lloyd George's view, to give the German Government every encouragement to stifle revolutionary movements, even if this involved the use of German troops commanded by German officers and using weapons which ought under the Treaty of Versailles to have been surrendered already to the Allies. He approved of the German Government's promptness in preparing to act.

The French had no such sympathies. Any manifestation of German strength was anathema to them. They wanted to be the arbiters of domestic German politics, and in particular of all events whose focal point was the Rhine. Having failed at Versailles to obtain a separate Rhineland State, they were nevertheless determined to impose the solutions which they preferred upon this area. They therefore refused to allow the German Government to move its troops. But allied dissension, together with the urgency of the situation, gave Germany both the encouragement and incentive to action. On 3 April 1920 eighteen thousand German troops moved into the Ruhr. Three days later, without consulting Britain, France occupied five Rhineland towns, including Frankfurt and Darmstadt.

That same morning the French Ambassador in London, Paul Cambon, saw Andrew Bonar Law, a member of the Cabinet and leader of the Conservative Party, to explain the French action.[4] He described the German movement of troops as "a grave violation of the treaty, and a serious menace to France." Bonar Law was not impressed. He pointed out to Cambon that this was probably the first time since the war had begun in 1914 that one ally had acted against the known wishes of another, without consultation. This created grave difficulties, as the British Government now found themselves, in Bonar Law's words, ". . . in the embarrassing position of having either to declare to the world that the unity of the alliance was broken, or to express approval of, and assume responsibility for, a policy which they held to be wrong and dangerous."

Two days later the Cabinet discussed the French action. Curzon was asked to communicate their collective disapproval to the French Government. He rebuked Cambon for a French announcement that their action followed consultation with Britain, a statement which implied that Britain had approved. He pointed out that Millerand had failed to inform him of the course of his negotiations with the Germans. Such methods, he insisted, were incompatible with the mutual understanding and common action "upon which the stability of the Alliance and the security of Europe alike depended." In a defiant mood, a crowd at Frankfurt had provoked

---

[4]*British Documents,* Series 1, vol. 9, No. 292. Account by Lord Curzon of the interview between Cambon and Bonar Law, dated 5 April 1920. See also No. 298, dated 6 April 1920, for the second interview between Cambon and Bonar Law.

some French troops, who opened fire and killed some eight people. Curzon made use of the incident to stress even further British disapproval:

I also pointed out to the Ambassador—holding in my hand the newspaper which recorded the unfortunate collision which had taken place in Frankfort . . . that this was precisely the kind of incident which we had anticipated from the appearance of French forces in the areas in question. I did not remind him, as I might have done, that the situation had doubtless been aggravated by the fact that the large majority of these forces appeared to be black.[5]

Here was a cause for complaint that was to re-occur during the second French occupation of the Ruhr in 1923. The use of Moroccan troops was regarded by many Englishmen as perfidy. Lloyd George considered it a political blunder which would accentuate Anglo-French hostility. The coloured troops were thought by Britons and Germans alike to be particularly vicious and insensitive. In the public mind they were associated with stories of violent assault and rape. The British public's suspicions of France were confirmed and strengthened by this use of "savage" troops, an action seen by some as a deliberate French policy intended to frighten the local inhabitants.

The British Cabinet were encouraged in their opposition to France when they discovered that the Italians and Japanese shared their views. British anger was turned, not primarily against the French action as such, but against all unilateral action. The British Government's hope was for peaceful change, which they thought was best obtained by co-operation and consultation. Powers acting alone could only disrupt the European harmony which peaceful change was expected to bring about. As Curzon pointed out in an urgent telegram to the British Ambassador in Paris, Lord Derby, which Derby was instructed to read to Millerand "without delay":

. . . as time goes on no power may be able to enforce the terms of the Treaty single-handed against a resuscitated Germany.

In these circumstances, His Majesty's Government wish to make it clear that so long as the French Government persist in taking independent action, they must themselves bear the whole responsibility.[6]

The French withdrew from the Ruhr, but the *Entente* was broken. No longer would French fears act as a check upon British action. No longer would the concept of allied solidarity stand in the way of a policy of Anglo-German reconciliation. The French occupation of the Ruhr seemed to confirm British suspicions of French irresponsibility, and made the need for an Anglo-German rapprochement appear more urgent. It seemed necessary to show Germany that she would be allowed to become an equal member of the European community; and this would clearly have to be done before French extremism further disturbed and embittered the European scene. For six years, when Englishmen talked of atrocities, they had meant atrocities attributed to German soldiers in Belgium. In 1920 the word gained a further association. In the public mind it became linked with stories of French atrocities in the Ruhr, perpetrated by coloured soldiers. This was considered a challenge, not only to the moral code, but also to racial unity. The thought of African troops as the instruments of a vindictive French policy went against the grain of English ideas of

---

[5] *British Documents*, series 1, vol. 9, No. 318. Account by Lord Curzon of his interview with Cambon, 8 April 1920.

[6] *British Documents*, series 1, vol. 9. No. 322. Lord Curzon to Lord Derby. Marked 'urgent', 8 April 1920.

decency. Slowly, almost imperceptibly, and yet by very definite gradations, the balance of sympathy was tilting towards Germany.

The remaining five Conferences of 1920 were a constant source of Anglo-French friction. At San Remo in April Lloyd George argued in favour of opening negotiations with Germany in order to fix a lump sum for reparations; but the French wanted to be able to increase the amount as Germany recovered economically.[7] At Lympne in June Lloyd George tried to cast the net of appeasement over Russia, pleading eloquently in favour of allied mediation in the Russo-Polish war; but the French spoke enthusiastically of sending military help to Poland.[8] At Lympne in August the French pressed for action against Russia, whose forces had then almost reached Warsaw, and against whom the armies of the newly independent Poland seemed incapable of much further resistance. Lloyd George explained his difficulty with stark clarity:

He did not wish the working classes to be able to say . . . that he missed any chance of making peace. If they could say so with truth, it would rot the navy, and it would rot the working classes and lead to the triumph of Bolshevism in England.[9]

The French were insistent, however, that the Bolshevik armies should be halted, and preferred to try to halt them on the Vistula than on the Rhine. Lloyd George then proposed a blockade of Russia, not by Britain and France alone, but "partly by se-curing the co-operation of the members of the League of Nations, and also of the United States and Germany." This was not what Millerand wanted. Not only did he suspect that any action in which League nations had to co-operate would never materialize, but he was alarmed by Lloyd George's inclusion of Germany in the draft. Nothing would induce him to co-operate with Germany against Russia, for German help would clearly throw a burden of obligation upon France which would weaken her ability to push Germany to the utmost limit of her capacity to pay reparations. Millerand told Lloyd George that: "He would prefer that the word [Germany] should disappear at once, otherwise he would have to enter a formal protest at the end of the document." Lloyd George agreed to alter the draft. But the British view of Germany had clearly changed from one of overt but distant sympathy to one of searching for means of working together.

Appeasement was never a mere sentimental attitude; it had many practical applications. The French took particular offence at an article on the subject of German help which had appeared in the *Evening News* on 28 July 1920, just before the Conference met. The author of the article, Winston Churchill, was Secretary of State for War and Air. He feared the imminent destruction of Poland, and the Russian armies poised on the German frontier:

It will be open to the Germans either to sink their own civilization in the general Bolshevist welter and spread the reign of chaos far and wide throughout the Continent; or, on the other hand, by a supreme effort of sobriety, of firmness, of self-restraint, and of courage—undertaken, as most great exploits have to be, under conditions of peculiar difficulty and discouragement—to build a dyke of peaceful, lawful, patient strength, and virtue against the

---

[7] The proceedings of the San Remo Conference are printed in *British Documents*, series 1, vol. 8, Nos. 1–20, pp. 1–252.

[8] The proceedings of the Lympne Conference are printed in *British Documents*, series 1, vol. 8, Nos. 26–30, pp. 307–33.

[9] *British Documents*, series 1, vol. 8, No. 84, p. 741, 8 August 1920.

flood of red barbarism flowing from the East, and thus safeguard her own interests and the interests of her principal antagonists in the West.

If the Germans were able to render such a service, not by reckless military adventure or with ulterior motives, they would unquestionably have taken a giant step upon that path of self-redemption which would lead them surely and swiftly as the years pass by to their own great place in the councils of Christendom, and would have rendered easier the sincere co-operation between Britain, France, and Germany on which the very salvation of Europe depends.[10]

Events in Europe seemed to conspire against France, and to shorten beyond Germany's wildest hopes the period when she would be approached once again as a potential ally rather than as a beaten foe. In September Lord Robert Cecil, Britain's most energetic supporter of the League of Nations, said that if Germany applied for admission to the League in 1921 he would support her request, and thought it would succeed.[11] In October the British Government decided that if Germany were unable to pay reparations at the scheduled time, Britain would not exercise her right under the Treaty of Versailles to seize the property of German nationals in England.[12]

This brazen decision was taken by the British Cabinet without consultation with France. It caused an immediate and justifiable outcry in France. Austen Chamberlain, the Chancellor of the Exchequer, explained in the House of Commons that the threat of seizing German assets had already resulted in much German money

staying out of England.[13] As London was the financial centre of the world, he felt that no obstacle should be placed in the way of its further expansion. It was clearly bad business to drive out even German money. The French were not mollified by this explanation. But when the French Chargé d'Affaires called on Lord Curzon to protest, Curzon repeated Chamberlain's statement, and proceeded to give copious examples of French hostility to Britain as shown in the Paris press. Curzon deplored the constant and shrill attacks on "British honour, British good faith, and British policy" and ended by warning the Chargé d'Affaires that:

Phlegmatic as the British people were, a time might come when they would say that, though they were convinced of the immense importance of friendship between France and this country, they were being asked to pay almost too high a price for it, if they were to continue to be subjected to incessant abuse.[14]

As 1920 drew to a close this warning was repeated in different forms on a variety of occasions. No amount of diplomatic tact was able to join the fragments of the *Entente* together. When, in November 1920, H. A. L. Fisher proposed in the League Assembly at Geneva that the League Council should at once invite all the League nations not to increase their armaments over a period of two years, prior to arranging for a general disarmament, it was France that took the lead in quashing the proposal. Among the powers France persuaded to support them were Poland and Rumania. France was looking eastwards, not northwards, for her security. Fisher wrote to his wife that "the French were very foolish not to let so harmless a

[10]*Evening News*, 28 July 1920.

[11] Harold Temperley, *The Second Year of the League*, pp. 42–3.

[12]*British Documents*, series 1, vol. 10, Nos. 386, 387, 397 and 398. The Germans were informed of this on 15 October 1920, a day before the French.

[13]*Hansard*, 28 October 1920. Chamberlain's statement is also printed in full in *British Documents*, series 1, vol. 10, No. 397, pp. 542–3.

[14]*British Documents*, series 1, vol. 10, No. 397, p. 546. Lord Curzon to Lord Derby, 29 October 1920.

resolution through." [15] But France felt that her only security against German recovery was to keep, and even to increase the level of her armaments, and to find eastern allies equally conscious of the importance of large armies and burgeoning armaments. The League became as much a scene of Anglo-French discord as were the inter-allied conferences. Quarrels arose on every issue, not solely through an inability to agree on technical points, but rather through differences of national outlook and tradition. Whether over the means of controlling the illegal international drug traffic, or halting the white slave trade, of protecting the Armenians from Turkish violence, or keeping Danzig out of exclusive Polish control, Anglo-French interests always seemed to clash.

The final breach of the year arose over reparations. In June 1920 the total amount payable by Germany had been reduced from £24,000 million, the sum decided upon in 1918 by the Hughes-Cunliffe Committee, to £13,450 million. It was decided, on a British initiative, to open discussions with the Germans on how this amount should be paid. A conference was arranged, to be held in Brussels in December. Lord D'Abernon, the British Ambassador in Berlin, wrote forcefully to Curzon early in November, warning him that the German economic situation was precarious and that the value of the Mark was in danger of collapsing. "It is in my judgement important," he wrote, "to keep the discussion at Brussels off the more or less Byzantine question of Germany's duty, and to confine it to the practical question of Germany's ability." [16] Lord Hardinge,

who had succeeded Derby as Ambassador in Paris, warned the French Minister for Foreign Affairs, M. Leygues, at the beginning of December, that "it was generally realized in England that it would be absolutely impossible to carry out the intention, at one time proclaimed by both the French and British Governments, to extract from Germany payment of the whole cost of the war." [17]

The Brussels Conference upheld the British view. While not fixing a final limit to German payments, as Lloyd George wanted, it did arrange a much more moderate scale of payments than that demanded by France. Germany was to pay £150 million a year for five years, after which the question would be reviewed. But the French refused to accept the opinion of financial experts, and, despite protests from Lloyd George, France obtained in May 1921 German acceptance under duress to a total sum of £6,600 million. The British disapproved, not primarily because of the size of the sum, which was the lowest yet agreed on, but mainly because the French had threatened to occupy the Ruhr again if the Germans refused to accept it. The Germans, however, gave way. But British irritation at the hectoring methods France had used remained.

On the Reparations Commission set up at Versailles, which was intended to have an American representative as a moderating influence, the British representative, Sir John Bradbury, was in a minority. He could always be outvoted by his French and Belgian colleagues. It was a galling position for Britain, and one in which the fundamental difference between the British and French positions was constantly forced into the open. Yet because of the

---

[15] Letter dated 15 November 1920. Quoted in Martin Gilbert, *Britain and Germany Between the Wars*, p. 25.

[16] *British Documents*, series 1, vol. 10, No. 401, p. 552. Lord D'Abernon to Lord Curzon, 4 November 1920.

[17] *British Documents*, series 1, vol. 10, No. 409, p. 558. Lord Hardinge to Lord Curzon, 2 December 1920.

composition of the Commission the British view could not prevail.

It was not French harshness alone which made the diplomacy of 1920 so acrimonious, and pushed Britain towards Germany. Equally harmful to the *Entente*, neither Lloyd George nor Curzon was temperamentally sympathetic to French fears. Both wanted to dictate to Europe. Neither wished to defer either to his own colleagues, or to other nations. Neither was easily persuaded to modify his opinions. Lloyd George was tenacious, and appeared impervious to the most vigorous of arguments; Curzon was volatile, and, having accepted a compromise, could veer back unexpectedly to his original position without qualms. Neither provided the moderating influence needed at the succession of conferences. Although both were the exponents of moderation, both presented their case with little chance of gaining adherents.

The alienation of France from Britain was a spur to appeasement. If Britain wished to have some influence over European affairs, she needed a power other than France with whom she could co-operate, and whose goodwill could be exerted on Britain's behalf. Germany was the obvious choice. By 1921 an Anglo-German rapprochement was becoming both possible and desirable. The danger of communism in Germany, either by internal revolution or Russian invasion, was receding. The Weimar Republic seemed capable of making parliamentary democracy work. The disarmament carried out under the terms of the Versailles Treaty prevented, or seemed to prevent, the rise of militarism. The Kaiser was securely in exile in Holland. Many hoped that British friendship would encourage Germany to persevere with her new form of Government, and to feel that the sacrifices made after the ar-

mistice had not been entirely in vain. Germany should be pleased at having gained Britain's respect, sympathy, and friendship. Britain's willingness to contemplate Anglo-German co-operation was part of the tradition of British foreign policy. Britain, from a position of strength, could make concessions without fear of weakening herself, or of being deceived. In Burke's words: "Peace implies reconciliation; and where there has been a material dispute, reconciliation does in a manner always imply concessions on the one part or the other. . . . The superior power may offer peace with honour and with safety."[18]

Lloyd George and his Government were clearly the superior power. Birkenhead, Bonar Law, Austen Chamberlain, Curzon, Churchill, and Lloyd George himself had all shown themselves interested in "peace with honour." Recognizing the weaknesses and even faults in the Versailles Treaty, they wished to create a post-war world in which the prevailing spirit of international relations would be that of Lloyd George's Fontainebleau Memorandum. The Germans had only once been Britain's enemy in war: there seemed no need to regard Anglo-German conflict as a fixed part of European affairs. France had been the traditional enemy from medieval times to the Napoleonic Wars. Germany had often provided cause for British respect and emulation. Lloyd George himself had drawn inspiration from German social legislation, and based much of his own radical programme upon it.

Appeasement in 1920 was a shrewd policy, designed to end the division of Europe into the warring camps of 1914. It was also a cautious policy, aimed at dissociating Britain from French hostility to all aspects

---

[18] Edmund Burke, *Speech on Conciliation with America*, 22 March 1775. Collected Works, 1815 edition, vol. 3, p. 34.

of German recovery. It was a policy which depended for its success upon European economic co-operation, and upon the revision of all clauses in the Versailles Treaty whose alteration could be shown to be conducive or even essential to European peace. It was a practical policy, one of whose aims was to stimulate trade and recreate the flourishing and confident business activity of the pre-war years. Lloyd George was the first active appeaser. But his success was limited to a single year, 1920. And it was seriously hampered by French intransigence.

A former editor-in-chief of the German Foreign Ministry Documents and an adviser to the Royal Archives, JOHN WHEELER-BENNETT (b. 1902) has written *Hindenburg: the Wooden Titan*, (1936), *Brest-Litovsk: the Forgotten Peace*, (1939), and *The Nemesis of Power: the German Army in Politics*, (1954). His study on Munich is one of the best written to date. Wheeler-Bennett believes that the way had already been prepared for a policy of appeasement by the time Hitler came to power in Germany. In the following selection he discusses the first trial of strength between the leaders of Britain and France and the German dictator. In spite of the Nazi regime's brutality and intransigence the two democracies hoped "the situation would settle down to a more normal condition which would lend itself to settlement by negotiations."*

John Wheeler-Bennett

The Road to Appeasement

"To avoid war should be the highest ambition of statesmanship," wrote Friedrich Gentz to King Frederick William III of Prussia in 1797, and thereby crystallized a verity. "War is a fearful thing," said Mr. Neville Chamberlain on an historic occasion, "and we must be very clear, before we embark upon it, that it is really the great issues that are at stake." The truth of these words is, if anything, more painfully clear in 1947 than in 1938.

It follows, therefore, that to appease, to placate—to agree with an adversary while we are in the way with him—becomes a fundamental purpose of all diplomacy, because it is a necessary condition of our civilized order which it is the purpose of that diplomacy to preserve and develop. At the

same time, in any but a strictly pacifist society, the use of force is regarded as legitimate, at any rate for self-defence, and a successful foreign policy must, therefore, oscillate between these two apparently opposite poles.

Why, then, has Appeasement acquired the invidious connotation which it bears to-day? Some might say, because it has come to be regarded as a unilateral act of policy, as distinct from a mutual agreement, in which each side concedes something to the view-point of the other. Yet this does not seem to be a wholly adequate explanation. Governments may make concessions unilaterally in pursuit of policy, whatever the principles of that policy may be. But such concessions must never involve the surrender of any fundamental principle upon the preservation of which the claim to loyalty and respect of governments rests. To surrender these is branded as "Appeasement" in the bad sense, and rightly so, for the means, in such cases, openly or covertly, betray the ends which they are called into being to promote. Surrender to blackmail is always damnable because it sets a higher value upon mere self-protection than upon principles, which, in fact, we know to be sacred and inviolable. Such appeasement is justly condemned because it is felt to be an act of treason against all we stand for—the purchase of life at the expense of those ultimate ends of which the pursuit alone makes life worth living. It is in this sense that men of honour are admired, because we consider that in no circumstances will they think it right to sacrifice principle to expediency.

In the past centuries men fought with zeal for such ends as the defence and extension of their religious faiths, for the dynastic interests of their monarchs, and for the retention or expansion of their possessions, but, with the gradual development of modern warfare towards totality, there came a growing inclination on the part of civilized peoples to restrict to the barest minimum the issues on which they would have recourse to the arbitrament of arms.

From this tendency evolved the desire for "Peaceful Change" and for the discovery of some method for the settlement of international disputes other than a resort to war with its sacrifice of human life, its destruction of social and economic order, and its inevitable consequences in ruin, disease and death. Parallel with this progression was a similar anxiety to localize and isolate such armed conflicts as did occur, on the principle that the fewer the Powers concerned in a war the less destructive its effects.

This combination of pacific propensities, which was prominent at the Congress of Vienna, resulted in the successful avoidance of a general war in Europe for the next hundred years. There were local wars, indeed, in which relatively few Powers were engaged, but there were many occasions on which issues, of a kind which might in times past have provoked hostilities, were settled by arbitration or diplomatic appeasement, and others in which the solution by pacific means of disputes and differences actually resulted in the promotion of better relations between the Powers concerned than had previously existed. As examples of the first of these categories may be cited the unilateral denunciation in 1870 by Russia of the Black Sea clauses of the Treaty of Paris, and the annexation by Austria-Hungary of the provinces of Bosnia and Herzegovina in 1908; while a striking example of the second is the Anglo-French Agreement of 1904, which provided the basis of a firm alliance between the two countries for the next thirty-seven years.

This gravitation toward peace had its defects as well as its virtues. Their general and sincere abhorrence of war afflicted the Powers with a certain systematic political myopia which obscured the danger inherent in, for example, the rise of German militarism. The desire to isolate war in this case outran wisdom, for it was clear, from the moment of Bismarck's declaration of the Policy of Blood and Iron in 1862, that Prussia openly regarded war as a definite instrument of policy in the fulfilment of her national ambitions. Thus Denmark was abandoned in 1864—"I see, my lord, that I can put aside the supposition that Britain will ever go to war on a point of honour," was the comment of Prince Gortschakov to Lord Napier on receiving the British refusal to participate in intervention against Prussian aggression—while

Austria-Hungary and France fought alone and disastrously in 1866 and 1870. There resulted the carefully planned emergence of the German Empire. While guided by the aged Prince Bismarck, who followed the policy of "limited objectives" and always knew when and where to call a halt, this new political manifestation did not prove itself an essential danger to peace, but it became an inevitable agent of destruction under the self-obsessed and irresponsible Wilhelm II.

Under the shadow of the then unparalleled ravages of the First World War, the peace-makers of Paris sought to repair the damage suffered by the machinery for pacific settlement, to strengthen and extend it beyond all previous limits, and to obviate the errors of the past by recognizing the truth that, since peace is indivisible, so must the means of preserving it be indivisible. Under the Covenant of the League of Nations the principle was acknowledged, for the first time, that a wrong done against one State constituted a wrong against all, and it was hoped that by the over-all guarantee of the League against aggression a potential aggressor would be deterred from committing his contemplated crime.

Alas for the imperfections of human nature; neither the peoples of the world nor their governments were sufficiently in earnest for this plan to become realized in any major degree. The powers of the old Adam of nationalism were too strong for the new international ideal to prevail against them. For a variety of reasons, familiar enough but too numerous to be dealt with here, the system of collective security, as visualized under the Covenant, never materialized in practice, and one by one, Japan, Italy, and Germany committed their acts of aggression unchecked and unpunished.

Yet, by a curious contradiction, the will to peace persisted, as strong and stronger than before, among the majority of nations—but it became the will to peace at almost any price. The same mixture of fear and blindness which had afflicted their fathers seventy years before, in regard to the rise of German militarism now hampered the peoples and governments of the world in assessing the dangers of its recrudescence in the form of National Socialism. The passionate will to peace—so right, so laudable, so understandable in itself; that same will which had, in Britain, promoted a unilateral reduction of armaments to a point barely compatible with the needs of national defence—now became the progenitor of a profound desire, not to prevent aggression, but to avoid war, and, if war should come, to keep out of it. In following this policy the governments were at one with their peoples, and in Britain, for example, there is no question but that Mr. Anthony Eden voiced the popular opinion of the majority when he declared, as Foreign Secretary, that "nations cannot be expected to incur automatic military obligations save for areas where their vital interests are concerned."

It is a tragic irony of history that this very will for peace was among the most important contributory factors to the Second World War, for it is clear that early and bloodless victories convinced Hitler that Britain and France would never oppose him by force, or that, if they did so, their opposition would prove negligible. Because of their horror of the concept of war as the *ultima ratio regum*, Britain and France had reduced their armaments and neglected their defences. Because they could not make up their minds as to what their "vital interests" really were, they did not—or would not—realize that they themselves were menaced by the rearmament of Germany, by the reoccupation of the Rhineland, by the unilateral abrogation of the Treaty of Locarno, by the annexation of Austria or by the crippling of Czechoslovakia. In the name of peace and appeasement they condoned injustice and aggression on the part of Germany because they believed themselves too weak to oppose her and because they hoped against hope that—in accordance with the Führer's promises—each act of depredation would be the last. Not until it was well-nigh too late did Britain and France come fully to realize that German ambitions constituted a direct threat to their own most vital interest of all—their way of life, their tradition of liberty and decency, their "deathless attachment to freedom"; when they had so realized, they fought—but for France it was too late.

What, then, is the answer, since all must be agreed that "to avoid war must be the highest ambition of statesmanship"?

It lies surely, first, in the proposition that disarmament must follow—and not precede—the establishment of an effective system of security; that never again must any peace-loving Power become so weak that, either individually or in alliance with others, it is unable to say "No" to a potential aggressor at the earliest symptom of his aggressive designs; that it should have it within its power to insist that disputes be settled in equity and justice. "The concessions of the weak are the concessions of fear," declared Edmund Burke in 1775, and this is as profoundly true to-day as it was one hundred and seventy years ago. Appeasement—a necessary and invaluable card in the game of diplomacy—must be played from strength and never from weakness.

The answer lies, secondly, in that, having the necessary force at our disposal, we should arrive at a broader recognition of our "vital interests," and a realization that the most vital of all, our way of life, to which we have ever pledged "our lives, our fortunes and our sacred honour," may be threatened by events farther afield than we are at first disposed to perceive.

It was not for Belgium or for Serbia that we fought in 1914; it was not for Czechoslovakia that we might have fought in 1938; it was not for Poland that we fought a year later; it was in defence of a principle, in the words of Mr. Duff Cooper, "that one Great Power should not be allowed, in disregard of treaty obligations, of the laws of nations and the decrees of morality, to dominate the continent of Europe." In defence of this principle we have fought many times in the past and must be prepared to fight again in the future, for on the day when we are not prepared to fight for it we shall have forfeited our liberties, our independence, and all the hopes and ideals which we have ever cherished.

Appeasement, then, must ever stop short of this point. But how to realize in time that the point has been reached? How to prevent Europe from again being plucked like an artichoke, leaf by leaf, until we ourselves remain the tastiest morsel of all—le fond d'artichaut?

To this question the answer was given one hundred and forty years ago:

Expressions like "The fate of this or that part of Europe does not concern us" or "we limit ourselves to the maintenance of order in such-and-such an area" and so on should never again pass the lips of a ruler or statesman.... The more vigorously and courageously injustice and force are attacked at their first appearance, the less often will it be necessary to take the field against them in battle.... The more sensitive is every part to the injuring of the whole, the less frequent will wars become [Friedrich Gentz].

These words, written in the face of Napoleonic aggression, were true after the First World War and are still true to-day. Their purport is clear beyond misunderstanding; peace is one and indivisible. In an imperfect world, from which the imperfections are not likely to be speedily removed, it must be recognized that, alongside the desire for change and rectification arising from the normal tendencies of evolution and progress, evil, predatory instincts, national passions and hatreds, will continue to exist. Appeasement has its rightful and appropriate place in the solution of problems and disputes by methods of "peaceful change" and pacific settlement, but is inadmissible in dealing with aggression.

Has the world learned its lesson, or are we, in effect, merely taking "an unconscionable time a-dying"? . . .

WHEN Adolf Hitler came to power in Germany on January 30, 1933, the continent of Europe was in the latter years of a period of which the watchwords—at least outwardly—had been "Peace, Retrenchment and Reform." This period, which had been inaugurated with the acceptance of the Dawes Plan for Reparation Payments in 1924, had reached its peak a year later in the Locarno Agreements of 1925, and its anti-climax in the Kellogg-Briand Pact for the Renunciation of War in 1928. The chief objective of policy among the European Powers had been to bring Germany back to the fold of the body politic of Europe, while seeking to violate as little as possible the provisions and safeguards of the Treaty of Versailles. This procedure became known as "Peaceful Change."

The European Powers, great and small, had, moreover, endeavoured to protect themselves against future aggression— whether from Germany or from any other source—by a system of bilateral and multilateral pledges, so that by the close of 1932 Europe was enmeshed by a web of alliances, pacts and treaties of mutual assistance, in addition to the general guarantees and instruments of the League of Nations. On paper the Continent was well insured against all forms of international

violence, but in reality all that this "Pactomania" had produced was a flimsy structure, destined to collapse at the first test of its strength.

Under the freezing winds of the Great Depression, the fortunes of "Peaceful Change" had withered and declined. The forces of nationalism, apparently dormant during the comparative peace and plenty of the 'twenties, revived with renewed vigour under the influence of economic disaster and were in full flower on both sides of the Franco-German border by the close of 1932. The *Annus Terribilis* of 1931 marks the first turning-point from peace to war, but it must be remembered that great progress had been made towards reaching an agreement between Germany and the Allied Powers before the inauguration of the Third Reich.

Within Britain and France there had matured strong forces of opinion which called for a revision of the Treaty of Versailles, by common consent, in Germany's favour. German economy, it was said, must be relieved from the crippling burden of reparation payments if Germany was not to relapse into economic chaos. Similarly, if the Allied Powers could not themselves agree upon a measure of disarmament, compatible with the general reduction envisaged at Versailles and to which the disarmament of Germany was specifically stated to be a preliminary measure, then Germany must be allowed to increase her military establishment beyond the restrictions imposed by the peace treaty to a level at which the Allied Powers could agree to reduce their own armaments, thus establishing an equality of status.

Above all, it was pointed out, unless concessions were made by the Allied Powers to the German Government of the day in the matter of treaty revision in order to strengthen their position so that they could, by their own success, check and harness the great wave of national awakening which was sweeping over Germany, the rising tide of National Socialism would carry Hitler to the supreme power in the German Reich.

The failure of Stresemann's Policy of Fulfilment to bring forth what the German people regarded as satisfactory results, and the alluring prospects promised under Hitler's Policy of Repudiation, were driving Germans of all ages, but more especially the youth of Germany, into the ranks of the National Socialist Party, which by the close of 1931 had achieved the position of the largest single party in the country, with a registered membership of over a million.

Unable to ignore these warnings of approaching disaster, the Allied Powers made shift to meet the situation by diplomatic methods: Concessions which, had they been made earlier to Heinrich Brüning, might have achieved their object, were made wholesale to the Government of the egregious Franz von Papen, which had virtually repudiated the reparation payments and withdrawn from the Disarmament Conference. In consequence the Lausanne Agreement of July 1932 abrogated the reparation clauses of the Treaty of Versailles—save for a final token payment of 3 milliard marks, which everyone tacitly agreed should never be made—and von Papen was able to announce to the German people that the "War Guilt" Clause (Article 231) had been erased from the Treaty of Versailles with the lapsing of Part VIII (Reparation), of which it formed the first article. Although this was a unilateral statement and found no echo either in the Lausanne Agreement or in the other European capitals, it remained unchallenged by any of the Allied Governments.

Similarly the Agreement of December 11, 1932, granted to the Government of General von Schleicher in the matter of rearmament that status for Germany of "equality of rights within a system which would provide security for all nations" which had been consistently refused to Brüning, and procured, thereby, the return of Germany to the Disarmament Conference.

Thus, when Hitler came to power, the way to treaty revision by peaceful means had already been cleared of its two most outstanding obstacles, and, had he elected to follow this same path, his achievement might have been more successful and more durable.

It was evident from the first, however, that the new régime in Germany had no pacific intentions. Though the Government declaration in the Reichstag on March 21, 1933, called for "a long-term consolidation of peace by the really great national Powers, in order to restore the mutual confidence of the peoples," a monument was almost immediately thereafter erected in West Prussia, looking towards the Corridor and bearing the inscription: "Never forget, Germans, of what blind hate has robbed you. Bide the hour which will expiate the shame of this bleeding frontier." This, it was felt, interpreted more accurately both the spirit and the policy of the new Germany.

As the spring drew on to summer, there was no neighbour of the Reich who was not in a ferment of anxiety, and the world at large was nauseated by the brutalities of the Brown Terror which convulsed Germany. At the Disarmament Conference the German delegates maintained an attitude of complete obduracy and intransigent non-co-operation, and on May 12, in a speech at Münster, Vice-Chancellor von Papen announced that "on January 30, 1933, Germany struck out the word 'pacifism' from her vocabulary."

The effect on public opinion in Britain and France of this terrifying phenomenon in Central Europe was one of bewilderment and confusion. Whereas the "anti-Germans" remained consistently hostile, the former Germanophiles became hopelessly divided between those who secretly admired the Nazi régime or feared it to the point of appeasement, and those who, while sincerely detesting the cruelties of National Socialism, retained a belief in the fundamental decency of the German people, and waited hopefully for "the other Germany" to rise up and expel the Nazi forces of evil. Some placed their faith in the Army, some in the Churches, some in the Radical and Communist elements of the Left.

As the revolution in Germany increased in fury and bestiality there followed a further shifting of political thought outside the Reich. Those who had always suspected Germany of malevolent intentions, ever since the signing of the Peace Treaty in 1919, now joined hands with those who had become "anti-German" since the Revolution, and made common cause in demanding that Germany should be restrained by force from her aggressive policies; the original "anti-Germans," because of their inherent phobia, and the "anti-Nazis," because of their belief that only by the military destruction of National Socialism could "the other Germany" be liberated from the thraldom under which its own strange lack of preparedness and comprehension of danger had placed it. These incongruous allies were united against the forces of appeasement, which, prompted by a strange amalgam of reluctance, misplaced confidence, and lack of understanding, struggled to maintain the peace of Europe by the method of giving in to the Nazis and even of condoning certain of their criminal actions.

Thus, as early as the summer of 1933, there were those in London and in Paris and in Warsaw who were advocating a preventive war on Germany for the preservation of peace.

In effect, however, the chief contributory factor to the bewilderment and division of counsel which afflicted all schools of thought in Britain and France from 1933 to 1939 was a fundamental ignorance of the German character and a complete inability to comprehend the lengths of evil, dishonesty and deception to which the Nazi mentality could extend. It seemed incredible to many in Britain and in France that the German people, who had but recently emerged from the depths of defeat, should again permit themselves to be led into the ways of aggression by a wanton adventurer. The capacity of the Germans for sheep-like conformity to leadership was not appreciated, nor the fact realized that this new political phenomenon combined all the guile of the old pre-war duplicity of Prussian diplomacy with a new and ruthless deceit of unplumbed depths.

For this reason, therefore, while there was an immediate reaction in Britain and in France against any further concession to Germany in the matter of treaty revision—and especially regarding the revision of the territorial provisions of the Peace Treaties—there was a general tendency among Governmental circles in both countries toward wishful thinking and to the hope that, when the first blast of Hitler's exuberance had been exhausted, the situation would settle down to a more normal condition which would lend itself to settlement by negotiation.

These illusions were fostered by the Führer's speech on May 17, 1933, before the Reichstag, which could scarcely have been equalled by Stresemann or Brüning. "No fresh European war," Hitler declared, "was capable of putting something better in the place of the unsatisfactory conditions which to-day exist. . . . The outbreak of such a madness without end would lead to the collapse of the existing social order in Europe." He then repeated the basis of Germany's claim to equality, but added: "Germany is at any time ready to assume further international security obligations if all nations are prepared to do so and Germany benefits thereby. Germany is also ready without further ado to dissolve her entire military forces and destroy the weapons left to her if other nations will do the same. If, however, they are not willing to carry out the disarmament stipulations of the Treaty of Versailles, then Germany must at least maintain her claim to equality."

The effect of the speech was a diplomatic and tactical victory for Hitler, who had suddenly extricated himself from the position of being responsible for the breakdown of the Disarmament Conference and had placed the onus for such a collapse—if such there should be—at the door of the Allied Powers. Nor was the Führer content with words. Two days after the speech, his representative at Geneva had withdrawn all previous objections raised by Germany and had accepted as a basis for discussion the Draft Treaty submitted by the British Government (May 19).

To the optimists in Europe the new development betokened a justification for their wishful thinking. Hitler had succeeded in his first diplomatic campaign and had established a balance on the credit side. He had given proof of his *Bundnisfähigkeit* ("pactworthiness") and had dispelled many of the reservations which the leaders in France and Britain had entertained in regard to entering into written agreements with him. It was now held that nothing could be lost in concluding a pact with Hitler, and indeed that the more agreements to which he could be persuaded to put his name the more difficult it would be for him to practise the aggression which all had feared. Forthwith, in a naïve attempt to contain the Führer by paper obligations, there was signed the Four-Power Pact between Britain, France, Germany and Italy (June 8, 1933), which was intended to provide not only the formula of success for the Disarmament Conference but also the foundation for a new Concert of Europe.

Alas for the hopes thus engendered; the advancing summer brought no hope of fulfilment. Nazi propaganda in Austria clearly aimed at the overthrow of the Federal Government and the union of that country within the Reich, and in this campaign the German Legation in Vienna made no secret of its connection with the Austrian Nazi Party.

Moreover, it soon became apparent, despite the Führer's pious asseverations, that Germany had made up her mind to rearm. . . . [The Nazis restored the army to its former place of glory. Germany became a nation in uniform. Beginning with their eleventh year, boys were trained to be future soldiers. At the same time, Germany increased its imports of strategic metals and planned to transform its industry for war production.]

To France it seemed as if her patience were being tried unduly highly, and to this M. Paul-Boncour made significant reference on September 3, at the unveiling of M. Briand's memorial at Trébenden. "How easy it is to observe the contrast between a peaceful manifestation such as this and the agitations which surge to the very boundaries of our territories," he declared, and added that, if French patience with Germany were due to a feeling of weakness, that would be grave; but France knew herself strong enough to resist violence, and the recent visit of the Premier to the frontier defences was the best reply to proceedings of which the least he could say was that "they deeply trouble the atmosphere of peace so necessary to European restoration."

In Great Britain the repercussions of the European situation were of a different nature, and produced among thinking people two divergent schools of thought, both of which were more long-sighted than the views expressed in Europe, and treated the question of disarmament in relation to the whole vast problem of Treaty revision. The one school held that, unless some specific guarantee were given, Europe would most certainly drift back to war which, as in 1914, would gradually engulf the whole world. It was maintained that, even though minor rectifications of the Peace Treaties were made, Germany would not be content, but would demand and would prepare to take more by force, unless it were made absolutely clear by Great Britain that she meant to oppose such unilateral revision, if need be also by force. It was thought, therefore, that, unless such additional guarantees of security were given, either France or Poland might precipitate war before Germany had had time to rearm, or that Germany, if given time, might re-establish a hegemony over Europe which would threaten the rest of the world as it had in 1914.

The view of the second school was far more isolationist in character. It urged that Great Britain should resolutely refuse to form part of any special system of European security, and that the main object of her policy should be to co-operate with the Dominions and the United States in trying to form a non-European or Oceanic *bloc*, actively interested in the prevention of war and prepared to carry out its obligations under the Covenant, "as these are generally understood to-day." Apart from these commitments Britain should be entirely unpledged to any special or automatic economic or military action.

This school of thought—and in this particular aspect it was surprising to find the Round Table Group and the Beaverbrook Press in a startling degree of agreement—

considered further that the provisions of the Locarno Treaty must in any case be reviewed, and that any special obligation which Great Britain might undertake on her own account in Europe as a modification of the Locarno system should be undertaken in the interests of her own security and should be limited to a renewal of the guarantee to Belgium and a declaration never to permit the return of Alsace-Lorraine to Germany. In no case, however, should Great Britain form part of a balance of power in Europe involving her inevitable liability to belligerency whenever a European war broke out.

There was no indication as to whether either of these views was held by the British Government, which still maintained a masterly silence on all subjects connected with foreign affairs, save that on September 16, 1933, at Cupar, in Fifeshire, the Foreign Secretary, Sir John Simon, vouchsafed a gleam from the dark lantern, and disclosed the fact that he was shortly going to Geneva "to find out if there was even now some way in which we can secure an agreed Disarmament Convention."

A blow was dealt the isolationists of Britain, however, by Mr. Stanley Baldwin, then Lord President of the Council, on October 6, when he described their views as "both crude and childish," and gave a categorical reaffirmation of Britain's pledges to France and Belgium. "What Great Britain has signed she will adhere to," he declared, but he added that the Treaty of Locarno was "the most difficult" of the agreements entered into since the war.

It remained, however, for M. Daladier, Premier of France, to voice the question which all Europe was asking. What did Germany want? he demanded at the Radical Party Congress at Vichy (October 10). Publicly the German Government proclaimed their desire for peace, and, by diplomatic channels, their wish to draw closer to France. Yet why was German youth trained for fighting? Why this refusal to take the first step towards disarmament? Why this demand for the right to construct material which would have to be destroyed soon afterwards if the Disarmament Convention were signed?

Events were now moving with great rapidity towards a climax. Though all now knew that a crisis was inevitable, few had any conception of what its magnitude and its gravity would be.

When the representatives of Britain, France, Italy and the United States met in Geneva on October 9 for the meetings of the Bureau and the General Commission of the Disarmament Conference, they had already agreed among themselves that, at the present juncture and in view of the evidence then forthcoming from the Reich, Germany could not be granted immediately that equality of status in armaments which she had demanded. A "probationary period" of five years was regarded as desirable and it was this proposal which was put before the German representatives on the night of October 11.

Hitler at once took energetic action. He summoned his Cabinet on October 13, haled the aged President von Hindenburg to Berlin from the seclusion of his East Prussian retreat, issued a statement that the Four Powers' proposals were "incompatible with the principle of international politics" and, on the following day (October 14), announced the formal withdrawal of Germany not only from the Disarmament Conference but also from membership in the League of Nations.

October 14, 1933, was a momentous date in world history. On that day the second or Locarno period in the years between the wars came to an end and the world entered upon an uneasy progress towards a new conflict; a period which finally terminated on September 1, 1939.

More important, however, is that this date marks the first trial of strength between Hitler and the former Allied Powers, a contest in which, to his intense surprise, he won an easy victory. To those who were in Berlin on that evening it was clearly apparent that the gravest anxiety and apprehension permeated every stratum of German official life, both political and military, and to this the Führer himself was no exception.

There was no more disturbed man in the Reich than Adolf Hitler in the days immediately succeeding October 14. He had taken his decision to withdraw from Geneva in full anticipation of some military action on the part of France and her allies, and every hour he expected news of a French occupation of the Ruhr, of Czech troops in the brown coal country of Saxony, or of a Polish invasion of East Prussia. Gradually, in the silence which reigned in Paris, in Prague and Warsaw, Hitler discovered that he had achieved a major diplomatic victory, which was to bring him a genuine expression of public support in the German elections of November 12. With the success of his first act of defiance the Führer had taken the measure of his opponents and forthwith conducted his policy accordingly.

Although British leaders desired to appease Mussolini, they disagreed over reasons and techniques. In any event, the result was failure. GEORGE W. BAER (b. 1935), an assistant professor at the University of California, Santa Cruz, singles out the foreign secretary, Sir John Simon, for a large share of the guilt. Simon, he believes, "was not prepared to undertake an effective appeasement of Mussolini by asserting British strength." This selection discusses also the Italian dictator's diplomatic maneuvering prior to his all-out attack on Ethiopia.*

George W. Baer

Ineffective Appeasement

In May 1936 Benito Mussolini proclaimed the establishment of an Italian empire in east Africa. Ethiopia was annexed to Italy; the last African country free from foreign domination had been conquered by the Italian army. Haile Selassie had fled to England; the king of Italy was invested with the title of emperor. But the conquest of Ethiopia was more than an incident in the later history of European imperialism in Africa. It was also of great importance in the history of Europe after the First World War.

Italy's invasion of Ethiopia in October 1935 posed a direct challenge to the postwar system of collective security as established by the League of Nations. This challenge was not met. The League of Nations failed to protect one of its members; Italy's war of conquest was permitted to succeed; and the League was discredited as a political institution. Its strongest members, Britain and France instead of upholding the Covenant, withdrew into defensive isolationism and began to pursue policies of appeasement. In these circumstances Germany was encouraged to rearm and to violate the treaties of Locarno and Versailles. Italy, having survived the limited sanctions imposed upon it by the League, was by 1936 moving away from its earlier association with the Western democracies and setting on a course that was to end with the Axis. "The Italian-Ethiopian affair," said Joseph Avenol, secretary-general of the League, was "a European poison.". . .

*Reprinted by permission of the publishers from George W. Baer, *The Coming of the Italian-Ethiopian War,* Cambridge, Mass.: Harvard University Press, Copyright, 1967, by the President and Fellows of Harvard College. Pp. vii, 87–95. Footnotes omitted.

From the beginning of 1935, two related problems faced Italian diplomats. One was to maintain the good will of Britain and France. The other was to prevent the League of Nations from acting on Ethiopia's appeals for help. If Britain and France were sympathetic, the League could be immobilized with no difficulty. For the League followed without much question wherever the two great Western democracies led.

Despite some disenchantment, Mussolini's confidence in the French-Italian entente turned out to be well placed. France supported Italy throughout the conflict, up to one crucial point at any rate. That point was reached when the shortcomings of Italian diplomacy and the boldness of Mussolini's ambitions met Britain's unexpectedly renewed interest in international morality. Should a decisive choice have to be made, France, as the French always knew, would have to opt for Britain. As General Gamelin said, "for us Italy is important; England is essential." On the other hand, the effects of this situation might be altered for Italy's behalf, and in such tacking Laval excelled. But this troublesome situation was not yet in the offing, and for the present it appeared that Britain was steering the same course as France. To keep the active sympathy of French officials, all Italian diplomacy had to do, it seemed, was not to alienate Britain.

By the end of January, as we shall see, Italy had won an important diplomatic victory over Ethiopia at Geneva. Following the Walwal incident, Ethiopia made an effort to invoke article 11 of the Covenant, declaring that a threat to the peace was at hand. To prevent the League from taking formal jurisdiction in the matter, Italy proposed as an alternative that direct arbitration only over the Walwal conflict take

place. By this tactic the Italians sought to bypass the League, to bypass the larger questions of war or peace and Italy's intentions in Ethiopia. Italy's proposal was accepted by Ethiopia at the urging of France and Britain. In the wake of this success, on 29 January 1935, three weeks after the accord with France, Italy approached the British government on the matter of Ethiopia.

There was a marked contrast between the two Italian moves. With France, Italy entered into a new era of diplomatic relations, the friendship sealed by apparently extravagant Italian concessions. Mutual need bound the two nations' together, and the entente was cemented by careful diplomatic attention in the months that followed. Toward Britain, Italy's behavior seemed almost casual. On 29 January Leonardo Vitetti, counselor to the Italian embassy in London, visited the Foreign Office for an informal conversation. Vitetti was instructed to let the British government know that Italian interest in east Africa was quickening and that agreement on its general direction had been reached with France. He informed the British of the secret understanding between Mussolini and Laval for a French economic *désistement* in Ethiopia.

Mussolini did not want the British to think they had been duped by a French-Italian understanding made behind their backs. It was important that the British learn of the French permissiveness, for this information might have an influence on future British policy. But the Italians did not at this time seek specific British approval of their plans, nor did they look for promises of a free hand. They did not even seek "good will" as such. Mussolini merely wanted to put London *au courant*, to maintain the illusion that Italy had acted in open frankness with its partners in the

1906 treaty and to assure Britain that its interests in Ethiopia would be protected. The British were not informed that Mussolini was planning to use force in Ethiopia, and Vitetti deliberately kept the Italian plans vague.

Vitetti was also instructed to suggest informally that an exchange of views might take place concerning the claims of Britain and Italy in east Africa. This was, Mussolini asserted later, an invitation to the British "to consider the possibility of specific agreements" for harmonious development of the two countries' interests in Ethiopia. But the invitation was casually tendered and Italy did not extend its exploratory démarche. The Italian purpose was not to initiate negotiations so much as to inform the British that lines of communication were open if the British cared to make use of them. Mussolini watched carefully for Britain's reaction. One object of broaching the subject at this time was to give the British an opportunity to clarify their own position on the matter of Ethiopia, for themselves as well as for Italy. There was general uncertainty in Rome as to what Britain's future policies would be both toward Europe and toward a conflict between Italy and Ethiopia. As long as the government seemed uncertain of its own course, any negotiation to bring Britain into prior agreements seemed unlikely to succeed. Mussolini also lacked the opportunity to bargain with the British that he had with the French. He made no further effort to open negotiations, but an invitation for discussion had been put forth. It remained for the British to accept.

Guariglia, in his speculation on Mussolini's motives, surmised that the Duce did not want to run the possibility of stirring up serious opposition in Britain before his own plans and preparations had been fully developed. Mussolini knew that an Italian war against Ethiopia would be very unpopular in Britain. What effect public opinion might have on the government was uncertain. For the moment, the British government was friendly enough toward Italy. Indecision was better than opposition, and, if this indecision lasted long enough, perhaps Italy might be able to present the British with a *fait accompli*. Mussolini therefore preferred to leave unsaid those facts which might cause premature hostility and force the British into a recalcitrant stand. He eschewed frank discussion and wanted to "let the sleeping dog lie."

This tactic of equivocation rested on the assumption that the British were, at least in the short run, friendly or indifferent enough not to interfere, or that, despite their feelings, they were unwilling to undertake large-scale resistance to the Italian invasion of Ethiopia. While waiting for a statement of governmental intention on which negotiations might be based, Mussolini counted on the pacifism of the British people to offset any hostile reaction against Italy. Before beginning his plans for the conquest of Ethiopia, Mussolini had ordered a statistical study of the age groupings of British citizens. The conclusions of the survey were that British society consisted mostly of "static" elements, the elderly and women, and that the British would seek peace and compromise rather than interrupt a quiet life for military resistance. With this in mind Mussolini judged that, once France had accepted Italian ambitions in east Africa, Britain's government would not create a stumbling block. The long tradition of compromise over Ethiopia might still be counted on as a guide to British policy. The treaty of 1906, recognizing most of Ethiopia as Italy's sphere of influence, was still in force, as was the bilateral agreement of 1925, and their import clearly was that Italy would be allowed to extend its influence throughout Ethiopia so long as no blatant violation of international law took place and no specifically British interest was endangered.

It was true that the British government wanted to keep Italy's friendship. Despite Mussolini's own confidence, however, it was not certain Italy could count on Britain once the design on Ethiopia was revealed not merely as economic penetration but as military conquest, a violation of the League Covenant. Aggression against Ethiopia, in the current context of international affairs, would be a direct challenge to the principles of the League. It was now difficult to separate a specific colonial action from its repercussions on the international scene, and a violation of the Covenant was not endorsed by any British-Italian agreement over Ethiopia. Although the British government may have been willing to give Mussolini as much latitude in Ethiopia as it could, it dared not act too far in opposition to British public opinion. Here is where Mussolini's assumptions and his policy of purposeful ambiguity ran into danger. The British people did not want war, as Mussolini correctly perceived, but they did feel strongly about the League. This fact was of the utmost importance, for it placed the League in the forefront of British policy making. Just because at the start of 1935 British public opinion appeared quiescent and peace-seeking, no one could be certain that, in the case of an unprovoked Italian war of conquest, a popular inclination to stand behind the League would not outweigh the pacifism. If it should and if the British government, uncommitted in prior agreements with Italy, should allow itself to be pushed into upholding the principles of the League and imposing military sanctions, the consequences for Italy and for Fascism would be disastrous.

This possibility worried the more prudent Italian diplomats. The risks of conducting a war fought on the far side of the Suez Canal, in the face of British control of the Mediterranean, the canal, the Red Sea, and the Indian Ocean, were enough to daunt even the most sanguine of the Italians. The military risk, as Neville Chamberlain later expressed it, was like tying a noose around one's neck and leaving "the end hanging out for anyone with a Navy to pull."

These dangers, however, still remained only possibilities. In January 1935 Mussolini deemed it sufficient diplomatic preparation merely to inform the British of his renewed interest in Ethiopia and to suggest further discussions as a matter of mutual colonial interest. This done, he left the next move up to Britain.

The decision on how to treat the Italian overture of 29 January rested with Sir John Simon, minister of foreign affairs. Simon realized, as he told Geoffrey Thompson in January, that "the Italians intended to take Abyssinia." Simon had no special love for Ethiopia, and he did not want to oppose Mussolini. He feared that British resistance would bring about the Duce's fall and leave Italy open to the Bolsheviks. For Britain's strategic needs, too, there was great value in having Italy as a friend. Simon did not believe that the protection of a remote and primitive African kingdom was worth the cost of losing this friendship, to say nothing of the much greater cost of a British-Italian war. Simon's overriding concern, then, as he told King George in February, was to handle the Italian-Ethiopian conflict "in a way which will not affect adversely Anglo-Italian relations." This approach to the coming crisis was conditioned by expedience, not by broader principles. Mussolini's plans for the conquest of Ethiopia were a direct and vital challenge to the ideals and political existence of the League of Nations. But to champion the League meant to oppose Italy and hence endanger Britain's interest in a stable and peaceful Mediterranean. This Simon was not willing to do. He did not believe enough in the principle of collective security or in its value to Britain to make a national sacrifice on its behalf.

On the other hand, Simon was not prepared to undertake an effective appeasement of Mussolini by asserting British strength, despite the fact that such a course would benefit both Britain and the cause of European peace and security. Mussolini later claimed that at this time he had been willing to "table his case." The door to negotiation was opened by Italy on 29 January, and there was a very real possibility that at this early stage, if the British took the initiative, a bargain for the peaceful settlement of Mussolini's colonial ambitions might be struck. Such an effort would enable the British to keep Italy's friendship and to prevent a major Italian challenge to the League. Robert Vansittart, the permanent secretary of the Foreign Office, saw Italy as a vital element in containing a rearmed Germany. Germany had to be deprived of "the one thing she needed to precipitate [a] conflict"—Italy as an ally. Mussolini was potentially trustworthy, Vansittart thought, and he could be bought. The question was: How, and at what price? Vansittart was furious with the French for giving Mussolini concessions so broad as to make it impossible for Britain to accept them. Yet something might be worked out, as far as the British were concerned, to appease the Fascist appetite. Mussolini refused to help the British along by suggesting a plan of his own for a modus vivendi with Ethiopia, but this did not mean that a solution could not be found if the British government had the will, the nerve, and the skill.

For example, the British as a first step might give Mussolini quiet and forceful warning that they would not tolerate military aggression against Ethiopia. This would be in line with the moral and political ideals of the League, and British control of the seas would lend substance to the warning. Stated at the outset before Mussolini had publicly committed his prestige to a military imperium, such a warning might deter Italy from invasion, give Mussolini sufficient reason to back down, and force him to limit his demands to claims which could be met either by the peaceful cession of territory in east Africa, parts of Ethiopia or British Somaliland, or by the peaceful economic penetration of Ethiopia with British and French cooperation. In the last instance the Ethiopians could be pacified with, say, the gift of an outlet to the sea at Zeila and further British guarantees of their territorial and political integrity. Such a plan would have been worth a try. If successful, an unjust war would be prevented. A critical challenge to the League would be forestalled. Britain would not have to choose between Rome and Geneva. And, with proper diplomatic care, Italy's friendship need not be irrevocably lost. As it was, no such plan was then proposed or even considered. The times cried out for creative statesmanship on the part of the British. But farsighted, imaginative, and courageous diplomacy was simply absent from the Foreign Office. "What we needed to steady [Mussolini] at this stage was a British statesman who would impress him, and we had not got one," wrote Vansittart. Sir John Simon let this opportunity slide by without any action on his part.

The British response to the overture of Vitetti on 29 January was to postpone a decision on the matter. Italy did not request an immediate or specific reply to its informal proposal, and so Britain did not offer any. Mussolini interpreted British muteness as tacit consent: "In the face of that silence there was only one road which remained open to me and I took it." From this time on, the development of the dispute put a reasonable diplomatic settlement increasingly out of reach. Mussolini hurled his army beyond Suez and thereby cut off the possibility of retreat. Positions moved to extremes and hardened. The British government thus missed the best opportunity to exercise effective diplomacy that the Italian-Ethiopian conflict was to offer.

Only Dino Grandi, the Italian ambassador in London, made a further effort at this time to have the Ethiopian question treated as an object of colonial agreement between the interested powers and not, as it was threatening to become, a subject of policy bound up in the anti-colonialist strictures of the new international morality. Grandi was a good Fascist who had come during his time at the Palazzo Chigi to think like an old-line diplomat, and he was eager to maintain British-Italian friendship. In February 1935, on his own initiative, he spoke several times with British officials. The British government, however, did not take up his proposals for negotiations, even though Grandi told Vansittart that he did not believe Mussolini had yet come to an irrevocable decision over Ethiopia. Anthony Eden considered this news "hopeful, almost a hint," but no action was taken. Another opportunity to reach a negotiated settlement with Mussolini was passed up, though Vansittart did give Grandi some cautions for the future. At a meeting on 27 February, Vansittart said that British public opinion would be hostile to any Italian colonial war in Ethiopia. Such a war would seriously jeopardize the new and important possibility of cooperation among Britain, France, and Italy to keep the peace in Europe. Simon in his turn made a small effort to point out a danger to Italy and informed Grandi that Britain would continue to allow Ethiopia to import arms across British Somaliland. Obviously rebuffed, Grandi did not press his proposals any further. The British were not ready to enter into negotiations, and he could not let it seem that British approval was considered a necessary preliminary to Italian action. Italy had decided to maintain as free a hand as possible in this affair.

At the beginning of March 1935, it became obvious that some policy had to be formulated by the British Foreign Office in the increasingly serious Italian-Ethiopian situation. And so the issue was referred to a committee. On 6 March a special interministerial commission under Sir John Maffey was secretly established to study the question of British interests in Ethiopia. The Italian preparations for invasion pushed forward. Mussolini had no assurance that Britain would allow him his conquest, but, all things considered, he did not fear the British, and English silence seemed as good as the French wink.

An associate professor of international relations at Lehigh University, HENDERSON B. BRADDICK (b. 1920) agrees with Baer that British policy was prompted more by concern for a general security of interests in the Mediterranean than by any special regard for the fate of Ethiopia. He attributes British failure to "the willingness of politicians to use foreign policy matters as expedient tactics in domestic politics and the disparity between the public and private attitudes of British leaders." The crisis that produced the Hoare-Laval Plan was essentially a clash between Fascist and British imperialisms in which both sides played a game of power politics, but where only the British were bluffing.*

Henderson B. Braddick

The Hoare-Laval Plan

The agreement between British Foreign Minister Sir Samuel Hoare and Pierre Laval, French Premier and Foreign Minister, in early December, 1935, was a major turning point in European international politics during the interwar period. It placed a premium on Fascist aggression in Ethiopia by proposing that Italy be given actual or *de facto* control over huge slices of the African country. Several volumes of memoirs published in the last few years throw new light on some aspects of the proposal itself and on the politics of Great Britain, Italy, and France toward the Italo-Ethiopian conflict, policies which at the height of the international crisis produced the Hoare-Laval Plan. In addition, the State Department documents, published and unpub-lished, are a mine of information on these matters.

Standard accounts of European international relations during the period tend to neglect the power politics which lie behind the Plan. And even in the most extensive treatments of the crisis, there are important gaps in this respect. It has been maintained, for example, that France prevented England from leading the League of Nations in imposing an oil sanction against Italy. The evidence, however, indicates that the British were just as reluctant to support this measure as the French.

The Hoare-Laval proposal for the settlement of the Italo-Ethiopian War cannot be understood without reference to the main lines of British, French, and Italian policies

*Henderson B. Braddick, "The Hoare-Laval Plan: A Study in International Politics," *The Review of Politics*, vol. IV, no. 3 (July, 1962), pp. 342–364. Footnotes omitted.

in the crisis as it developed. Ethiopia had been a target of Italian expansionism for many decades and, beginning in 1928, the Fascist Government had pursued a policy of economic and political penetration with considerable vigor, though with little success. Indeed, by the end of 1934, the Italians believed that British influence in the country was becoming so powerful that within a few years they might virtually be forced out. They had information concerning negotiations between Ethiopia and Great Britain about the establishment of a British protectorate and the cession of part of Ethiopia to British Somaliland. Moreover, there is evidence that British authorities supported an Ethiopian military demonstration in November, 1934, before Wal Wal, a military outpost which the Italians had held for a number of years near the disputed Ethiopian-Italian Somaliland frontier. The demonstration was made by a large Ethiopian military escort of a joint Ethiopian-British commission, engaged in surveying the boundary between British Somaliland and Ethiopia. While Wal Wal was located some 50 miles from the Italian Somaliland frontier accorcording to most maps, even Italian ones, it was also about 100 miles from the Ethiopian-British Somaliland frontier as it then stood.

Immediately after the Wal Wal incident, Mussolini ordered his military forces to be ready for a campaign against Ethiopia to begin not later than October, 1935. The possibility of such action had been considered seriously by the Duce since 1933; and although military preparations had been begun in 1934, it was apparently the Wal Wal affair that precipitated his decision. Of course, he would have been satisfied if the other powers had handed Ethiopia to him; he had no desire to waste limited Italian resources on protracted military campaigns. In any event, he had to show that he meant business.

On their side, the British became concerned about the implications of the steady Italian military build-up in Africa. This concern, however, related less to an independent Ethiopia than to the security of British interests in East Africa and the Near East. While there was anxiety over the safety of the headwaters of the Blue Nile at Lake Tsana in Ethiopia, Italian preparations suggested that Mussolini intended to pursue the grandiose policy which he had publicly proclaimed in March, 1934:

I could give you the details of a plan up to 1945 but I prefer to point out to you the historical objectives towards which our generation and the generations to follow should be directed during the present century. Let us calmly consider a plan that reaches the nearby millennium, the year 2000. It is only a question of sixty years. The historical objectives of Italy have two names: Asia and Africa. South and East are the cardinal points that should excite the interest and the will of Italians. There is little or nothing to do towards the North and the same towards the West, neither in Europe or beyond the Ocean. These two objectives of ours are justified by geography and history. Of all the large Western Powers of Europe, Italy is the nearest to Africa and Asia. A few hours by sea and much less by air are enough to link up Italy with Africa and with Asia.

For generations Britain had assiduously extended and consolidated her influence in the Near East and East Africa; the maintenance of her predominance there was an imperative of British foreign policy. Thus, the Italo-Ethiopian controversy led to a crisis between Fascist and British imperialisms, for British imperial and commercial policy could not countenance a substantial augmentation of Italian power in these areas or in the Mediterranean.

It was of importance to Mussolini that some sort of understanding be worked out with Britain if possible, because the vital logistical line from Italy to Somaliland and Eritrea was vulnerable to British sea power along most of its length, especially at the bottleneck of Suez. While Italian military strength in Africa accumulated, spokesmen in Rome made statements to the effect that Italy did not intend to interfere with British interests. Such statements were probably discounted in Whitehall and produced little more than a warning against the use of force.

The British Foreign Office did not consider Italy as a first-rate diplomatic power; the Italian international political position was particularly weak at the moment because of German pressure on Austria where Italian influence was paramount. In London, Mussolini was regarded as having an intense dislike and fear of Hitler. Furthermore, it was believed that the Italians were apprehensive about the possibility of German forces on the Brenner. After all, had not an Italian military demonstration at the northern frontier saved Austria from Hitler in 1934, and would the Duce risk the Austrian *status quo* by committing Italian arms in Ethiopia? In any case, there was considerable doubt in London whether Italian financial and military resources could sustain an overseas adventure.

It is likely that Sir John Simon, British Foreign Minister during the first half of 1935, felt no need to bargain with Italy, an inferior power, about the developing Anglo-Italian problem in Africa. Simon's strategic plan in the existing situation was evidently to maintain freedom of action and a measure of the initiative *vis-à-vis* Italy by refusing to inform the Italians as to what Britain would do about Italian ambitions in Ethiopia. At the same time, he exerted considerable diplomatic pressure on the Fascist Government, particularly in the League of Nations, to settle the Wal Wal incident and other differences with Ethiopia peacefully. In this way he demonstrated the predominance of British power in Anglo-Italian relations to the peoples of Africa and the Near East. With regard to Ethiopia itself, there is good evidence that the country was rapidly and quietly moving into the British orbit. Simon's international policy and League action gave the impression that Britain had won the first round in an Anglo-Italian diplomatic contest. Instead of weakening before this pressure, Mussolini mobilized further military resources and sent new military units to Libya, near the Egyptian frontier. He instructed his delegate at the League to maintain an attitude of complete intransigence.

This was the situation confronting Sir Samuel Hoare, who succeeded Simon as British Foreign Minister in early June, 1935. He decided that an effort had to be made to deal with the Italian leader. It was not successful. In the first place, the decision to send Anthony Eden, then Minister for League of Nations Affairs, as the emissary to carry the British proposal to Mussolini, was not a happy one. Mussolini regarded the Geneva organization as primarily an instrument of British and French politics and Eden as the British Minister charged with the mission of enlisting League support for British policy against him. The proposal would have given Ethiopia the important commercial advantage of an outlet on the Red Sea through British Somaliland. But in return, Italy was to receive only the desert province of Ogaden and undefined economic concessions. Mussolini rejected the idea out of hand. In fact, Rome interpreted the proposal as likely to advance

British political and economic interests in Ethiopia and not those of Italy. The result was an exacerbation of Anglo-Italian relations, rather than an amelioration of tension. Eden said that he had been treated like a pickpocket, while the Italian view was that the proposal was a trap. Furthermore, secret documents which Mussolini's agents had purloined from the British Embassy reinforced his suspicion that London was playing a double game with him over Ethiopia.

Mussolini was infuriated by the attitude of the British. He argued that he merely intended to do in Ethiopia what they had done in Egypt or the French in Morocco; he was particularly angered at their policy of pressure against him while condoning Japanese expansion in Manchuria. Japanese grievances against the Chinese in Manchuria evoked considerable sympathy in England and were in many respects similar to those held by Italy against the Ethiopians. In both cases, the weaker states violated existing economic agreements. Chiang Kai-shek and Haile Selassie had made progress in unifying and strengthening their countries, a development that might diminish foreign privileges. Japanese in China and Italians in Ethiopia were subjected to indignities, the Japanese because of hate, the Italians because of scorn. "There is a large Ethiopian party," reported the American Minister in Addis Ababa, "which looks with contempt on the Italians and believes, probably fatuously, that it is more than a match for any Italian army if but given the chance to fight. This Ethiopian contempt for the Italians will doubtless survive through the present and perhaps through another generation." He also wrote that to "mislead an Italian is probably the Ethiopian idea of a highly satisfying practice and diversion, particularly as Italian resentment

does not appear since the Battle of Adowa in 1896 to have taken any positively threatening or potentially dangerous form."

Following the Duce's rejection of their June proposals, the British attempted to align France behind British policy. As might be expected, Laval had his own ideas on this matter. Earlier in the year he had concluded an agreement with Mussolini to defend the independence of Austria and led the Italian dictator to believe that he could proceed with his intended penetration of Ethiopia. There is evidence that Laval even made promises of French financial assistance for the enterprise. Details of an Italo-French military agreement, especially regarding Austria, were worked out shortly thereafter. Also, Laval had entered into a defensive military understanding with Soviet Russia. Though he had been successful in organizing the Continent against Germany, it is not clear whether Laval's activities were designed entirely for the purpose of containing German expansion. There are indications that he may have had in mind the alternative of bargaining with Hitler, for example over Eastern and Central Europe, from a more powerful situation of strength.

Meanwhile, the British had concluded a naval agreement with Germany. This accord permitted German naval construction (in violation of the Versailles Treaty) up to thirty-five per cent of British strength in being. Such action can be explained in part as an effort to "restore" the Continental balance of power and as a manifestation of British isolationism. The naval agreement strengthened the German position with regard to the French alliance system and suggested to Mussolini that Italy must look to its own devices for protection against German expansionism. Under these conditions it could hardly be expected that Laval would respond with great enthusiasm to British proposals for French cooperation against the Italian Duce. While the naval agreement strengthened the German position against France, the Italo-French understanding strengthened Italy against Britain in East Africa and against Germany over Austria. British Conservative leadership, 1934–38, had no particular objection to an alteration of the Austrian *status quo*, provided it was not accomplished by violence. Nazi penetration of Austria, it was believed, would accentuate Italian dependence on England. With regard to the Austrian question, the Franco-Italian agreement tended to prevent the British from assuming an advantageous middle position between Italy and Germany.

Following orthodox British policy, Whitehall would press Italy only as far as it could lead another Continental power. But France under Laval had no intention of seriously endangering the Franco-Italian alliance or of risking war with Italy for the sake of British interests in the Mediterranean and Africa. On the other hand, the French Premier saw in the situation possibilities of promoting French interests, as he interpreted them. He hoped to maintain the Italian commitment against Germany intact while extracting a guarantee of Austrian independence from the British, the *quid pro quo* for a measure of support against Italy in the present crisis. His cynical maneuvers alienated both London and Rome. The British had no more intention of exposing themselves to the danger of fighting Germany for the French position in Central and Eastern Europe than did Laval of fighting Italy for British interests. Furthermore, Britain exploited her middle position between France and Germany by telling Laval flatly that if France did not cooperate against Italy, Britain might withdraw from Continental affairs. This

was a threat; it was also very close to being a policy. The British were protected by the Anglo-German Naval Treaty, and there was a conviction that the direction of German dynamism lay in east and southeast Europe where British interests were minor. Laval felt compelled to make some concessions to British demands. Italy hardly posed a mortal danger to Great Britain, but a remilitarized Germany did positively threaten France. Yet close cooperation between Britain and France was virtually impossible because each Government suspected the other. Mussolini made the most of Anglo-French differences and worked hard to prevent Laval from going completely into the British camp.

Such were the national policies of the three powers when another effort was made in August, 1935, to settle the Italian dispute with Ethiopia by peaceful means. On this occasion, Britain and France proposed a scheme that would have permitted Italian colonial settlement in parts of Ethiopia and a measure of Italian political and economic penetration of the rest. These last privileges were to be exercised under the supervision of the League, a body in which French and British influence was paramount. Consequently, Mussolini sensed another trap and flatly rejected the proposal; his anger at Laval and antipathy for the British increased accordingly.

Mussolini's attitude led the British Cabinet to apply more pressure against Italy, using the British fleet and the collective security apparatus of the League of Nations. A large armada of warships was sent into the Mediterranean and Sir Samuel Hoare made an electrifying speech before the League: apparently proponents of collective security action against Italy had found a champion. However, the fleet which steamed into the Mediterranean had only a short supply of antiaircraft ammunition and Valetta, the capital of Malta and only a short distance from Italian air fields, was without air defense. There was concern in London about the maneuverability of heavy British vessels in narrow seas. Consequently, the British Chiefs of Staff advised the Cabinet that the country was dangerously over-extended. This warning came before the fleet was sent into the Mediterranean and before Hoare's speech. In a word, therefore, the dramatic naval show of force was simply bluff.

There are indications that British policy in the League of Nations was not only that of bluff, but Machiavellian as well. On the day preceding Hoare's speech before the League Assembly, he and Laval had agreed that the League should take no action that would bring the danger of war with Italy. In any case, Whitehall believed that the League States probably would not follow British leadership in the matter anyway because few of their immediate and vital national interests were involved in the crisis. Why then did the British foreign policy planners decide to place the matter before the League and risk a rejection of British policy? The risk was taken because the political strategists of the Conservative Party were convinced that the Government had to endorse collective security against Italy in order to win an immediately forthcoming general election. Moreover, there is strong evidence that the Conservative leadership was of the opinion that Hoare's efforts in the League would fail. The views of both Hoare and Neville Chamberlain on this point are most instructive. Apparently, Chamberlain helped Hoare draft the League of Nations speech. The two men told L. S. Amery that sanctions would not involve the danger of war with Mussolini because only mild economic measures would be taken and that either Mussolini would succumb

to British pressure or the French would back out. Chamberlain told Lord Lloyd virtually the same thing, adding that anything was better than being drawn into a war in which Britain was too weak to fight. Should the sanctions program collapse, the Conservative Party could tell the electorate that it had done its best. However, as an instrument of collective security, the League of Nations would be destroyed.

While the British exerted themselves to mobilize the League in the name of collective security, they also made further efforts to bargain with the Duce. New proposals for the settlement of the Italo-Ethiopian dispute at the expense of Ethiopia were made to Mussolini between September 12 and 18. In this carrot and stick politics, while the stick became heavier, the carrot also became sweeter, but not appetizing enough from the Italian viewpoint. Mussolini buried the proposal by calling it "not only unacceptable but derisory." Consequently, there was no settlement and Fascist Italy invaded Ethiopia on October 3. Britain led the League in adopting a program of limited economic sanctions.

The British objective was to isolate Mussolini politically and make him more amenable to a settlement on British terms. But neither Britain nor France had any intention of adopting measures which might bring hostilities with Italy. On the other hand, because of the Anglo-French public commitment to collective security, an opportunity was presented to the smaller states to press for really effective sanctions. And the question of an embargo on oil and other strategic raw materials was raised by small power delegates at Geneva in mid-October. The small states tended to support collective security through the international organization because it offered a measure of protection for them against predatory great powers. League support for British leadership gave Whitehall some surprise. Britain and France were faced with the possibility that their hands might be forced. They had gone on record in support of an oil sanction, but Mussolini let it be known that the imposition of this sanction might bring an attack on the British fleet in the Mediterranean. He later boasted to the Germans that he was convinced that the British, a satiated and pacifistic people, would not risk a showdown with him. But Mussolini's politics were largely the politics of prestige; and it is more likely that the only way out, as he saw it, was to risk marching forward. Whatever Mussolini's motivations, his policy presented an acute dilemma to the British policy makers. The Conservative Party was returned to power in the election of November 14 partly because of its platform of support for League action against Italy, but, as has been noted, British service chiefs warned the Cabinet that Britain was not prepared for war. There was a further difficulty in the minds of some. Anglo-Italian hostilities might lead to the fall of Mussolini; Fascist Italy was looked on as a bulwark against a Red Italy.

By November, it was clear that the whole matter would soon come to a head, probably when the League met to decide on the oil sanction proposal. The obvious resolution of the British dilemma was to achieve a negotiated settlement with Italy beforehand, procure the acquiescence of Ethiopia, present it to the League as an agreement among the three powers and Ethiopia, and confidently expect ratification. In this way the principal internal and external political objectives of the Government in the situation would be achieved. Since negotiations leading to an agreement would be authorized by the League and the agreement ratified by the League, sufficient *pro forma* and procedural support for the Covenant would be given to fulfill the election promise of the Conservative Party.

If the position of the British leadership in the developing crisis was dangerous, that of the Italian Duce was precarious. Influential groups in Italy were working for his overthrow. Except for France under Laval, Italy was nearly isolated in the international community. Britain had been successful in aligning the League States behind its public policy, and the American Administration was doing what if felt it could to encourage effective League action against Italy. Responsible officials in Washington intimated that in the event of hostilities between Italy and England growing out of the Italo-Ethiopian war, the provisions of the Neutrality Act would not be extended to England. Hitler went so far as to offer German war equipment to the British. He probably wanted a bargain giving German support for sanctions against Italy in return for British support of his designs on Austria. There was some sympathy for this idea in London.

The Italians were aware that Laval was not to be relied upon in spite of his undertakings made at Rome earlier in the year, and it is clear that he intended to extract the maximum advantage for himself and for France from the crisis. His political position had been strengthened by the fact that both Britain and Italy had acquiesced in his role as an intermediary. Knowing that Laval was subjected to enormous pressure by the British, Rome renewed assurances that Italy would stand at the side of France against Germany. The Italians also heavily subsidized sections of the French press in order to influence French public opinion. To this pressure, Laval responded in kind. He gave the British the impression that he was pro-Italian, while causing the Italians to fear an Anglo-French deal at their expense. By this strategy, he sought to force each side to lower its demands so that a peaceful settlement, which was his objective, could be achieved. This would give all three powers more freedom of action to face the greatest threat to Europe: German militaristic revisionism.

Peaceful settlement of the Anglo-Italian dispute and of the Italo-Ethiopian War was in accordance with the interests of all three governments, as interpreted by those chiefly responsible for foreign policy formulation. And negotiations to this end began in Paris late in October, 1935, continued intermittently in November, and finally concluded with the Hoare-Laval Plan in early December. Consideration of oil sanctions by the League was postponed at the initiative of Laval to permit the working out of an agreement. During this period, each of the powers increased pressure on the others for the purpose of maximizing the satisfaction of national interests in a settlement. Britain urged the adoption of an oil sanction against Italy as a political tactic and, to guard against the possibility of an Italian "mad dog" attack against their fleet, sought to form a naval coalition in the Mediterranean with France as a member. The formation of such a coalition, however, was undesirable from Laval's standpoint because it would greatly strengthen the British hand in the Anglo-Italian crisis and diminish his influence as holder of the political balance of power between the two. There was apprehension in Paris that mobilization of the French fleet might bring serious internal disturbances; Laval, however, warned Mussolini that France would come to the assistance of Britain in case of an Italian attack. At the same time, he refused to make any positive commitment to Britain. On their part, the British attempted to increase their bargaining power in Paris by refusing consistently to give significant support for French security against Germany beyond that already on the books. They warned Laval, as already noted, that failure to support British policy against Mus-

solini might result in their withdrawal from Continental affairs.

Mussolini countered the British threat of oil sanctions with his own threat against the British fleet. He was fully aware of the danger of an oil embargo to his campaign in Ethiopia and told Hitler in 1938 that had one been imposed, he would have had to withdraw in a week. The Duce made strenuous efforts to prevent an Anglo-French agreement at his expense. Laval was informed that Italy stood squarely behind the Franco-Italian accord of January against Hitler, but that it would be a dead letter if Laval made a deal with England in the present crisis. On his side, Laval told the Italian negotiator in Paris that unless Italy agreed to British proposals, he would resign.

Such were the pressures exerted by the three powers on each other during the course of the conversations in Paris that led to the Hoare-Laval Plan. Sir Maurice Peterson, head of the Ethiopian Department of the Foreign Office, began negotiations on the British side. He was authorized to offer the concessions Mussolini had turned down in August, but began the discussions by proposing a solution, even less favorable from the Italian point of view, based on the plan which the Duce had rejected in June. Obviously, nothing could be accomplished on this basis and Peterson was given a new set of instructions. By this time, Whitehall was convinced that Mussolini would win in Ethiopia and the General Staff felt that there was nothing the Army could do about it. Possibly the British were impressed by the fact that General Badoglio, frequently regarded as the finest staff officer in Europe, was taking over command of the Italian forces in Africa.

In Paris, bargaining began in greater earnest. Mussolini had already let Laval know his minimum terms; but the latter, in dealing with the British, raised them. Because of their distrust of Laval, the British made an attempt in the first days of December to deal with Mussolini directly and sent more acceptable proposals to Rome. The decisive negotiations, however, continued in Paris where Sir Samuel Hoare and Sir Robert Vansittart took over from Peterson.

There is no need to make a detailed examination of the Hoare-Laval Plan here. An analysis of its provisions can be found in Arnold Toynbee's *Survey of International Affairs, 1935,* Volume II. With one minor exception, Italy was permitted to annex all the territory she had occupied in the north and southeast of Ethiopia. In addition, she was given a vast area in the south and central part of the country for economic exploitation. At the last moment, Laval insisted that this area be larger than even Mussolini demanded in his minimum terms. Peterson had tentatively set the western boundary of the zone of economic exploitation along the 40th meridian. The French negotiator St. Quentin had advocated the 38th, while Mussolini demanded the 37th. Then Laval suddenly insisted that Hoare agree to the 35th, as he did. Finally, the proposal envisaged that Ethiopia should receive the port of Assab in Eritrea, an adjacent Italian colony, together with a strip of territory connecting the port with Ethiopia. There is evidence of an Anglo-French understanding at Laval's insistence that the Ethiopians were not to build a railroad in this corridor, since it would compete with the French-owned Addis Ababa-Djibouti line, Ethiopia's only railway contact with a sea port.

Such were the principal provisions of the Hoare-Laval Plan. It gave the aggressor more than he had, but less than he could take. The taking, however, would require a substantial investment of men, time, and money. Laval was in frequent telephonic communication with Mussolini, and it was understood that the Duce was favorably inclined toward the proposal. It marked the collapse of the British politics of rigorous pressure against Italy. Mussolini had called the British bluff, and the British were unwilling to run the risk that he was not bluffing. Settlement of the Anglo-Italian crisis would very likely have proceeded according to the Plan or something similar, but allegedly Laval arranged matters so that it was leaked to the press. Vansittart suggests that Laval's purpose was to destroy the proposal by exposing it to the public opinion which he anticipated would be hostile. However, Laval was perturbed and apparently surprised by the adverse reaction in Great Britain, and called Vansittart to the Quai d'Orsay in the middle of the night to explain the situation. If Laval was indeed responsible for the leak, it was more likely that he feared a bilateral settlement of the crisis without French participation. He knew that both governments were angry with him; he could hardly have been ignorant of the London-Rome exchange of views just a few days before. Therefore, he might have considered it expedient to have the proposal publicized as promptly as possible so that he could make the maximum capital in domestic and international politics of his successful role as mediator between Italy and England. In any case, a certain amount of Anglo-Italian animosity was probably desirable to Laval; it gave him an advantageous bargaining position with respect to both.

The Hoare-Laval Plan was accepted by the British Cabinet, then rejected following an explosion of public indignation against it. After all, the new Government had been elected on the basis of a platform which included a promise of support for collective security through the League. Hoare became the scapegoat and resigned, but was soon back in the Cabinet as First Lord of the Admiralty, and a few years later joined Neville Chamberlain, Sir John Simon, and Viscount Halifax as a member of the Inner Cabinet which shaped the course of British foreign policy in the year before World War II.

The victory of Mussolini in the crisis with England firmly established Italy as a great power. This status was acquired in the usual way: by inflicting a defeat on another great power. Here the defeat was political; it was nonetheless real, for the political battle was fought with great intensity on both sides. The outcome of the crisis could hardly have been more tragic. Formulation of the Hoare-Laval Plan destroyed the League as a collective security organization, for it showed that British and French support for collective action against Italy was largely a sham. Thereafter, small states in the League became more fearful of being drawn into the games of the big powers; they looked outside the League for security. The Plan's premature exposure in Paris as well as the orientation of French policy in the crisis confirmed opinions in London that France was unstable and untrustworthy. Repudiation of the Plan prevented a possible reconciliation between Italy and the Western powers. It was Hitler who exploited these divisions, marching into the Rhineland in March, 1936. Thereafter he maneuvered to maintain them, for unity of policy against him would have frustrated his grandiose dreams. Following the collapse of the Plan, the oil sanction proposal was gradually shelved and Mussolini's legions entered Addis Ababa in May, 1936. In the meantime, Japan took advantage of the turmoil in Europe to make a further penetration of North China.

Is it possible to account for the failure of British policy which was manifested in the Hoare-Laval Plan and its reception in England? A hypothesis can be suggested on the basis of available evidence. It is that the foreign policy decision-making process was impaired by amateurism, debility, and indifference in high places, the willingness of politicians to use foreign policy matters as expedient tactics in domestic politics, and the disparity between the public and private attitudes of British leaders toward the crisis. There was a tendency in London not to take the Italians very seriously, politically, economically, or militarily. Apparently, the Conservative policy makers believed that Italy must inevitably bend before the British will. The history of English relations with Italy since unification would indeed tend to support this view; as late as 1923, Mussolini had evacuated Corfu following British pressure. Nevertheless, this was more supposition than a calculated evaluation. It would appear that the attitude prevented a realistic appraisal of Mussolini's determination and Italian strength in 1935 until after the Cabinet had made a public policy commitment based on an invalid estimate of Italian weakness. Then the election promises of the Conservatives and press campaigns in both countries made an alteration of this policy very difficult. Hence the secrecy of the Anglo-French conversations in Paris and the uproar which in England followed the disclosure of the Plan.

In the first months of the crisis, Ramsay MacDonald, the Prime Minister, was so infirm that at times he was practically inarticulate; his mind, writes Vansittart, being "no longer equal to public tests." MacDonald's Foreign Minister, Simon, would not say either yes or no to the Italians regarding their ambitions in East Africa. British prestige was so high that there was no need to bolster its military underpinnings; complacency was general in 1935. A change in the government was imminent and Simon's foreign policy drifted along. MacDonald was succeeded by Stanley Baldwin who was more willing to endorse foreign policy as a tactical maneuver in domestic policies to win an election than to give direction to foreign policy matters *per se*. He had little interest in or knowledge of foreign affairs and was inclined to temporize when faced with difficult policy decisions. According to A. L. Rowse, he said some years later that he was physically incapable of holding office. When Hoare left for Paris in early December, 1935, to negotiate the Plan, the burden of Baldwin's instructions was to prevent war by whatever means. This was not foreign policy; it was an acknowledgment of political bankruptcy.

Such being the attitudes and capabilities of Baldwin, it was particularly unfortunate that his Foreign Minister, Hoare, came to office with little experience in the foreign field. Secretary of State for India in the preceding MacDonald Cabinet, he was utterly exhausted after guiding the Government of India Act through the House of Commons. The critical negotiations with Laval in December were conducted by a man so overworked that he was subject to what Baldwin called "fainting fits." As a matter of fact, Hoare stopped in Paris while en route to Switzerland for a rest leave to repair his health. This inexperienced and exhausted Foreign Secretary found himself in the fall and early winter of 1935 face to face with the most serious challenge to British imperial and prestige interests by a European power since World War I. He had little guidance from his chief whose eyes were fixed on the November elections. Moreover, the same preoccupation prevented the Cabinet from giving much attention to the crisis in the critical months of October and November.

Hoare did have the assistance of Anthony Eden, then Minister for League of Nations Affairs. But there is no evidence that Eden played a prominent role in foreign policy making during this period. He was the Government's spokesman in Geneva for the public policy of support for the League. The Permanent Under Secretary in the Foreign Office was Sir Robert Vansittart, a man of exceptional brilliance and experience who wrote at the end of his life that "I can recall no major issue on which my advice was taken." The principal preoccupation of Vansittart during this period was to prevent Austria from falling into the hands of Hitler. He had long since taken the measure of Nazism as an ominously powerful and disruptive force in European affairs, as evidenced by an extraordinary memorandum which he wrote shortly after Hitler came to power. While he was anti-German, he was certainly not pro-Italian and furthermore was among those who in the first part of the crisis held a dim view of Italian capabilities. When it became evident, however, that Mussolini regarded the danger of an imminent Nazi penetration of Austria as less serious to Italian interests than a failure of the Ethiopian adventure, Vansittart was willing to sacrifice Ethiopia to Mussolini in the hope that the latter would resume his role as the protector of Austria. Actually, Mussolini probably regarded his position against Germany over Austria as stronger in 1935 than in 1934 because of the alliance with Laval's France. During the Austrian crisis of 1934, neither Britain nor France gave much political support to his military demonstration at the Brenner. The Duce believed that Hitler would require several years more to complete his war preparations. This would give Italy a short time in which to augment her power and prestige through colonial enterprises in order to face the international crisis he saw looming over the European horizon. In the meantime, he threatened to deal with Hitler by making it clear that Italy, alone, would not undertake the preservation of Austrian independence.

When the crisis came to a head in early December, 1935, therefore, Baldwin wanted compromise and peace with Italy at almost any price for want of a policy, while Vansittart accepted compromise to support a policy of promoting the containment of Germany. He thought it vital to prevent Austria from falling into Hitler's hands either through Italian weakness or an Italo-German bargain. Compromise and settlement with Italy, however, were made impossible because the British public had elected a government which had publicly committed itself to the coercion of Italy through the League. British policy therefore fell between two stools. One difficulty was that the collective commitment of the Government was more domestic than foreign policy and that it could not be openly and dramatically repudiated. Another was that the global security requirements of Britain exceeded by far its existing military strength. This was a principal malaise of the democracies during the 1930's. Anglo-Italian hostilities in the Mediterranean might have permitted either Japanese action in North China, an area of important British commercial interests, or German aggression in Europe. But it was not until late October or early November that such military consider-ations became decisive factors in policy formation. Until that time it was felt that Italy could be coerced into a settlement in spite of military deficiencies.

This account must close on a tentative note. The failure of British pressure on Mussolini in Paris is largely to be explained by the unwillingness of Britain to test his threat of armed reprisal in the event of an oil sanction. British military unpreparedness was undoubtedly the prime factor here. However, it is to be noted that while Baldwin received an authorization to rearm in the November elections, he proceeded very slowly in this direction. One is struck, moreover, by the totality of Hoare's capitulation in the Paris negotiations. There are indications that more subterranean currents were at work in shaping policy. At the end of November and the first days of December, British industrial and financial interests exerted strong pressure on the Cabinet to avoid a conflict and the oil sanction which might precipitate it. The identity of such interests can only be the subject of speculation. But it may be noted that the International Petroleum Cartel, which had controlled roughly 75 per cent of the Italian market since 1928, would certainly be apprehensive about the upsetting effects of an oil sanction.

While Britain and France moved to accommodate Mussolini, the United States remained aloof. What were the obligations of that country in the crisis? HERBERT FEIS (b. 1893) believes that in failing to intervene in Europe to halt aggressions the United States was evading her basic responsibility. In failing to use her power to act as the balancer of power, she committed, at the least, a sin of omission. Feis, a member of Princeton's Institute for Advanced Studies and a former member of the State Department policy planning staff, has written extensively on foreign policy: *The Road to Pearl Harbour* (1950), *The China Tangle* (1953), *Churchill, Roosevelt, Stalin* (1957), *Foreign Aid and Foreign Policy* (1964), and *Seen from E.A.* (1947), from which this selection is taken.*

Herbert Feis

The American Circuit of Indecision

During the whole period—in which Italian aggression was prepared and begun—Washington was an important station in the circuit of indecision. It is time to take account of what had been occurring there.

To the Italian dictator the American course was of the utmost importance. He seems to have felt assured that the mistrust pervading the relations between the states of Europe would prevent collective action to check him, unless some outside power bolstered the attempt. There was only one country strong enough and free enough to turn the balance of events against him, if it so willed—the United States.

The peoples of Europe prayed that the Americans would provide the supporting strength to defend them against the demanding threats that issued from Rome and Berlin. Over all the roads of Europe apparitions appeared at dawn and night— of dirty, haggard men in muddy uniforms limping towards the trenches, of exhausted and frightened women and children trudging out of destroyed towns. To the imaginative, the throats of Mussolini and Hitler poured forth not human words, but mud and lice and pieces of bloody flesh.

The governments of Europe did not give way to such fantasies or tremors. But as they probed to see how much they could rely on one another in any joint effort to check Mussolini, they peered in the direction of the United States. They knew the state of American opinion well enough to

*From *Seen from E.A.*, by Herbert Feis. Copyright 1946 by Indiana University. Reprinted by permission of Alfred A. Knopf, Inc. Pp. 218–232.

realize that the United States would not keep in regular step with them. They accepted the evidence that the American people were bent upon believing that European quarrels were of little concern to them and beyond their power to reconcile. They responded to intimations that if openly asked to act with the League, the American government would look the other way. But as soon as the League began to consider ways and means of halting Italian aggression, two most practical questions arose in regard to American policy: First, if economic sanctions were applied, would the United States render them futile by supplying economic aid to Italy? Second, if as an outcome of the use of sanctions, Italy attacked members of the League, would the United States be an indifferent and difficult neutral, a benevolent friend, or an ally?

The League members were left to the end to guess the full answers to these questions. They were compelled by use of the telescope to discern what they could from obscure actions and smoky explanations.

During the summer months of 1935, when Italian intentions were becoming obvious, neither the American people nor the American government were moved to take any step that might seriously deter Mussolini. Many Americans sensed uneasily that deadly evil was being given a new passport into the world. But the country as a whole either misunderstood or evaded the coming crisis. We restricted ourselves to some half measures gauged, at one and the same time, to absolve us of any charge of defeating collective action and lessen the chance of being drawn into dispute with any belligerent. A wish to avoid responsibility, rather than any positive will to play a part in defeating aggression, governed our swaying policy.

The request, made in July by the Ethiopian government that we invoke the pact of Paris against Italy, had met only sympathetic evasion. The State Department, during the following week, pursued a conventional diplomatic course. In various ways it made plain to the Italian government that it was disturbed by the dangerous drift of events. It dwelt upon the rewards and virtues of peace and urged Italy to be moderate. But at the same time it discreetly took care to see that the foreign offices of Great Britain and France did not misinterpret these *démarches*. Ways were found to make sure that they were not to be taken as a promise for a new attempt to draw us into joint responsibility.

While the failure of the League at mediation was becoming plain, the President on July 24 responded to intensely active agitation throughout the country. He asked Congress to consider "neutrality" legislation. A few days thereafter (July 26), he lapsed into the remark that the Italo-Ethiopian dispute was not of direct concern to the United States. On August 1, he expressed the hope that the Council of the League would succeed in settling the issues that had arisen. This wish could have been met as well by a settlement that gave in to Italy as by a firm refusal to do so. These actions were expressions of a transient half belief that the United States might wisely pursue an isolated course—no matter who gained power and mastery elsewhere.

But they also suited a purpose. That was to keep control of the making of foreign policy in the face of an effort, within Congress and outside, to impose upon the Executive rigid rules of isolation, amounting almost to nonintercourse. It was feared that any overt measure of encouragement to the League to repress Italy would strengthen the position of the advocates of isolation.

It was deemed certain that any action that aligned the United States with the League, even before it was known whether

Great Britain and France would defend the principles of the League, would provoke a bitter internal conflict. In their earlier days, many of the officials that were now compelled to decide how to act in this crisis of aggression had witnessed closely the failure and death of Woodrow Wilson. The popular mood seemed far more averse to any venture in co-operation than in 1919. They were afraid of repeating his failure.

Several groups in Congress vied with each other in order to secure the credit for the new policy of peace. The Senate Committee on Foreign Relations, the House Committee on Foreign Affairs, and the group of extreme isolationists led by Nye and Clarke, each sprang forward with a program designed to keep us clear of foreign strife. All refused to admit that the American people had an earnest concern with any foreign dispute, or a possible great interest in its outcome. It was as though they thought there could be no rights or wrongs of consequence to us outside the Western Hemisphere, no purpose ever in taking up arms, no hope of trustful co-operation between nations.

The Senators in their visits to the White House met no opposition to their plans for the enactment of some new form of neutrality legislation. The Secretary of State and some of his staff smouldered with doubt in regard to what was under way. But this was permitted to appear only as a faint glow. The Senate combinations seemed strong enough to defeat any Secretary of State on this question, and, if his opposition was vigorous, to destroy him. Therefore, such powers of persuasion as he possessed were gently employed towards trying to obtain in the prospective legislation some discretion for the Executive. But that is exactly what the extreme and powerful isolationist and anti-British wing of the Senate was determined to deny.

Congress passed and the President signed the Neutrality Resolution in August 1935 while the League was permitting Italy to complete its military measures. The timing of our action was influenced by discernment that Italy was about to break the world's peace; and that the League would either have to knuckle down or to fight. In either event, embarrassing difficulties were foreseen—which, it was thought, might be "shooed" away by *prior* proclamation of our isolation.

Despite the enthusiastic furor with which the Neutrality Resolution was rushed through Congress, a sense remained in many minds that the subject had not been thoroughly considered. Therefore, it was made effective only until February 29, 1936. This temporary legislation was counted upon by its advocates to guarantee the good behavior of the President during the prospective recess of Congress. . . .

The Neutrality Resolution made it mandatory upon the President, on finding that a state of war existed to prohibit the sale or export of "arms, ammunition, and implements of war" to all belligerents. Americans were left free to trade in all other products—including many no less essential for war. The dividing line was arbitrary. It reflected the fact that not even the isolationist Senators were ready to push their theory of peace to the point where it might seriously disturb American economic life.

The actual substance of the Neutrality Resolution had little immediate importance. Its passage, nevertheless, had great significance. For it seemed to reveal what the American attitude would be toward the critical issues that were shaping up in the Italo-Ethiopian dispute. It seemed to mean, first, that if foreign countries found themselves at war—whether in support of their obligations as members of the League or in self-defense—they could not count upon the United States to supply weapons. And second, if they refused, as a sanction, to trade with the aggressor, it was doubtful whether the United States would do the same. In that case, the whole idea of economic sanctions grew hollow; only blockade could prevail, and that meant war.

True, this was a hasty interpretation of the ultimate significance of the passage of the resolution; palmistry, rather than penetration. But only those with deep insight into the intelligence and moral nature of the American people could have been expected to dispute it. Ironically this interpretation was longer maintained in Berlin than in London; it contributed to fatal German misjudgment of the ultimate American course.

The passage of the Neutrality Resolution dampened the spirit of resistance to Mussolini. As reported by Birchell in the *New York Times* of August 26, the resolution "disappointed and even discouraged many here (London) who had hoped for United States cooperation in compelling the truculent to keep the peace. Coming during a period when the League members were wavering between their conciliation efforts and proposals to apply collective punitive action to Italy, it must have justified doubt in those circles of European government, as to the wisdom or significance of such punitive action."

But it is also certain that the action of the American government was not the main reason for the hesitation of the League. Almost none of its members were ready to fight Italy.

A strong element in British opinion clamored for collective action. But many of its public advocates seemed to infer that this form of action was a sort of magical prescription that would safely and painlessly dispose of any evil-doer. They seemed to think that condemnatory words, if hurled in unison, would halt dictators. Few spokesmen asked their fellow countrymen bluntly if they were willing, if need should be, to go to war against the Blackshirts. And the British military establishment, even its navy, was unready for immediate action. Nervousness seems to have entered even into the paneled rooms of the admiralty. The mementos of past valor and victories did not entirely dissipate fear that the Italian fleet might be able to gain control over the eastern Mediterranean and the direct route to India. Or if that fear was dismissed, the thought was left that a damaged fleet might someday soon have to deal with a stronger enemy. In the Foreign Office there was a great reluctance to smash the Stresa front, which had been formed against Germany by such hard diplomatic labors. The hope lingered that Italy might be retained as a useful ally.

And France was resisting all suggestion of pressure on Italy with a firmness that aroused mistrust, as well it might. The government of Laval showed itself determined to avoid any quarrel with Italy that would rupture their relations. He was prepared, if need be, to sacrifice the League in favor of his understanding with Mussolini. French opinion was wavering and divided. There were many—especially among the Left parties—who were devoted believers in the cause of the League, friends of all that was humane, and enemies of all that was cruel. But they were mostly men skilled only in the argument and appeal of the classroom or political meetings; they had not yet lived in the maquis and been toughened to the use of arms; and they did not control French opinion or their government. Fear of Germany reconciled many Frenchmen to Laval's open effort to serve Mussolini; fear of Russia brought approval from many others; fear of again experiencing the dreadful sorrow and suffering of war, most of all. Laval could warn that there would be civil war in France if that country was called upon to fight Italy. His opponents could not threaten that there would be civil war if the League bowed before Fascism.

This was the main gambit of doubt and deception that kept England wavering and France evasive. It was why they and the other countries of Europe failed to form a quick and effective combination in the League to halt Italy. However, each item of doubt gained extra weight because of the judgment that the United States would either stand aside, or even make such an attempt more difficult and dangerous. The passage of the Neutrality Resolution confirmed that possibility.

In the interval between the passage of the Neutrality Resolution and the Italian invasion of Ethiopia, American policy continued to be as elusive as notes dancing in air. The Italian proclamations of defiance were becoming noisier and noisier. Reports on the tangled talks between the British and French governments produced complete uncertainty in Washington as to what to expect at Geneva. The American government supplemented the confusion of counsel in Europe by diffuse and inconclusive explanations of its own. The Secretary of State on September 12 circulated a detailed account of the record of the American government, vis-à-vis the Italian-Ethiopian dispute. This was intended both as a defense for our policy and an indirect means of renewing our plea that peace should not be broken. Its long explanations left only a sense of emptiness. It did not affect the course of events in any way. Nor did the repetition of the plea for peace which was made by the President on the following day.

The vague utterances were disregarded. The American multigraph machine failed.

Hoping it knew not what, the American government waited for the next event. It waited uneasily. For the perception that only collective action could really safeguard future peace for the United States, though dismissed, would not quit the mind. A vague realization that the outcome of the League crisis would affect our future would not fade.

Alas, when the wait was ended by the Italian invasion of Ethiopia on October 3, it was succeeded only by a greater agony of indecision. . . .

We had missed any chance decisively to influence events before the crisis. We had remained aloof while they shaped into an Italian threat not only against Ethiopia but against the whole League system. Then on the very eve of the clash we merely issued a statement urging all countries to support economic and world peace. Its inchoate stream of language seemed to suggest that the ultimate causes of the episode were economic and that if only trade barriers were removed, the aggressive pressure for political change would vanish. It was as though we thought that by holding up high the scales of abstract justice disputants would come into court and bring their sins with them. Circumstances of the moment did not justify the thought.

Now events began to compel the government to move from the court of comment to the field of decision. Of the many aspects of the problem before the American government only one was clear. It was agreed by all that the President was bound to recognize that war had come and apply the Neutrality Resolution. But the problem arose as to when to do so. Italy had issued no declaration of war; that country was still hoping that the world would shut its ears to the noise of exploding bombs. The League of Nations was in a state of pause. Should the American government be the first to affirm that war existed? There was room for query as to what immediate consequences might flow from that formal action. Would it make it more difficult for Italy to draw back? Would it embarrass last-minute efforts of the League to halt the fighting by conciliation?

Behind these perplexities lay further ones. If the government applied the Neutrality Resolution and did nothing more, how might the later conduct of Italy and the League be affected? Would this step be taken to mean that we intended otherwise to ignore the Italian aggression, to give up all thought of dealing with it? Would this be a true reading of what the country might later decide to do? The executive was in no position to encourage hope that we would help effectively in any joint effort to stop Italy, but most Americans were ready to applaud the efforts of other countries to do so. Would an unsupplemented announcement of American neutrality give reluctant members of the League an acceptable reason for inaction? Would it enable them to place the blame for failure of the League upon the United States?

The government craved a course of action that would be without consequence on external events. It wished for a line that could neither be attacked as calculated encouragement to the League to proceed with sanctions against Italy, nor used by unwilling members of the League as an excuse for not doing so. The lawyers of the State Department labored to supply a garment of formulas within which we could shrink.

Their task was made more difficult by the knowledge that Congress would insist that we deal with *all* belligerents on the same terms. Suppose the executive action went outside the Neutrality Resolution and tried, for example, to repress the flow of American war materials to Italy. Would

it find itself driven to deny them also to England and France, if these countries found themselves at war with Italy?

The meetings of disturbed officials during the days that followed the invasion of Ethiopia were a convention hall of these queries. Every single one of them paraded around under its own banner. The President was away from Washington. Views had to be discussed over the telephone and telegraph when he could be reached.

On the one point that was clear, decision was prompt. The President and the Secretary of State concluded to recognize that war existed without waiting for the League to do so, and to place the mandatory provisions of the Neutrality Resolution into effect. It was their plain duty under the law so to act. The possibility that this precedent might later be regretted would have to be disregarded. Immediate application of the resolution had still another attraction to minds caught in a multiple spray of cold doubt; it would serve as a proof of the contention that had been carefully maintained by the State Department that American action was independent of that of other nations.

This decision was made in the face of an urgent plea of the American Minister at Geneva to delay. He was opposed to an American declaration that war existed before the Council of the League affirmed it. He feared the stain of responsibility on our cuff if we moved our hand first.

During the days of October 4 and 5, when the proclamations were being prepared, forecasts in Washington of what the Council might decide to do were scant and confused. The British government was in the direct line of conflict. Thus, when the proclamations were ready, it was thought a reasonable precaution and courtesy to afford it a chance to object to their immediate issuance. No objection was made.

The President proceeded to declare that

"a state of war unhappily exists between Ethiopia and the Kingdom of Italy." One proclamation was issued prohibiting shipment of arms, ammunition, and implements of war to the belligerents. Another requested American citizens not to travel on the ships of belligerents and stated that if they did so it was at their own risk.

In announcing this action, and in all later expositions of our course throughout the espisode, the State Department emphasized that they were taken in entire independence of other countries. Any suggestion that heed was being taken of events at Geneva was indignantly denied; and contention that it was our duty to prevent Italian aggression was answered with silence. The country was repeatedly informed that the government had but one thought or aim—to "keep out of war."

This explanation of the basis of our policy was irritating to all except those American officials who were in the center of the buffeting storm. It was immune from direct objection. It conformed to the prevailing American opinion that joint action with other countries would "involve" us in war. It made it possible to avoid a debate that would almost certainly have been lost;

whether or not the security and welfare of the United States demanded a concert of action with foreign powers.

Here in this Ethiopian dispute were born the verbal formulas that were used to explain and defend many important actions of the Executive during the troubled years ahead—first, that they were independently conceived and taken, and second, that they were designed solely to keep the United States out of war. By their use it was possible for American diplomacy to achieve a measure of freedom from the restraints of ignorance and lethargy. But they failed ever to direct the full force of American influence or power to prevent developments that made war inevitable. Friends were left without assurance. Foes could form the belief that the American instinct for greatness, hatred of evil, and shrewdness had lapsed. But the bitter unwillingness of American opinion to mingle in foreign disputes exacted from their leaders this insufficient and misleading version of the realities they had to take into account.

Hauling up this confused and confusing banner, then, in the summer of 1935, we marched towards events.

A master of St. Catherine's and a vice-chancellor of Oxford, ALAN BULLOCH (b. 1914) discusses the effect of the Ethiopian crisis on Adolf Hitler. Like Wheeler-Bennett, Bulloch sees that appeasement of the German Führer began before appeasement of the Duce, but he writes that the Ethiopian crisis provided Hitler "with the opportunity to extend his power outside the German frontiers of 1914." Each dictator profited from the other's actions: Hitler profited from British and French concern over Mussolini's acts in the Mediterranean, and Mussolini profited from British and French concern about Hitler's rearmament program. Bulloch's study of Hitler has been described as one of the best books written on Nazi Germany.*

Alan Bulloch

The Crisis and Hitler

[Hitler's ideas for aggressive war] did not depend upon the triumphs of 1938–41 for their conception. They can be traced from the pages of *Mein Kampf,* through the conversations recorded by Rauschning in 1932–4, up to the talks in the Führer's H.Q. in 1941–2 and Himmler's wartime addresses to the S.S. But in 1933–4, in the first year or two after Hitler had come to power, the prospects of accomplishing even the annexation of Austria, still less of overrunning Russia, appeared remote. Germany was politically isolated. Economically, she was only beginning to recover from the worst slump in her history. Her army, limited to the hundred thousand men permitted by the Treaty, was easily outnumbered by that of France alone. A move in any direction—in the west,

against Austria, Czechoslovakia, or Poland—appeared certain to run into the network of alliances with which France sought to strengthen her security. So impressed were the German diplomats and the German generals with the strength of the obstacles in Germany's way that up to 1938, and indeed up to the Battle of France in 1940, their advice was always on the side of caution.

Hitler, on the other hand, became more and more sure of himself, more and more contemptuous of the professionals' advice. He was convinced that he had a far keener appreciation of political—or military—factors than the High Command or the Foreign Office, and he dazzled them by the brilliant success of the bold tactics he adopted. Hitler took office as Chancellor

*From pp. 319–321, 330–341 in *Hitler, A Study in Tyranny,* Completely Revised Edition, by Alan Bulloch. Copyright ©1962 by Alan Bulloch. Reprinted by permission of Harper & Row, Publishers, and the Hamlyn Publishing Group Limited. Footnotes omitted.

without any previous experience of government. He had never even been a Reichstag deputy, leave alone a minister. He had no knowledge of any country outside Germany and Austria, and spoke no foreign language. His sole experience of politics had been as a Party leader and agitator. He knew nothing and cared less for official views and traditions; he was suspicious of anyone who might try to instruct him. In the short run, these were assets. He refused to be impressed by the strength of the opposition his schemes were likely to meet, or to be restricted to the conventional methods of diplomacy. He displayed a skill in propaganda and a mastery of deceit, a finesse in exploring the weaknesses of his opponents and a crudeness in exploiting the strength of his own position which he had learned in the struggle for power in Germany and which he now applied to international relations with even more remarkable results.

This is not to suggest that Hitler, any more than Bismarck in the 1860s, foresaw in 1933 exactly how events would develop in the course of the next decade. No man was more of an opportunist, as the Nazi-Soviet Pact shows. No man had more luck. But Hitler knew how to turn events to his advantage. He knew what he wanted and he held the initiative. His principal opponents, Great Britain and France, knew only what they did not want—war—and were always on the defensive. The fact that Hitler was ready to risk war, and started preparing for it from the day he came to power, gave him a still greater advantage. Disinclined to bestir themselves, the British and the French were eager to snatch at any hope of avoiding a conflict and only too ready to go on believing in Hitler's pacific assurances. . . .

From the summer of 1934 the principal object of the Western Powers' diplomacy was to persuade Germany to sign a pact of mutual assistance covering Eastern Europe. Just as the Locarno Pact included France, Germany, Belgium, Great Britain, and Italy, each undertaking to come to the immediate aid of France and Belgium, or Germany, if either side were attacked by the other, so this Eastern Locarno would include Russia, Germany, Poland, Czechoslovakia, and the other states of Eastern Europe and would involve the same obligation of automatic assistance in the case of an attack.

Hitler had no intention of entering into any such scheme: it was not aggression that he feared, but checks upon his freedom of action. His preference—for obvious reasons—was for bilateral agreements, and if he were to sign a multilateral pact of non-aggression it would only be one from which all provisions for mutual aid had been removed, a statement of good intentions unsupported by any guarantees to enforce them. German opposition, which had already been made clear in 1934, was powerfully assisted by that of Poland. Pilsudski was highly suspicious of Russia and anxious that Poland should not be pushed into the front line of an anti-German combination—which could only mean that Poland would be either the battleground of a new clash between her two neighbours or the victim of a deal concluded between them at her expense, as happened in 1939. Polish quarrels with Lithuania and dislike of Czechoslovakia added further reasons to his reluctance to enter any such all-embracing project. Pilsudski, and his successor Beck, saw the only way out of Poland's difficulties as a policy of balancing between Moscow and Berlin, a policy which fatally overestimated Poland's strength, and fatally underestimated the danger from Germany.

Hitler courted the Poles assiduously, constantly urging on them the common interest Poland and Germany had in opposing Russia. "Poland," he told the Polish

Ambassador in November 1933, "is an outpost against Asia. . . . The other States should recognize this role of Poland's."

Göring, who was used by Hitler in the role of a candid friend of the Poles, spoke even more plainly when he visited Warsaw at the end of January 1935. He began his conversations in the Polish Foreign Ministry by mentioning the possibility of a new partition of Poland by agreement between Germany and Russia. But he did this only to dismiss it as a practical impossibility: in fact, he continued, Hitler's policy needed a strong Poland, to form a common barrier with Germany against the Soviet Union. In his talks with Polish generals and with Marshal Pilsudski, Göring "outlined far-reaching plans, almost suggesting an anti-Russian alliance and a joint attack on Russia. He gave it to be understood that the Ukraine would become a Polish sphere of influence and North-western Russia would be Germany's." The Poles were wary of such seductive propositions, but they were impressed by the friendliness of the German leaders, and in the course of 1935 relations between the two governments became steadily closer. Göring visited Cracow for Pilsudski's funeral in May. The same month Hitler himself had a long conversation with the Ambassador, and after a visit of the Polish Foreign Minister, Colonel Beck, to Berlin in July the communiqué spoke of "a far-reaching agreement of views." The attention Hitler paid to Polish-German relations was to repay him handsomely.

Meanwhile, the British and French Governments renewed their attempts to reach a settlement with Germany. The Saar plebiscite in January 1935 had produced a ninety per cent vote for the return of the territory to Germany. The result had scarcely been in doubt, although the Nazis cried it up inside Germany as a great victory and the destruction of the first of the Versailles fetters. The removal of this issue between France and Germany, which Hitler had constantly described as the one territorial issue dividing them, seemed to offer a better chance of finding the Führer in a more reasonable mood.

The proposals which the British and French Ambassadors presented to Hitler at the beginning of February 1935 sketched the outline of a general settlement which would cover the whole of Europe. The existing Locarno Pact of mutual assistance, which applied to Western Europe, was to be strengthened by the conclusion of an agreement to cover unprovoked aggression from the air. At the same time it was to be supplemented by two similar pacts of mutual assistance, one dealing with Eastern Europe, the other with Central Europe.

Hitler faced a difficult decision. German rearmament had reached a stage where further concealment would prove a hindrance. It seemed clear from their proposals that the Western Powers would be prepared to waive their objections to German rearmament in return for Germany's accession to their proposals for strengthening and extending collective security. Against that Hitler had to set his anxiety to avoid tying his hands, and his need of some dramatic stroke of foreign policy to gratify the mood of nationalist expectation in Germany which had so far received little satisfaction. On both these grounds a bold unilateral repudiation of the disarmament clauses of the Treaty of Versailles would suit him very much better than negotiations with the Western Powers, in which he would be bound to make concessions in return for French and British agreement. Could he afford to take the risk?

Hitler's first reply showed uncertainty. He welcomed the idea of extending the original Locarno Pact to include attack from the air, while remaining evasive on the question of the proposed Eastern and Danubian Pacts. The German Government invited the British to continue discussions, and a visit to Berlin by the British Foreign Minister, Sir John Simon, was arranged for 7 March. Before the visit could take place, however, on 4 March the British Government published its own plans for increased armaments, basing this on "the fact that Germany was . . . rearming openly on a large scale, despite the provisions of Part V of the Treaty of Versailles." The British White Paper went on to remark "that not only the forces, but the spirit in which the population, and especially the youth of the country, are being organized, lend colour to, and substantiate, the general feeling of insecurity which has already been incontestably generated." Great indignation was at once expressed in Germany, and Hitler contracted a "chill" which made it necessary to postpone Sir John Simon's visit. On the 9th the German Government officially notified foreign governments that a German Air Force was already in existence. This seems to have been a kite with which to test the Western Powers' reaction. As Sir John Simon told the House of Commons that he and Mr Eden were still proposing to go to Berlin and nothing else happened, it appeared safe to risk a more sensational announcement the next week-end. On 16 March 1935, the German Government proclaimed its intention of re-introducing conscription and building up a peacetime army of thirty-six divisions, with a numerical strength of five hundred and fifty thousand men.

Four days before, the French Government had doubled the period of service and reduced the age of enlistment in the French Army, in order to make good the fall in the number of conscripts due to the reduced birth-rate of the years 1914–18.

This served Hitler as a pretext for his own action. He was able to represent Germany as driven reluctantly to take this step, purely in order to defend herself against the warlike threats of her neighbours. From the time when the German people, trusting in the assurances of Wilson's Fourteen Points, and believing they were rendering a great service to mankind, had laid down their arms, they had been deceived again and again in their hopes of justice and their faith in the good intentions of others. Germany, Hitler declared, was the one Power which had disarmed; now that the other Powers, far from disarming themselves, were actually beginning to increase their armaments, she had no option but to follow suit.

The announcement was received with enthusiasm in Germany, and on 17 March, Heroes Memorial Day *(Heldengedenktag)*, a brilliant military ceremony in the State Opera House celebrated the rebirth of the German Army. At Hitler's side sat von Mackensen, the only surviving field-marshal of the old Army. Afterwards, amid cheering crowds, Hitler held a review of the new Army, including a detachment of the Air Force. So widespread was German feeling against the Treaty of Versailles, and so strong the pride in the German military tradition, that German satisfaction at the announcement could be taken for granted. Everything turned on the reaction abroad to this first open breach of the Treaty's provisions. Hitler had anticipated protests, and was prepared to discount them; what mattered was the action with which the other signatories of the Treaty proposed to support their protests.

The result more than justified the risks he had taken. The British Government, after making a solemn protest, proceeded to ask whether the Führer was still ready to receive Sir John Simon. The French appealed to the League, and an extraordinary session of the Council was at once summoned, to be preceded by a conference between Great Britain, France, and Italy at Stresa. But the French Note, too, spoke of searching for means of conciliation and of the need to dispel the tension which had arisen. This was not the language of men who intended to enforce their protests. When Sir John Simon and Mr Eden at last visited Berlin at the end of March they found Hitler polite, even charming, but perfectly sure of himself and firm in his refusal to consider any pact of mutual assistance which included the Soviet Union. He made a good deal of the service Germany was performing in safeguarding Europe against Communism, and, when the discussion moved to German rearmament, asked: "Did Wellington, when Blücher came to his assistance at Waterloo, first ask the legal experts of the Foreign Office whether the strength of the Prussian forces exceeded the limits fixed by treaty?" It was the Englishmen who had come to ask for cooperation and Hitler who was in the advantageous position of being able to say "no," without having anything to ask in return. The very presence of the British representatives in Berlin, after the announcement of 16 March, was a triumph for his diplomacy.

In the weeks that followed, the Western Powers continued to make a display of European unity which, formally at least, was more impressive. At Stresa, on 11 April, the British, French, and Italian Governments condemned Germany's action, reaffirmed their loyalty to the Locarno Treaty and repeated their declaration on Austrian independence. At Geneva the Council of the League duly censured Germany and appointed a committee to consider what steps should be taken the next time any State endangered peace by repudiating its

obligations. Finally, in May, the French Government, having failed to make headway with its plan for a general treaty of mutual assistance in Eastern Europe, signed a pact with the Soviet Union by which each party undertook to come to the aid of the other in case of an unprovoked attack. This treaty was flanked by a similar pact, concluded at the same time, between Russia and France's most reliable ally, Czechoslovakia.

Yet, even if Hitler was taken aback by the strength of this belated reaction, and if the Franco-Russian and Czech-Russian treaties in particular faced him with awkward new possibilities, his confidence in his own tactics was never shaken. He proceeded to test the strength of this new-found unity; it did not take long to show its weaknesses.

On 21 May Hitler promulgated in secret the Reich Defence Law which placed Schacht in charge of economic preparations for war and reorganized the commands of the armed forces under himself as Supreme Commander of the Wehrmacht. But this was not the face that Hitler showed in public. On the evening of the same day, he appeared before the Reichstag to deliver a long and carefully prepared speech on foreign policy. It is a speech worth studying, for in it are to be found most of the tricks with which Hitler lulled the suspicions and raised the hopes of the gullible. His answer to the censure of the Powers was not defiance, but redoubled assurances of peace, an appeal to reason, justice and conscience. The new Germany, he protested, was misunderstood, and his own attitude misrepresented.

No man ever spoke with greater feeling of the horror and stupidity of war than Adolf Hitler.

The blood shed on the European continent in the course of the last three hundred years bears no proportion to the national result of the events. In the end France has remained France, Germany Germany, Poland Poland and Italy Italy. What dynastic egoism, political passion and patriotic blindness have attained in the way of apparently far-reaching political changes by shedding rivers of blood has, as regards national feeling, done no more than touched the skin of the nations. It has not substantially altered their fundamental characters. If these States had applied merely a fraction of their sacrifices to wiser purposes the success would certainly have been greater and more permanent. . . . If the nations attach so much importance to an increase in the number of the inhabitants of a country they can achieve it without tears in a simpler and more natural way. A sound social policy, by increasing the readiness of a nation to have children, can give its own people more children in a few years than the number of aliens that could be conquered and made subject to that nation by war.

Collective security, Hitler pointed out, was a Wilsonian idea, but Germany's faith in Wilsonian ideas, at least as practised by the former Allies, had been destroyed by her treatment after the war. Germany had been denied equality, had been treated as a nation with second-class rights, and driven to rearm by the failure of the other Powers to carry out their obligation to disarm. Despite this experience, Germany was still prepared to cooperate in the search for security. But she had rooted objections to the proposal of multilateral pacts, for this was the way to spread, not to localize, war. Moreover, in the east of Europe, Hitler declared, there was a special case, the existence of a State, Bolshevik Russia, pledged to destroy the independence of Europe, a State with which a National Socialist Germany could never come to terms.

What Hitler offered in place of the "unrealistic" proposal of multilateral treaties was the signature of non-aggression pacts with all Germany's neighbours. The only exception he made was Lithuania, since Lithuania's continued possession of the German Memelland was a wrong which the German people could never accept, and a plain denial of that right of self-determination proclaimed by Wilson. Germany's improved relations with Poland, he did not fail to add, showed how great a contribution such pacts could make to the cause of peace: this was the practical way in which Germany set about removing international misunderstandings.

Hitler supported his offer with the most convincing display of goodwill. The fact that Germany had repudiated the disarmament clauses of the Treaty of Versailles did not mean that she had anything but the strictest regard for the Treaty's other provisions—including the demilitarization of the Rhineland—or for her other obligations under the Locarno Treaty. She had no intention of annexing Austria and was perfectly ready to strengthen the Locarno Pact by an agreement on air attack, such as Great Britain and France had suggested. She was ready to agree to the abolition of heavy arms, such as the heaviest tanks and artillery; to limit the use of other weapons—such as the bomber and poison gas—by international convention; indeed, to accept an over-all limitation of armaments provided that it was to apply to all the Powers. Hitler laid particular stress on his willingness to limit German naval power to thirty-five per cent of the strength of the British Navy. He understood very well, he declared, the special needs of the British Empire, and had no intention of starting a new naval rivalry with Great Britain. He ended with a confession of his faith in peace. "Whoever lights the torch of war in Europe can wish for nothing but chaos. We, however, live in the firm conviction that in our time will be fulfilled, not the decline, but the renaissance of the West. That Germany may make an imperishable contribution to this great work is our proud hope and our unshakable belief."

Hitler's mastery of the language of Geneva was unequalled. His grasp of the mood of public opinion in the Western democracies was startling, considering that he had never visited any of them and spoke no foreign language. He understood intuitively their longing for peace, the idealism of the pacifists, the uneasy conscience of the liberals, the reluctance of the great mass of their peoples to look beyond their own private affairs. At this stage in the game these were greater assets than the uncompleted panzer divisions and bomber fleets he was still building, and Hitler used them with the same skill he had shown in playing on German grievances and illusions.

In *Mein Kampf* Hitler had written: "For a long time to come there will be only two Powers in Europe with which it may be possible for Germany to conclude an alliance. These Powers are Great Britain and Italy." The greatest blunder of the Kaiser's Government—prophetic words— had been to quarrel with Britain and Russia at the same time: Germany's future lay in the east, a continental future, and her natural ally was Great Britain, whose power was colonial, commercial, and naval, with no territorial interests on the continent of Europe. "Only by alliance with England was it possible (before 1914) to safeguard the rear of the German crusade. . . . No sacrifice should have been considered too great, if it was a necessary means of gaining England's friendship. Colonial and naval ambitions should have been abandoned."

Although Hitler's attitude towards Britain was modified later by growing contempt for the weakness of her policy and the credulity of her governments, the idea

of an alliance with her attracted him throughout his life. It was an alliance which could only, in Hitler's view, be made on condition that Britain abandoned her old balance-of-power policy in Europe, accepted the prospect of a German hegemony on the Continent and left Germany a free hand in attaining it. Even during the war Hitler persisted in believing that an alliance with Germany on these terms was in Britain's own interests, continually expressed his regret that the British had been so stupid as not to see this, and never quite gave up the hope that he would be able to overcome their obstinacy and persuade them to accept his view. No British Government, even before the war, was prepared to go as far as an alliance on these terms, yet there was a section of British opinion which was sufficiently impressed by Hitler's arguments to be attracted to the idea of a settlement which would have left him virtually a free hand in Central and Eastern Europe, and Hitler, if he never succeeded in his main objective, was remarkably successful for a time in weakening the opposition of Great Britain to the realization of his aims. The policy of appeasement is not to be understood unless it is realized that it represented the acceptance by the British Government, at least in part, of Hitler's view of what British policy should be.

The speech of 21 May had been intended to influence opinion in Great Britain in Hitler's favour. The quickness of the British reaction was surprising. During his visit to Berlin in March Sir John Simon had been sufficiently impressed by a hint thrown out by the Führer to suggest that German representatives should come to London to discuss the possibility of a naval agreement between the two countries. Hitler must have been delighted to see the speed with which the British Foreign Minister responded to his bait, and in his speech of 21 May he again underlined his willingness to arrive at such an understanding. Even Hitler, however, can scarcely have calculated that the British Government would be so maladroit as to say nothing of their intentions to the Powers with whom they had been so closely associated in censuring Germany's repudiation of the Versailles disarmament clauses in the previous weeks.

Early in June Ribbentrop, whom Hitler now began to use for special missions, flew to London. Despite the brusque and tactless way in which he refused to permit discussion of the Führer's offer, he returned with the British signature of a naval pact. This bound the Germans not to build beyond thirty-five percent of Britain's naval strength, but it tacitly recognized Germany's right to begin naval rearmament and specifically agreed by an escape-clause that, in the construction of U-boats, Germany should have the right to build up to one hundred per cent of the submarine strength of the British Commonwealth. The affront to Britain's partners, France and Italy, both of whom were also naval powers, but neither of whom had been consulted, was open and much resented. The solidarity of the Stresa front, the unanimity of the Powers' condemnation of German rearmament, was destroyed. The British Government, in its eagerness to secure a private advantage, had given a disastrous impression of bad faith. Like Poland, but without the excuse of Poland's difficult position between Germany and Russia, Great Britain had accepted Hitler's carefully calculated offer without a thought of its ultimate consequences.

In September the Führer attended the Party's rally at Nuremberg. For the first time detachments of the new German Army took part in the parade and Hitler glorified the German military tradition: "in war the nation's great defiance, in peace the splendid school of our people. It is the Army which has made men of us all, and when we looked upon the Army our faith in the future of our people was always reinforced. This old glorious Army is not dead; it only slept, and now it has arisen again in you."

Hitler's speeches throughout the rally were marked by the confidence of a man sure of his hold over the people he led. The Reichstag was summoned to Nuremberg for a special session, and Hitler presented for its unanimous approval the Nuremberg Laws directed against the Jews, the first depriving Germans of Jewish blood of their citizenship, the second—the Law for the Protection of German Blood and German Honour—forbidding marriages between Germans and Jews and the employment of German servants by Jews. These laws, Hitler declared, "repay the debt of gratitude to the movement under whose symbol [the swastika, now adopted as the national emblem] Germany has recovered her freedom."

The same month, while Hitler at Nuremberg was making use of the power he held in Germany to gratify his hatred of the Jews, a quarrel began at Geneva which was to provide him with the opportunity to extend his power outside the German frontiers of 1914.

The alliance with Mussolini's Italy to which Hitler already looked at the time he wrote *Mein Kampf* had hitherto been prevented by Mussolini's Danubian ambitions, and the Duce's self-appointed role as the patron of Austrian independence. After the murder of Dollfuss, Mussolini had been outspoken in his dislike and contempt for the "barbarians" north of the Alps, and he had cooperated with the other Powers in their condemnation of Germany's unilateral decision to rearm. Mussolini, however, had long been contemplating a showy success for his régime in Abyssinia. It may be that he was prompted by uneasy fears that his chances of expansion in Europe would soon be reduced by the growth of German power; it may be that he was stimulated by a sense of rivalry with the German dictator; it is almost certain that he hoped to profit by French and British preoccupation with German rearmament to carry out his adventure on the cheap.

Abyssinia had appealed to the League under Article 15 of the Covenant in March. So far the dispute had been discreetly kept in the background, but in September the British Government, having just made a sensational gesture of appeasement to Germany by the Naval Treaty of June, astonished the world for the second time by taking the lead at Geneva in demanding the imposition of sanctions against Italy. She supported this by reinforcing the British Fleet in the Mediterranean. To the French, who judged that Germany, not Italy, was the greater danger to the security of Europe, the British appeared to be standing on their heads and looking at events upside down.

There was only one assumption on which British policy could be defended. If the British were prepared to support sanctions against Italy to the point of war, thereby giving to the authority of the League the backing of force which it had hitherto lacked, their action might so strengthen the machinery of collective security as to put a check to any aggression, whether by Italy or Germany. The outbreak of hostilities between Italy and Abyssinia in October soon put the British intentions to the test. The course pursued by the Baldwin Government made the worst of both worlds. By insisting on the imposition of sanctions Great Britain made an enemy of Mussolini and destroyed all hope of a united front against German aggression. By her refusal to drive home the policy of sanctions, in face of Mussolini's bluster, she

dealt the authority of the League as well as her own prestige a fatal blow, and destroyed any hope of finding in collective security an effective alternative to the united front of the Great Powers against German aggression.

If the British Government never meant to do more than make a show of imposing sanctions it would have done better to have followed the more cynical but more realistic policy of Laval and made a deal with Italy at the beginning. Even the Hoare-Laval Pact of December 1935 would have been a better alternative than allowing the farce of sanctions to drag on to its inconclusive and discreditable end. For the consequences of these blunders extended much farther than Abyssinia and the Mediterranean: their ultimate beneficiary was, not Mussolini, but Hitler.

Germany at first confined herself to a policy of strict neutrality in the Abyssinian affair, but the advantages to be derived from the quarrel between Italy and the Western Powers did not escape Hitler. If Italy lost the war, that would mean the weakening of the principal barrier to German ambitions in Central and Southeastern Europe. On the other hand, if Italy proved to be successful, the prospects for Hitler were still good. His one fear was that the quarrel might be patched up by some such compromise as the Hoare-Laval Pact, and when the Polish Ambassador in Berlin saw him two days after the announcement of the terms of the Hoare-Laval Agreement he found him highly excited and alarmed at this prospect. The further development of the dispute, however, only gave him greater cause for satisfaction. Not only was the Stresa front ended and Italy driven into a position of isolation, in which Mussolini was bound to look more favourably on German offers of support, but the League of Nations suffered a fatal blow to its authority from which, after its previous failure to halt Japanese aggression, it never recovered. French confidence in England was further shaken, and the belief that Great Britain was a spent force in international politics received the most damning confirmation.

The events of 1935 thus provided an unexpected opportunity for Hitler to realize his Italian plans: as Mussolini later acknowledged, it was in the autumn of 1935 that the idea of the Rome-Berlin Axis was born. No less important was the encouragement which the feebleness of the opposition to aggression gave Hitler to pursue his policy without regard to the risks. "There was now, as it turned out," writes Mr Churchill, "little hope of averting war or of postponing it by a trial of strength equivalent to war. Almost all that remained open to France and Britain was to await the moment of the challenge and do the best they could."

A foreign correspondent and radio commentator,
WILLIAM L. SHIRER (b. 1904) was well known for his
previous books on Germany (*Berlin Diary,* 1941, and *End of
a Berlin Diary,* 1947) before he wrote his National Book
Award winning *The Rise and Fall of the Third Reich* (1960).
Like Bulloch an advocate of the "war was planned" school
of history, Shirer blasts Chamberlain for his "fanatical
insistence on giving Hitler what he wanted." This selection
and the two that follow show the difficulty of separating
any discussion of the Czechoslovak crisis from a
consideration of its results. Shirer believes that Germany
was totally unprepared to go to war in 1938, and if she
had done so, she would have been quickly defeated.*

William L. Shirer

The Surrender at Munich

In this baroque Bavarian city where in
the murky back rooms of rundown little
cafés he had made his lowly start as a politician and in whose streets he had suffered
the fiasco of the Beer Hall Putsch, Adolf
Hitler greeted, like a conqueror, the heads
of governments of Great Britain, France
and Italy at half past noon on September
29.

Very early that morning he had gone to
Kufstein on the former Austro-German
frontier to meet Mussolini and set up a
basis for common action at the conference.
In the train coming up to Munich Hitler
was in a bellicose mood, explaining to the
Duce over maps how he intended to "liqui-
date" Czechoslovakia. Either the talks
beginning that day must be immediately

successful, he said, or he would resort to
arms. "Besides," Ciano, who was present,
quotes the Fuehrer as adding, "the time
will come when we shall have to fight side
by side against France and England."
Mussolini agreed.

Chamberlain made no similar effort to
see Daladier beforehand to work out a
joint strategy for the two Western democracies with which to confront the two fascist dictators. Indeed, it became evident to
many of us in contact with the British and
French delegations in Munich as the day
progressed that Chamberlain had come to
Munich absolutely determined that no
one, certainly not the Czechs and not even
the French, should stand in the way of his
reaching a quick agreement with Hitler.

*From William L. Shirer, *The Rise and Fall of the Third Reich* (New York: Simon & Schuster, Inc.,
1960), pp. 559–563, 568–577. Copyright © 1959, 1960, by William L. Shirer. Reprinted by permission of
Simon & Schuster, Inc., and Martin Secker & Warburg Limited. Footnotes omitted.

In the case of Daladier, who went around all day as if in a daze, no precaution was necessary, but the determined Prime Minister took no risks.

The talks, which began at 12:45 P.M. in the so-called Fuehrerhaus in the Koenigsplatz, were anticlimactic and constituted little more than a mere formality of rendering to Hitler exactly what he wanted when he wanted it. Dr. Schmidt, the indomitable interpreter, who was called upon to function in three languages, German, French and English, noticed from the beginning "an atmosphere of general good will." Ambassador Henderson later remembered that "at no stage of the conversations did they become heated." No one presided. The proceedings unfolded informally, and judging by the German minutes of the meeting which came to light after the war, the British Prime Minister and the French Premier fairly fell over themselves to agree with Hitler. Even when he made the following opening statement:

He had now declared in his speech at the Sportpalast that he would in any case march in on October 1. He had received the answer that this action would have the character of an act of violence. Hence the task arose to absolve this action from such a character. Action must, however, be taken at once.

The conferees got down to business when Mussolini, speaking third in turn—Daladier was left to the last—said that "in order to bring about a practical solution of the problem" he had brought with him a definite written proposal. Its origins are interesting and remained unknown to Chamberlain, I believe, to his death. From the memoirs of François-Poncet and Henderson it is obvious that they too were ignorant of them. In fact, the story only became known long after the violent deaths of the two dictators.

What the Duce now fobbed off as his own compromise plan had been hastily drafted the day before in the German Foreign Office in Berlin by Goering, Neurath and Weizsaecker behind the back of Foreign Minister von Ribbentrop, whose judgment the three men did not trust. Goering took it to Hitler, who said it might do, and then it was hurriedly translated into French by Dr. Schmidt and passed along to the Italian ambassador, Attolico, who telephoned the text of it to the Italian dictator in Rome just before he entrained for Munich. Thus it was that the "Italian proposals," which provided the informal conference not only with its sole agenda but with the basic terms which eventually became the Munich Agreement, were in fact German proposals concocted in Berlin.

This must have seemed fairly obvious from the text, which closely followed Hitler's rejected Godesberg demands; but it was not obvious to Daladier and Chamberlain or to their ambassadors in Berlin, who now attended them. The Premier, according to the German minutes, "welcomed the Duce's proposal, which had been made in an objective and realistic spirit," and the Prime Minister "also welcomed the Duce's proposal and declared that he himself had conceived of a solution on the lines of this proposal." As for Ambassador Henderson, as he later wrote, he thought Mussolini "had tactfully put forward as his own a combination of Hitler's and the Anglo-French proposals"; while Ambassador François-Poncet got the impression that the conferees were working on a British memorandum "drawn up by Horace Wilson." So easily were the British and French statesmen and diplomats, bent on appeasement at any cost, deceived!

With the "Italian" proposals so warmly welcomed by all present there remained but a few details to iron out. Chamberlain, as perhaps might have been expected from an ex-businessman and former Chancellor of the Exchequer, wanted to know who would compensate the Czech government for the public property which would pass to Germany in the Sudetenland. Hitler, who, according to François-Poncet, appeared somewhat pale and worried, and annoyed because he could not follow, as Mussolini could, the talk in French and English, replied heatedly there would be no compensation. When the Prime Minister objected to the stipulation that the Czechs moving out of the Sudetenland could not even take their cattle (this had been one of the Godesberg demands)—exclaiming, "Does this mean that the farmers will be expelled but their cattle will be retained?"—Hitler exploded.

"Our time is too valuable to be wasted on such trivialities!" he shouted at Chamberlain. The Prime Minister dropped the matter.

He did insist at first that a Czech representative ought to be present, or at least, as he put it, be "available." His country, he said, "could naturally undertake no guarantee that the [Sudeten] territory would be evacuated by October 10 [as Mussolini had proposed] if no assurance of this was forthcoming from the Czech government." Daladier gave him lukewarm support. The French government, he said, "would in no wise tolerate procrastination in this matter by the Czech government," but he thought "the presence of a Czech representative, who could be consulted, if necessary, would be an advantage."

But Hitler was adamant. He would permit no Czechs in his presence. Daladier meekly gave in, but Chamberlain finally won a small concession. It was agreed that a Czech representative might make himself available "in the next room," as the Prime Minister proposed.

And indeed during the afternoon session two Czech representatives, Dr. Vojtech

Mastny, the Czech minister in Berlin, and Dr. Hubert Masarik, from the Prague Foreign Office, did arrive and were coolly ushered into an adjoining room. There, after they had been left from 2 P.M. to 7 to cool their heels, the roof figuratively fell in on them. At the latter hour Frank Ashton-Gwatkin, who had been a member of the Runciman mission and was now on Chamberlain's staff, came to break the bad news to them. A general agreement had been reached, the details of which he could not yet give to them; but it was much "harsher" than the Franco-British proposals. When Masarik asked if the Czechs couldn't be heard, the Englishman answered, as the Czech representative later reported to his government, "that I seemed to ignore how difficult was the situation of the Great Powers, and that I could not understand how hard it had been to negotiate with Hitler."

At 10 P.M. the two unhappy Czechs were taken to Sir Horace Wilson, the Prime Minister's faithful adviser. On behalf of Chamberlain, Wilson informed them of the main points in the four-power agreement and handed them a map of the Sudeten areas which were to be evacuated by the Czechs at once. When the two envoys attempted to protest, the British official cut them short. He had nothing more to say, he stated, and promptly left the room. The Czechs continued to protest to Ashton-Gwatkin, who had remained with them, but to no avail.

"If you do not accept," he admonished them, as he prepared to go, "you will have to settle your affairs with the Germans absolutely alone. Perhaps the French may tell you this more gently, but you can believe me that they share our views. They are disinterested."

This was the truth, wretched though it must have sounded to the two Czech emissaries. Shortly after 1 A.M. on September

30 Hitler, Chamberlain, Mussolini and Daladier, in that order, affixed their signatures to the Munich Agreement providing for the German Army to begin its march into Czechoslovakia on October 1, as the Fuehrer had always said it would, and to complete the occupation of the Sudetenland by October 10. Hitler had got what had been refused him at Godesberg. . . .

What Chamberlain and Daladier at Munich had neglected to give Germany in Czechoslovakia the so-called "International Commission" proceeded to hand over. This hastily formed body consisted of the Italian, British and French ambassadors and the Czech minister in Berlin and Baron von Weizsaecker, the State Secretary in the German Foreign Office. Every dispute over additional territory for the Germans was settled in their favor, more than once under the threat from Hitler and OKW to resort to armed force. Finally, on October 13, the commission voted to dispense with the plebiscites which the Munich Agreement had called for in the disputed regions. There was no need for them.

The Poles and the Hungarians, after threatening military action against the helpless nation, now swept down, like vultures, to get a slice of Czechoslovakia territory. Poland, at the insistence of Foreign Minister Józef Beck, who for the next twelve months will be a leading character in this narrative, took some 650 square miles of territory around Teschen, comprising a population of 228,000 inhabitants, of whom 133,000 were Czechs. Hungary got a larger slice in the award meted out on November 2 by Ribbentrop and Ciano: 7,500 square miles, with a population of 500,000 Magyars and 272,000 Slovaks.

Moreover, the truncated and now defenseless country was forced by Berlin to install a pro-German government of obvious fascist tendencies. It was clear that from now on the Czechoslovak nation existed at the mercy of the Leader of the Third Reich.

The Consequences of Munich

Under the terms of the Munich Agreement Hitler got substantially what he had demanded at Godesberg, and the "International Commission," bowing to his threats, gave him considerably more. The final settlement of November 20, 1938, forced Czechoslovakia to cede to Germany 11,000 square miles of territory in which dwelt 2,800,000 Sudeten Germans and 800,000 Czechs. Within this area lay all the vast Czech fortifications which hitherto had formed the most formidable defensive line in Europe, with the possible exception of the Maginot Line in France.

But that was not all. Czechoslovakia's entire system of rail, road, telephone and telegraph communications was disrupted. According to German figures, the dismembered country lost 66 per cent of its coal, 80 per cent of its lignite, 86 per cent of its chemicals, 80 per cent of its cement, 80 per cent of its textiles, 70 per cent of its iron and steel, 70 per cent of its electric power and 40 per cent of its timber. A prosperous industrial nation was split up and bankrupted overnight.

No wonder that Jodl could write joyfully in this diary on the night of Munich:

The Pact of Munich is signed. Czechoslovakia as a power is out . . . The genius of the Fuehrer and his determination not to shun even a World War have again won the victory without the use of force. The hope remains that the incredulous, the weak and the doubtful people have been converted, and will remain that way.

Many of the doubtful were converted and the few who were not were plunged into despair. The generals such as Beck, Halder, and Witzleben and their civilian advisers had again been proved wrong. Hitler had got what he wanted, had achieved another conquest, without firing a shot. His prestige soared to new heights. No one who was in Germany in the days after Munich, as this writer was, can forget the rapture of the German people. They were relieved that war had been averted; they were elated and swollen with pride at Hitler's bloodless victory not only over Czechoslovakia but over Great Britain and France. Within the short space of six months, they reminded you, Hitler had conquered Austria and the Sudetenland, adding ten million inhabitants to the Third Reich and a vast strategic territory which opened the way for German domination of southeastern Europe. And without the loss of a single German life! With the instinct of a genius rare in German history he had divined not only the weaknesses of the smaller states in Central Europe but those of the two principal Western democracies, Britain and France, and forced them to bend to his will. He had invented and used with staggering success a new strategy and technique of *political warfare,* which made actual war unnecessary.

In scarcely four and a half years this man of lowly origins had catapulted a disarmed, chaotic, nearly bankrupt Germany, the weakest of the big powers in Europe, to a position where she was regarded as the mightiest nation of the Old World, before which all the others, Britain even and France, trembled. At no step in this dizzy ascent had the victorious powers of Versailles dared to try to stop her, even when they had the power to do so. Indeed at Munich, which registered the greatest conquest of all, Britain and France had gone out of their way to support her. And what must have amazed Hitler most of all—it certainly astounded General Beck, Hassell and others in their small circle of

opposition—was that none of the men who dominated the governments of Britain and France ("little worms," as the Fuehrer contemptuously spoke of them in private after Munich) realized the consequences of their inability to react with any force to one after the other of the Nazi leader's aggressive moves.

Winston Churchill, in England, alone seemed to understand. No one stated the consequences of Munich more succinctly than he in his speech to the Commons of October 5:

We have sustained a total and unmitigated defeat ... We are in the midst of a disaster of the first magnitude. The road down the Danube ... the road to the Black Sea has been opened ... All the countries of Mittel Europa and the Danube valley, one after another, will be drawn in the vast system of Nazi politics ... radiating from Berlin ... And do not suppose that this is the end. It is only the beginning ...

But Churchill was not in the government and his words went unheeded.

Was the Franco-British surrender at Munich necessary? Was Adolf Hitler not bluffing?

The answer, paradoxically, to both questions, we now know, is No. All the generals close to Hitler who survived the war agree that had it not been for Munich Hitler would have attacked Czechoslovakia on October 1, 1938, and they presume that, whatever momentary hesitations there might have been in London, Paris and Moscow, in the end Britain, France and Russia would have been drawn into the war.

And—what is most important to this history at this point—the German generals agree unanimously that Germany would have lost the war, and in short order. The argument of the supporters of Chamberlain and Daladier—and they were in the great majority at the time—that Munich saved the West not only from war but from defeat in war and, incidentally, preserved London and Paris from being wiped out by the Luftwaffe's murderous bombing has been impressively refuted, so far as concern the last two points, by those in a position to know best: the German generals, and especially those generals who are closest to Hitler and who supported him from beginning to end the most fanatically.

The leading light among the latter was General Keitel, chief of OKW, toady to Hitler and constantly at his side. When asked on the stand at the Nuremberg trial what the reaction of the German generals was to Munich he replied:

We were extraordinarily happy that it had not come to a military operation because . . . we had always been of the opinion that our means of attack against the frontier fortifications of Czechoslovakia were insufficient. From a purely military point of view we lacked the means for an attack which involved the piercing of the frontier fortifications.

It has always been assumed by Allied military experts that the German Army would have romped through Czechoslovakia. But to the testimony of Keitel that this would not have been the case must be added that of Field Marshal von Manstein, who became one of the most brilliant of the German field commanders. When he, in his turn, testified at Nuremberg (unlike Keitel and Jodl, he was not on trial for his life) on the German position at the time of Munich, he explained:

If a war had broken out, neither our western border nor our Polish frontier could really have been effectively defended by us, and there is no doubt whatsoever that had Czechoslovakia defended herself, we would have been held up by her fortifications, for we did not have the means to break through.

Jodl, the "brains" of OKW, put it this

way when he took the stand in his own defense at Nuremberg:

It was out of the question, with five fighting divisions and seven reserve divisions in the western fortifications, which were nothing but a large construction site, to hold out against 100 French divisions. That was militarily impossible.

If, as these German generals concede, Hitler's army lacked the means of penetrating the Czech fortifications, and Germany, in the face of France's overwhelming strength in the west, was in a "militarily impossible" situation and further, since, as we have seen, there was such grave dissension among the generals that the Chief of the Army General Staff was prepared to overthrow the Fuehrer in order to avert a hopeless war—why, then, did not the French and British general staffs know this? Or did they? And if they did, how could the heads of government of Britain and France be forced at Munich into sacrificing so much of their nations' vital interest? In seeking answers to such questions we confront one of the mysteries of the Munich time which has not yet been cleared up. Even Churchill, concerned as he is with military affairs, scarcely touches on it in his massive memoirs.

It is inconceivable that the British and French general staffs and the two governments did not know of the opposition of the German Army General Staff to a European war. For, as already noted here, the conspirators in Berlin warned the British of this through at least four channels in August and September and, as we know, the matter came to the attention of Chamberlain himself. By early September Paris and London must have learned of the resignation of General Beck and of the obvious consequences to the German Army of the rebellion of its most eminent and gifted leader.

It was generally conceded in Berlin at this time that British and French military intelligence was fairly good. It is extremely difficult to believe that the military chiefs in London and Paris did not know of the obvious weaknesses of the German Army and Air Force and of their inability to fight a two-front war. What doubts could the Chief of Staff of the French Army, General Gamelin, have—despite his inbred caution, which was monumental—that with nearly one hundred divisions he could overwhelm the five regular and seven reserve German divisions in the west and sweep easily and swiftly deep into Germany?

On the whole, as he later recounted, Gamelin had few doubts. On September 12, the day on which Hitler was thundering his threats against Czechoslovakia at the closing session of the Nuremberg rally, the French generalissimo had assured Premier Daladier that if war came "the democratic nations would dictate the peace." He says he backed it up with a letter expressing the reasons for his optimism. On September 26, at the height of the Czech crisis following the Godesberg meeting, Gamelin, who had accompanied the French government leaders to London, repeated his assurances to Chamberlain and tried to substantiate them with an analysis of the military situation calculated to buck up not only the British Prime Minister but his own wavering Premier. In this attempt, apparently, he failed. Finally, just before Daladier flew to Munich, Gamelin outlined to him the limits of territorial concessions in the Sudetenland which could be made without endangering French security. The main Czech fortifications, as well as the rail trunk lines, certain strategic branch lines and the principal defense industries must not be given to Germany. Above all, he added, the Germans must

not be permitted to cut off the Moravian Gap. Good advice, if Czechoslovakia was to be of any use to France in a war with Germany, but, as we have seen, Daladier was not the man to act on it.

A good deal was said at the time of Munich that one reason for Chamberlain's surrender was his fear that London would be obliterated by German bombing, and there is no doubt that the French were jittery at the awful prospect of their beautiful capital being destroyed from the air. But from what is now known of the Luftwaffe's strength at this moment, the Londoners and the Parisians, as well as the Prime Minister and the Premier, were unduly alarmed. The German Air Force, like the Army, was concentrated against Czechoslovakia and therefore, like the Army, was incapable of serious action in the West. Even if a few German bombers could have been spared to attack London and Paris it is highly doubtful that they would have reached their targets. Weak as the British and French fighter defenses were, the Germans could not have given their bombers fighter protection, if they had had the planes. Their fighter bases were too far away.

It has also been argued—most positively by Ambassadors François-Poncet and Henderson—that Munich gave the two Western democracies nearly a year to catch up with the Germans in rearmament. The facts belie such an argument. As Churchill, backed up by every serious Allied military historian, has written, "The year's breathing space said to be 'gained' by Munich left Britain and France in a much worse position compared to Hilter's Germany than they had been at the Munich crisis." . . . All the German military calculations a year later bear this out, and subsequent events, of course, remove any doubts whatsoever.

In retrospect, and with the knowledge we now have from the secret German documents and from the postwar testimony of the Germans themselves, the following summing up, which was impossible to make in the days of Munich, may be given:

Germany was in no position to go to war on October 1, 1938, against Czechoslovakia *and* France and Britain, not to mention Russia. Had she done so, she would have been quickly and easily defeated, and that would have been the end of Hitler and the Third Reich. If a European war had been averted at the last moment by the intercession of the German Army, Hitler might have been overthrown by Halder and Witzleben and their confederates carrying out their plan to arrest him as soon as he had given the final order for the attack on Czechoslovakia.

By publicly boasting that he would march into the Sudetenland by October 1 "in any case," Hitler had put himself far out on a limb. He was in the "untenable position" which General Beck had foreseen. Had he, after all his categorical threats and declarations, tried to crawl back from the limb on his own, he scarcely could have survived for long, dictatorships being what they are and his dictatorship, in particular, being what it was. It would have been extremely difficult, if not impossible, for him to have backed down, and had he tried to do so his loss of prestige in Europe, among his own people and, above all, with his generals would most likely, have proved fatal.

Chamberlain's stubborn, fanatical insistence on giving Hitler what he wanted, his trips to Berchtesgaden and Godesberg and finally the fateful journey to Munich rescued Hitler from his limb and strengthened his position in Europe, in Germany, in the Army, beyond anything that could have been imagined a few weeks before. It also added immeasurably to the power of the Third Reich vis-à-vis the Western democracies and the Soviet Union.

For France, Munich was a disaster, and it is beyond understanding that this was not fully realized in Paris. Her military position in Europe was destroyed. Because her Army, when the Reich was fully mobilized, could never be much more than half the size of that of Germany, which had nearly twice her population, and because her ability to produce arms was also less, France had laboriously built up her alliances with the smaller powers in the East on the other flank of Germany—and of Italy: Czechoslovakia, Poland, Yugoslavia and Rumania, which together, had the military potential of a Big Power. The loss now of thirty-five well-trained, well-armed Czech divisions, deployed behind their strong mountain fortifications and holding down an even larger German Force, was a crippling one to the French Army. But that was not all. After Munich how could France's remaining allies in Eastern Europe have any confidence in her written word? What value now were alliances with France? The answer in Warsaw, Bucharest and Belgrade was: Not much; and there was a scramble in these capitals to make the best deal possible, while there was still time, with the Nazi conqueror.

And if not a scramble, there was a stir in Moscow. Though the Soviet Union was militarily allied to both Czechoslovakia and France, the French government had gone along with Germany and Britain, without protest, in excluding Russia from Munich. It was a snub which Stalin did not forget and which was to cost the two Western democracies dearly in the months to come. On October 3, four days after Munich, the counselor of the German Embassy in Moscow, Werner von Tippels-

kirch, reported to Berlin on the "consequences" of Munich for Soviet policy. He
thought Stalin "would draw conclusions";
he was certain the Soviet Union would
"reconsider her foreign policy," become
less friendly to her ally France and "more
positive" toward Germany. As a matter of
fact, the German diplomat thought that
"the present circumstances offer favorable
opportunities for a new and wider German
economic agreement with the Soviet
Union." This is the first mention in the
secret German archives of a change in the
wind that now began to stir, however faint-
ly, over Berlin and Moscow and which,
within a year, would have momentous consequences.

CHARLES LOCH MOWAT (b. 1911) formerly a
professor at the University of Chicago and editor of the
Journal of Modern History, currently is teaching at the
University at Bangor, Wales. His study on Britain between
the wars is the standard work on that period. In the
following selection he considers the popularity of the policy
of appeasement and discusses also the important question
of rearmament. To what extent did Britain profit
militarily by the delay of war from 1938 to 1940? He
comes to conclusions different from those of Shirer, finding
that the "breathing spell . . . was decisive for Britain's
rearmament."*

Charles Loch Mowat

The Popularity of Munich

Neville Chamberlain succeeded to a
barren heritage. The rearming of the army
and navy, the expansion of the Royal Air
Force were only just beginning. The might
of Germany, on the other hand, was growing great, and the pause in its aggressive-
ness which had followed the reoccupation
of the Rhineland was unlikely to last much
longer. Moreover, the three militarist powers, Germany, Italy and Japan, were now
linked together: the Berlin-Rome "axis" of
November 1936 and the German-Japanese
Anti-Comintern pact of 1936 were merged
into a triangle on November 6, 1937. Following this, Italy left the League of Nations in December, as Germany and Japan
had done long since. The peace of the
world was crumbling: there was war in

China, there was bitter fighting in Spain.
Could the ruins be shored up and peace
preserved? Chamberlain was determined
to make a new attempt.

There were still three possible methods
of keeping the peace (apart from the
method of the pacifist); collective security
through the League, an alliance of the
anti-axis powers outside the League, and
the appeasement of the dictators. The first
was ignored by Chamberlain and not
strongly advocated by his critics. In none
of the crises of these latter years did the
League play a part: no longer did it earn
either the blessings of its friends or the
curses of its enemies. "What country in
Europe today if threatened by a large Power, can rely on the League of Nations for

*Reprinted from *Britain Between the Wars, 1918–1939* by Charles Loch Mowat, pp. 589–594, 619–622,
625–632 by permission of The University of Chicago Press and Methuen and Co. Ltd., London. Copyright
1955 by The University of Chicago. Footnotes omitted.

protection?" asked Neville Chamberlain in March 1938; he answered "None."

Alliances or arrangements with the anti-axis powers seemed no more promising. In the United States there was plenty of indignation at Nazi terrorism and Japanese aggression; but the Neutrality Act of 1935, which was replaced by a permanent measure in 1937, forbade the export of war materials to all belligerents and required countries at war to pay cash for any essential materials from the United States and to carry them away in their own ships. President Roosevelt, in a famous speech in Chicago on October 5, 1937, preached cooperation by the peace-loving nations and damned the dictators; but his hint that the United States should join in a "quarantine" of the aggressors evoked nothing but alarmed disclaimers from the public. Soviet Russia, a member of the League and an ally of France, was another candidate for British friendship; but Chamberlain distrusted it as a "half-Asiatic" country, unreliable in its military strength and more concerned to embroil other countries in war than to defend their liberty. In these feelings he was not alone: the great purges of 1937, and particularly the decimation of Russian generals and other officers, convinced the average man of the military weakness which was also the burden of confidential reports from official observers to the government. And, in any case, the old hatred of Bolshevism was far from dead, despite the cooings of Litvinov at Geneva.

There remained France and its system of alliances in the Little Entente. Cooperation with France was, indeed, inescapable; but with Neville Chamberlain, unlike Austen Chamberlain and Henderson, it was never cordial. France, with its fussy hankerings for its own security, had spoiled the peace treaties and perverted the purposes of the League; now the same distrust would block a general pacification. What made it worse, France was no longer a strong military power, and its government, in the hands of Leon Blum and the Popular Front, was as suspect by many British Conservatives as it was by business and conservative circles in France. The stay-in strikes, the civil unrest, and the introduction of the five-day week in the time of the Popular Front all justified a lack of confidence which was not greatly moderated when Blum's government was succeeded by that of Chautemps on June 21, 1937.

How much to be preferred was the policy of appeasement, of seeking the friendship of Germany and of dividing Italy from Germany. "The appeasement of Europe as a whole" had been Eden's object in March 1936; a "general scheme of appeasement" was Chamberlain's object two years later, and was not abandoned until March 1939. In one sense it was Chamberlain's own policy, and a very personal one; but it rested on illusions which were very widely shared. Chamberlain's hatred of war was passionate, his fear of its consequences shrewd. He believed, unlike the indolent but canny Baldwin, that much could be accomplished by personal diplomacy in conference; that there "must be something in common" between different peoples since "we are all members of the human race"; that there was a human side to the dictators, which could be appealed to, especially in *tête-à-tête* discussions ("an hour or two *tête-à-tête* with Musso might be extraordinarily valuable in making plans for talks with Germany"). He shared the fatal view of the times that discussion could change the nature of facts and the course of events. To make a general settlement he would go very far, even though at first he was sceptical of the chances of success: "I don't believe myself that we could purchase peace and a lasting settlement by handing over Tanganyika to the Germans, but if I did, I would not hesitate for a moment." The trouble was that such a policy, and especially when applied to other lands than Tanganyika, sacrificed Britain's real interests and ignored questions of right and wrong. It also involved negotiations with the Nazi tyrants of Germany whom so many of the British people not merely distrusted as liars but loathed as bestial persecutors of Jews and of Christians.

Yet until after Munich there was no question that appeasement was popular, despite its many critics. It had the greater part of the press behind it: in particular *The Times* (which was often ahead of the game), the *Daily Express* of Lord Beaverbrook and the *Daily Mail* of Lord Rothermere, and the fulminations of J. L. Garvin in the *Observer*. Lloyd George returned from a visit to Hitler at Berchtesgaden in September 1936 enthusiastic for Hitler's work for Germany and for his peaceable intentions—though he was later undeceived. The alternative to appeasement was war—or so the critics were told; and no one advocated that. Certainly not the Labour party; nor Tory imperialist critics such as Churchill, exiled from office because of his views on India and generally distrusted as a "warmonger." In retrospect everyone was against appeasement; at the time not so many. One could salve one's conscience by enjoying Low's stinging cartoons and the asininities of Colonel Blimp: the savage taunt against the "empire on which the sun never sets," the picture of the "Shiver Sisters Ballet, 1938," in which Lord Lothian, Geoffrey Dawson, Lady Astor and Garvin danced to Goebbels' baton. One could complain of the "Clivedon set" without having to produce evidence that the Astors, Lothian, Dawson and their friends really made policy at week-end parties at Cliveden. A more serious complaint was of the uncritical admiration of Nazi Germany by members of the upper class, such as Lord Londonderry. The German Embassy, particularly during Ribbentrop's term as ambassador in 1936–38, was the scene of lavish parties at which many transient converts to a snobbish pro-Germanism were made.

One argument for the policy of appeasement was that the Dominions supported it. They had little chance to do otherwise: their acquiescence was an effect rather than a cause of the policy it served to excuse. Since the war, and particularly since the Chanak episode, their policy had been one of no commitments—and certainly they were not going to be bound by Britain's commitments. Uninstructed as to the course of a personal and secretive diplomacy, soothed by urbane pronouncements by British leaders, they naturally opposed involvement in war and rejoiced that appeasement was keeping the threat of war at a distance. If Czechoslovakia was far away from England, it was a long way farther from Canada or Australia.

Dislike of the policy of appeasement was increased by circumstances partly incidental, partly essential to it—the character and methods of Neville Chamberlain. There was a quality of "self-sufficient obstinacy" about him; and his rather forbidding features, his dark clothes, his harsh voice, above all his umbrella, made him seem more narrow and smug, and his policies more sinister, than was really the case. He did not, except during the crisis of Munich, court popularity—indeed, his acclaim at that time is a measure of the nation's temporary suspension of judgment in the shock of calamity suddenly looming ahead and as suddenly removed. Rather, he invited opposition by his impatience of criticism, and his tendency to ignore parliament and to evade debate. Within his Cabinet he was master, not only in giving a strong lead to his colleagues as chairman, but in keeping in close touch with their

work in the departments. His was a personal government in a very different sense
from Baldwin's and in some ways like that
of his *bête noire*, Lloyd George. Leading decisions, when not made by Chamberlain
alone, were made by an inner cabinet consisting of himself, Lord Halifax, Simon
(Chancellor of the Exchequer) and Hoare
(Home Secretary). Ministers, even of the
inner circle, were kept in the dark about
his intentions, or learned of them only
through his close friend (though a minor
minister) Sir Kingsley Wood.

Nowhere were Chamberlain's activities
more intrusive than in foreign policy. He
distrusted the officials of the Foreign Office and was ready to circumvent them by
his personal diplomacy, intervening not
only more than Baldwin, whose indifference to foreign affairs was abnormal, but
more than the usual and natural concern
of the Prime Minister with foreign affairs
would justify. He leaned heavily on the
advice of Sir Horace Wilson, a civil servant
whose title was Chief Industrial Adviser to
the government. Wilson, who had been
Permanent Secretary in the Ministry of
Labour and was adept in industrial conciliation, was advanced through J. H.
Thomas' friendship and won Chamberlain's favour for his services at the Ottawa
conference. Very hard-working, rigidly self-
controlled, never rushed, quick to master
documents, skilful in talking round difficulties, always ready to play for safety and
to find the soothing formula which each
party will accept in his own sense and both
agree to long enough to compromise the
issue—no matter how disastrously: he reinforced Chamberlain's weaknesses—his tunnel vision and his faith in talk round a
table—and from the best of motives was the
worst of advisers in foreign affairs. Yet
Chamberlain relied on him heavily, gave
him an office adjoining his own, and for

three years went for a walk with him daily
in the park.

The stage was quickly set for the new
policies. One of Ribbentrop's first successes
in London had been to procure the recall
of Sir Eric Phipps from the British embassy
in Berlin; Phipps, a veteran diplomatist
with no illusions about Nazi Germany, was
transferred to Paris. His successor at Berlin, and a much more acceptable figure
there, was Sir Nevile Henderson, who had
been ambassador in Buenos Aires. Before
leaving for Berlin in May 1937, Henderson
had a cordial talk with Chamberlain, with
whom he worked very closely thereafter,
though as an appeaser he was often ahead
of his master and certainly of the Foreign
Office. "Guarantee us peace and peaceful
evolution in Europe, and Germany will
find that she has no more sincere, and, I
believe, more useful friend in the world
than Great Britain," he told the Anglo-
German Fellowship. Soon this friendship
would be proffered in advance of any
guarantee. . . .

Before blaming Chamberlain for the
evils of the Munich settlement we must
remind ourselves that he was not alone in
his enthusiasm for it. He was deluged with
letters of praise from people at home and
abroad, high and low, from the King, from
General Smuts, from the kitchen-maid of
the Chamberlain family. *The Times* declared that "no conqueror returning from a
victory on the battlefield had come
adorned with nobler laurels." A popular
journalist (Godfrey Winn) had written before the Munich conference: "Praise be to
God and to Mr. Chamberlain. I find no
sacrilege, no bathos, in coupling those two
names." Most of the press was nearly as
enthusiastic; and the vehement defence of
the Munich settlement continued until the
end of the year, though more and more the

subject became one causing bitter divisions, in society as in politics, in bar-rooms and in clubs. The chief defenders in the government, beside Chamberlain, were Simon, Hoare, Inskip, and Lord Maugham (who succeeded Lord Hailsham as Lord Chancellor in March 1938).

Criticism, however, was not lacking from the first. Talk of peace for our time seemed to be belied by the recruiting posters, the balloon-barrage, the distribution of gas masks, the A.R.P. activities which continued after Munich. Books about Czechoslovakia and the European situation, such as Douglas Reed's *Disgrace Abounding* and a Penguin Special, *Europe and the Czechs,* which enjoyed a very large sale, stirred—or rather echoed—second thoughts about Munich. The sacrifice of Czechoslovakia was a sin not expiated until Britain had gone through her own lonely ordeal in 1940–41. Before parliament met again, on October 3, Duff Cooper, the First Lord of the Admiralty, had resigned in protest, and there were signs of revolt among some of the "young Turks" of the Conservative party. Professor R. W. Seton-Watson had circulated a memorandum among members of parliament describing some of the pressures to which the Czechoslovakian government had been exposed from its friends, and this, though rather too vigorously contradicted by Hoare, had had its effect.

The Commons debated the Munich agreement for four days (October 3–6). Chamberlain reiterated his belief that his action had avoided war, and that he had been right in taking it; his purpose since taking office had been "to work for the pacification of Europe," even though "the path which leads to appeasement is long and bristles with obstacles" (October 3). Simon asked critics if they would, if they could, undo what had been done, and "fling the world into the cauldron of immediate war." Few took up this challenge. Attlee condemned the settlement as one of Britain's greatest diplomatic defeats and a bitter humiliation; a gallant and democratic people had been "betrayed and handed over to a ruthless despotism"; brute force had triumphed, and Hitler had won dominance over Europe without firing a shot. Churchill foretold doom. "We have sustained a total and unmitigated defeat," the fruits of five years of "uninterrupted retreat of British power." He concluded:

And do not suppose that this is the end. This is only the beginning of the reckoning. This is only the first sip, the first foretaste of a bitter cup which will be proffered to us year by year unless by a supreme recovery of moral health and martial vigour, we arise again and take our stand for freedom as in the olden time.

Duff Cooper gave an explanation of his resignation. If war had come over Czechoslovakia it would have been, as in 1914, to prevent one country from dominating the continent "by brutal force." "For that principle we must ever be prepared to fight, for on the day when we are not prepared to fight for it we forfeit our Empire, our liberties and our independence."

Despite these criticisms, there was no doubt that the government would be sustained in parliament, as it was supported by a majority of the people outside. Opposition came from the Liberals and the Labour party, and from some thirty Conservatives: Eden, Cranborne and their followers, and Churchill, Amery, Robert Boothby, Duncan Sandys, Harold Macmillan, Brendan Bracken, Lord Lloyd, Lord Cecil. In the Commons such critics abstained from voting, and the government carried the motion of approval by 366 votes to 144. In November the Duchess of Atholl resigned her seat in protest against the government's foreign policy, and ran for re-election as an Independent, but was defeated.

Yet it was soon clear that whatever else had been saved by the Munich agreement, Czechoslovakia had been abandoned even more shamefully than had at first appeared. The so-called international commission which was to delimit the fifth and last zone which the Germans were to occupy, and to supervise other arrangements, consisted of two German generals, the British, French and Italian ambassadors in Berlin, and a Czech representative. To decide which districts should, on an ethnographical basis, be included in this fifth zone, the Germans insisted that the census of 1910 be used, thus greatly and unjustifiably increasing their "take": the Czech representative appealed for help to the British and French ambassadors and was coldly ignored. The Germans took what they wanted without let or hindrance. Poland and Hungary presented claims to Czechoslovakian territory also, and these were settled, not by a four-power conference which the Munich agreement had promised, but by an "award," in the case of Hungarian claims, made by Ribbentrop and Ciano, the Italian foreign minister, at Vienna on November 2. The British government accepted this exclusion placidly, and the "guarantee" which had been given for Czechoslovakia's new frontiers was allowed to fade away, until on March 2, 1939, in response to a query about it, the German government insolently stated that even to raise the question was an unwarranted and undesirable interference in Germany's sphere of influence. All Czechoslovakia got from Great Britain was a loan of £30 millions, which provoked rude comparisons with a certain thirty pieces of silver, and the balance of which, remaining in London after Germany extinguished what little survived of Czechoslovakia in March 1939, was, amid the stupe-fied disgust of the public, handed over to the German government.

What was left, then, of Chamberlain's gifts from Munich? The democratic powers had lost, to Hitler, the strategic position of Czechoslovakia, her fortified frontiers, her 21 regular divisions and 15 or 16 second-line divisions; they had lost a just cause, they had lost their good name, they had lost the support of the smaller powers, they had exchanged, in the event, the possible assistance of Russia for a cold and fatal neutrality on her part. As it became clearer that in spite of all this they would still, in all likelihood, have to fight, only two points of justification remained: when war came, the country entered it with greater unity than it would have done in 1938 and with much greater support from the Dominions; and it entered it with greater strength, because the breathing spell which it won was decisive for Britain's rearmament. The last argument was inconsistent with the earlier claim that Chamberlain had brought back "peace for our time." . . .

In the months following the Munich settlement as much energy was devoted to rearmament as to appeasement, inconsistent though they were. Britain had begun to enlarge the air force, in a very modest way, in 1934; rearmament became an official policy in 1935, and policy was translated into practice in 1936. The pace, however, remained leisurely until after Munich: Treasury control exercised its normal restraints; rearmament must not lead to the "sacrifice" of British commerce or prejudice policies of conciliation; the public was not ready for large programmes. Rearmament was still thought of as a deterrent to aggressors, not as a preparation for war.

Between the beginning of 1936 and the end of 1938 the main progress made was in the enlargement and re-equipment of the R.A.F. New types of aircraft began to appear: their prototypes were first seen by the public in 1936, and represented the fruits of Lord Londonderry's term at the Air Ministry: the Wellington, Hampden and Blenheim bombers, the Spitfire and Hurricane fighters, on which Britain's survival in 1940 largely rested. The Spitfire was the last and most beautiful of the designs of R. J. Mitchell: an attempt to translate the flight of birds into the lines of an aeroplane which his tragically short life only just permitted him to realise. Under Lord Swinton the Air Ministry became very busy. A new programme, Scheme F, approved by the Cabinet in February 1936, provided for the construction of 8000 planes in three years as compared with 3800 which the previous programmes would have produced in two years: this allowed for a much greater reserve of planes. The strength of the R.A.F. was expanded, and the Royal Air Force Volunteer Reserve was inaugurated.

Even these developments were necessarily slow in producing results; a new and warlike temper was needed, and appeared after the *Anschluss*—six months before the new spirit, born of Munich, began to transform the rearmament of the two older services. After a tug-of-war between Swinton and Simon, the Chancellor of the Exchequer, financial restraints were practically given up, and industrial capacity became the chief limitation. The new programme, Scheme L, approved on April 27, 1938, provided for 12,000 new planes in two years (the figure was raised to 17,500 just before the war began). This involved close planning of production with the aircraft companies. The production staff of the Air Ministry was strengthened by the appointment of Air-Marshal Sir Wilfrid Freeman as Air Member for Development and Production, and Ernest Lem-

on (of the L.M.S. Railway) as Director-General of Production. The expansion of aircraft factories and the construction of shadow factories were pushed forward; sub-contracting was developed; the potential of the aircraft industry was so increased that in 1939 deliveries exceeded expectations. In April, the first mission for the purchase of planes went to the United States: 400 planes were ordered as a result, to the benefit of the American aircraft industry's war potential. When war came, the R.A.F., with the industrial strength on which it depended, was better prepared than the army or navy. This was not enough, however, to save the government from severe criticism in a debate on air strength on May 12, 1938; as a result of which Lord Swinton was replaced by the brisk and more genial figure of Sir Kingsley Wood, the Minister of Health (succeeded in turn by Walter Elliot).

Progress was much slower in the other services. The navy, which had less lost ground to recover, began a modest programme of expansion in 1935, designed to supplement its "one-power standard" (the power being Japan) by new vessels, chiefly cruisers and destroyers, to provide protection against German depredations on commerce during a war in Europe. This was slightly accelerated in 1936. The army had been the most neglected of the services. The regular army consisted of five divisions, of which one (divided into two in 1938) was mobile; but only two were fully equipped by October 1938. Mechanisation was more of a theory than a practice: it was not until 1938 that the army possessed its peacetime complement of wheeled vehicles and half the needed number of tracked vehicles. Its greatest limitation was, however, in the idea of its use: it served a doctrine of limited liability, under which it was expected to provide for home defence and for imperial garrisons, but not

British and German Expenditure on Armaments

	1934 (£ millions)	1938 (at 1934 prices)	Increase (per cent)
Great Britain	99.1	350.0	250
Germany	280.0	1600.0	470

Estimated Annual Expenditure on Rearmament in Great Britain, 1934–39 (£ millions)

	Total	Factory construction (Royal Ordnance Factories and others)	Army	Navy	R.A.F.
1934	37.2	–	6.9	20.9	9.4
1935	42.6	–	8.5	24.2	9.9
1936	60.7	–	12.5	29.6	18.6
1937	104.2	1.5	21.4	42.0	39.3
1938	182.2	8.7	44.3	63.2	66.0
1939	273.1	12.7	67.6	82.9	109.9

to produce an expeditionary force nor support commitments on the continent of Europe. This, among other things, meant that the chief effort in its re-equipment was devoted to its tasks in anti-aircraft defence. There was, none the less, an important expansion of the arms industry after 1936 under a new official, the Director-General of Munitions Production, Engineer Vice-Admiral Sir Harold Brown: new Royal Ordnance Factories and private arms factories were built, and in 1937 the stockpiling of strategic materials was begun. Moreover the enlargement and re-equipment of the Territorial Army increased the efficiency of the regular army also.

Such measures of rearmament, large and indeed unprecedented in their cost in peacetime, were much less than those of Germany. In 1938 Germany was spending £1710 millions, or a quarter of her national income, on armaments, Great Britain £358 millions, 7 per cent of her national income. The increase in expenditure on armaments in Great Britain, great as it was (250 per cent more than the figure for 1934), was less than Germany's (470 per cent); by 1938 Britain's expenditure exceeded that of France, a reversal of the situation in 1934.

Such expenditures put a heavy strain on the budget. For 1938 total expenditure was estimated at £944 millions, compared with £862.8 millions in 1937; of this the defence services accounted for £253 millions (plus £90 millions to be provided by borrowing). The standard rate of income tax was raised from 5s. to 5s. 6d. in the £. In the last peacetime budget, that of 1939, expenditure was estimated at £942 millions, of which defence demanded £250 millions (plus £380 millions to be found by borrowing). The limit on borrowing for defence was raised from £400 millions to £800 millions. On this occasion surtax rates and death duty on the larger estates were increased. Actual expenditures were, of course, higher than the estimates.

The war-scare over Czechoslovakia revealed to the public some—though not necessarily the most serious—of the deficiencies in the country's defences. Most serious seemed to be the anti-aircraft defences: the cupboard was almost bare, and could hardly provide for London, let alone any other city: only 44 of the larger (3.7 inch) A.A. guns ordered were available; and there were only 60 fire pumps in London. Nor did the spirit of urgency produced by the crisis pass with Chamberlain's return from Munich: indeed the unanimity with which increased efforts in rearmament were called for was a measure of the confidence which friend and foe put in "peace for our time." In the year of peace which remained many deficiencies were made good, though not so much as a result of new plans as of the carrying forward, more or less to schedule, of those already made. The R.A.F.'s programmes were now being achieved in full measure. The navy's main addition was in the construction of trawlers and escort vessels for protection against mines and submarines. A list of reserved occupations promised the proper husbanding of man-power in January 1939. Financial restraints on defence measures thawed rapidly. And in April 1939, Chamberlain even agreed to the creation of a Ministry of Supply, though without responsibility for the requirements of the Admiralty and R.A.F. It began to function in July, though Chamberlain's choice of minister, Leslie Burgin (a National Liberal who had been Minister of Transport) did not inspire enthusiasm. All these developments expressed a change of spirit: rearmament in preparation for war, and no longer as a safeguard for peace. Yet it still fell short of the full mobilisation of the country's resources. It was based on the supposition that resources could be built up over two years: by the summer of 1940 Britain would be ready for war; before

then she must begin no premature military action.

One great change there was: in the conception of the army's function. The idea of "limited liability" was dropped early in 1939, thanks to Leslie Hore-Belisha (the War Secretary) and Halifax. The defence of Britain was understood to involve the defence of France. Anglo-French military conversations were resumed on a serious level. A British expeditionary force was to be prepared, consisting of 19 infantry and 2 cavalry divisions; in the event 4 divisions were ready by September 1939, and 6 by January 1940. The army was to be raised to 32 divisions (the six regular divisions and 26 Territorial divisions) by bringing the Territorial Army to full strength and doubling its size; these decisions were made on March 29 and April 21, 1939. The final measure was the introduction, for the first time during peace, of conscription.

How far did the progress of rearmament after Munich justify the settlement on the ground, of which its apologists came to make so much, that the time gained was greatly, even indispensably, to Britain's advantage? Stocks of rifles, guns, tanks were increased: in October 1938, only two army divisions were fully equipped; by September 1939 there was equipment for five. Industrial mobilisation had a year more in which to pick up momentum. The provision of anti-aircraft guns increased fourfold, to about two-fifths of the estimated "ideal" requirements. The chain of 20 radar stations, first proposed by Robert Watson-Watt in 1935, was completed: even during the Munich crisis it had been in operation in the Thames estuary. And the number of modern planes, of the necessary speed and fire power, which Britain possessed had increased. In September 1938, the R.A.F. had five squadrons of Hurricanes and one of Spitfires; a year later it had 26 squadrons equipped with one or the other. The expansion of Germany's air force was nearly complete in 1938, Britain's was beginning; the disparity between the two was therefore reduced in the year which followed as far as quality of planes was concerned, though it was increased in the comparative size of the two forces. It was Britain's monthly output of planes which was the hopeful sign: in 1938 it was over 200 a month, in 1939 over 600. It was in the strengthening of her air power that the breathing spell afforded by Munich was of supreme value to Great Britain.

have won easily the bases in France and the Low Countries from which to raid England on a large scale. Whether the gains of the Munich year are held to outweigh the losses will depend on one's judgment of the value of a year in increasing Britain's air power and industrial potential for war—an increase which came, not so much from what was done in the year, as from the greater length of time in which programmes of production already begun could gain momentum.

In one other sphere there was a gain. After Munich, Britain's civil defences were put in order. The work of A.R.P. (Air

British and German Air Strength, 1938–39

| | German | | Britain (home strength) [a] | |
	1938	1939	1938	1939
First-line aircraft	2847	3609	1854	1978
Totals of new aircraft production in year	5235	8295	2827	7940

[a] France had 1735 first-line aircraft in 1939.

So far so good. What was lost, by not fighting in September 1938, were the 36 Czech divisions, and the fact that at that time Germany had only 13 divisions on her western front. A year later Germany could dispose most of her forces in the west after the fall of Poland and by that time had greatly strengthened her fortifications in the west (the Siegfried Line). In 1938 Germany had between 21 and 51 fully-equipped divisions, by 1939, 106; yet in that year French strength had not increased and that of the British army not very much. Churchill claimed that in 1938 France still possessed military superiority over Germany; by 1939 the reverse was true. In 1938 Britain was weaker in the air than in 1939; but Germany could not then

Raid Precautions) had begun in 1935, under the Home Office: doctors, air-raid wardens, policemen had been given training, volunteer workers recruited, handbooks prepared. Late in 1937 the Air Raid Precautions bill was enacted, imposing A.R.P. duties on the local authorities at the charge, up to 90 per cent of the cost, of the national government. In late October 1938, Sir John Anderson, the distinguished civil servant, was made Lord Privy Seal with responsibility for civil defence, and new plans were made and put into action. Emergency fire services and transport services were prepared, and 400,000 small steel shelters (Anderson shelters) ordered for use in private houses and gardens (plans for deep air raid shelters were rejected). In January 1939, the government's *Guide to National Service* was distributed to every household in the kingdom, and everyone was urged to volunteer for service of some sort. Plans for evacuation of people from the cities, especially children and hospital patients, were completed—a task falling chiefly to Walter Elliot and the Ministry of Health. The calls which war was likely to make upon all, civilians and soldiers alike, were clear, even exaggeratedly so, as 1939 opened.

Under the pressure of events Labour slowly and doubtfully abandoned its opposition to rearmament. Belief in pacifism, disarmament, collective security had been gradually undermined, partly by the events in Spain, Austria, Czechoslovakia, partly by the efforts of such leaders as Dalton and Bevin, respectively chairman of the Labour party and of the T.U.C. in 1937. The Parliamentary Labour Party abandoned direct opposition to the estimates of the service departments—and hence to rearmament—in July 1937, when it decided by a vote of 45 to 39 to abstain in such votes in future; even this change,

however, was resisted by Attlee, Morrison, Greenwood, so great was their distrust of Chamberlain's policies. The next statement of the National Council of Labour on foreign policy, *International Policy and Defence*, issued in July 1937, still talked of restoring the League, of disarmament and the avoidance of an arms race; but it added that the country must be strong enough to defend itself and fulfil its part in collective security, and that until conditions improved a future Labour government would not reverse the policy of rearmament. This report was adopted by overwhelming majorities by the T.U.C. in September and by the Labour party conference at Bournemouth in October 1937: both actions were taken to imply support for rearmament. A circular of the National Council of Labour in March 1939, was more specific: "rearmament is necessary, and indeed unavoidable in the interests of self-defence alone." Labour had shown on the eve of Munich that it would accept, even welcome, a strong policy; and in this, despite its opposition to conscription, it remained firm.

The Origins of the Second World War (1961) by A. J. P.
TAYLOR (b. 1906) is one of the most controversial books
on the subject today. Currently a fellow of Magdalen
College, Oxford, Taylor has written widely; his works
include a biography of Bismarck, a history of the
Hapsburg empire, and a survey of European diplomacy
during the half century prior to World War I. Taylor is at
his best when challenging traditional interpretations. His
judgments that Hitler was more opportunist than
warmonger, that the Czech President Beneš deliberately
heightened tension to provoke British and French support,
that the Czechoslovak crisis of 1938 was of British making,
differ radically from earlier generally accepted
interpretations.*

A. J. P. Taylor

Hitler's Opportunism

After partitioning the Ottoman empire
in Europe in 1913, Pasich, the prime minister of Serbia, is reputed to have said:
"The first round is won; now we must prepare the second against Austria." The second round duly came a year later, though
it was not of his making. Everyone in Europe felt much the same in March 1938
after the *Anschluss*. The Austrian round
was over; the Czechoslovak round was due
to begin. It was not necessary to prepare
this second round. Geography and politics
automatically put Czechoslovakia on the
agenda. As an ally of France and the only
democratic state east of the Rhine, she was
a perpetual reproach to Hitler, thrust far
into German territory. Nor was it easy to
sustain her. The Italians, if they wished,

had direct access to Austria. Czechoslovakia was cut off on every side. Germany
divided her from France; Poland and Rumania from Soviet Russia. Her immediate
neighbours were hostile: Hungary bitterly
"revisionist"; Poland, though an ally of
France, also revisionist because of Tešin,
which the Czechs had acquired after the
first World war, and blindly confident in
her own non-aggression pact with Germany. There could be no question of "aid-
ing" Czechoslovakia. It was full-scale European war or nothing.

The question of Czechoslovakia would
have been less immediate if geography
alone had been in play. Even her democracy and her alliances might not of themselves have provoked the crisis. But

*From *The Origins of the Second World War* by A. J. P. Taylor. Copyright © 1961 by A. J. P. Taylor.
Reprinted by permission of Hamish Hamilton Ltd. and Atheneum Publishers. Pp. 151–159, 187–191. Footnotes omitted.

Czechoslovakia had a canker at her heart. Despite appearances, she was a state of nationalities, not a national state. Only the Czechs were genuine Czechoslovaks; and even they interpreted this to mean a centralised state of Czech character. The others—Slovaks, Hungarians, Ruthenes, and above all Germans—were national minorities: sometimes quiescent, sometimes discontented, but never convinced adherents of the existing order. The three million Germans (loosely, though wrongly, called Sudetens) were closely linked to the Austrians by history and blood. The *Anschluss* stirred them to ungovernable excitement. Maybe they would have been wiser to remain contented with their lot—free, though not equal, citizens in a democratic community. But men are not wise when they hear the call of nationalism. The great German state—powerful, united, nationalist—lay just across their borders. Their Austrian cousins had just joined it. They wished to join it too. No doubt, in a muddled way, they also wished to remain in Czechoslovakia; and never considered how the two wishes could be reconciled. But the German national movement in Czechoslovakia, however confused, was a fact; and those who wanted to "stand by Czechoslovakia" never explained how they would deal with this fact. Hitler did not create this movement. It was waiting for him, ready—indeed eager—to be used. Even more than in the case of Austria, Hitler did not need to act. Others would do his work for him. The crisis over Czechoslovakia was provided for Hitler. He merely took advantage of it.

Hitler undoubtedly wished to "liberate" the Germans of Czechoslovakia. He was also concerned, in more practical terms, to remove the obstacle which a well-armed Czechoslovakia, allied to France and Soviet Russia, raised against German hegemony. He was by no means clear how this

could be done. Like everyone else in Europe, he overrated French strength and French resolution. A direct German attack on Czechoslovakia would, he thought, provoke a French intervention. His initial solution, as he had revealed at the conference of 5 November 1937, was to hope for a conflict in the Mediterranean between France and Italy. Then, as he put it some time in April 1938, "we return with Czechoslovakia in the bag"; but, if Italy failed to move, "return with bag empty." This plan, too, rested on a miscalculation: it overrated Italy's capacity for aggression. But, whether the Mediterranean war came off or not, it was worth while preparing the situation in Czechoslovakia by encouraging the Sudeten movement. It is as certain as anything can be that Hitler did not intend to overthrow the French system in Europe by a frontal assault. "Munich" still dominated his mind; and at this time Munich meant for him not the triumphant conference of September 1938, but the disastrous Nazi rising of November 1923. He meant to succeed by intrigue and the threat of violence, not by violence itself. On 28 March he received the Sudeten representatives and appointed Henlein, their leader, his "viceroy." They were to negotiate with the Czechoslovak government; and, in Henlein's words, "we must always demand so much that we can never be satisfied." The movement was to remain legal and orderly; the Czechs must be given no excuse to crush it by force. Perhaps the Czechs would put themselves in the wrong; perhaps the French would be preoccupied or would lose their nerve. In the spring of 1938 Hitler did not see his way clearly. He screwed up the tension in the hope that something would give somewhere.

Hitler's antagonist, President Benes of Czechoslovakia, had a similar aim. He, too, wished to screw up the tension, though in hope of exactly the opposite result. Faced with a crisis, the French, and the British also, would, he hoped, come to their senses; they would stand by Czechoslovakia; Hitler would draw back, and this humiliation would not only arrest his march to the domination of Europe—it might even bring down the Nazi régime in Germany itself. Benes had behind him twenty years of diplomatic experience and diplomatic success. He was the Metternich of democracy, with the same self-confidence; the same ingenuity of method and argument; with the same exaggerated reliance also on treaties and international rights. He handled the Sudeten problem much as Metternich handled the Italian problem a century earlier: insoluble at home, it could only be settled on the international field. Benes was as ready to negotiate with the Sudetens as they were to negotiate with him, and with equally little hope of a successful outcome. Perhaps even with less; for concessions to the Germans in Czechoslovakia would bring demands from the other national minorities, to the ruin of the existing state. Benes and the Sudetens alike negotiated solely with their ear cocked on British and French opinion. The Sudeten leaders tried to give the impression that they were merely asking for equal treatment within Czechoslovakia. Benes tried to force them into an open demand for her dissolution. Then, he believed, the Western Powers would assert themselves. He judged these Powers from his years in France during the first World war, and from his later experiences when they dominated the League of Nations at Geneva. Like most people, including Hitler, he failed to recognise their present weakness, both moral and material—that of France in particular.

Benes had limitations of his own. Czechoslovakia's alliances looked formidable on paper. There was the alliance for mutual defence with France made in 1925; the alliance with Soviet Russia of 1935, which however only operated if France acted first; and the Little Entente with Rumania and Yugoslavia, directed against Hungary. Benes did not make the most of this position. He deliberately neglected the alliance with Soviet Russia. To his mind, it was a supplement to the French alliance, not a substitute for it. Others might speculate, usually with some scepticism, whether Soviet Russia would aid Czechoslovakia even if France remained neutral. Benes did not raise the question. He was a westerner, the heir of Masaryk, who had won Czechoslovakia's independence with Western, not with Russian, assistance. He told Newton, the British minister: "Czechoslovakia's relations with Russia had always been and would remain a secondary consideration. . . . His country would always follow and be bound to Western Europe." The Spanish civil war gave additional warning against defending "democracy" with Russian backing. But Benes did not need this warning: his mind was made up long before. Even if he were tempted, there were strong restraining forces within Czechoslovakia. The Czech Agrarians, the largest party in the government coalition, dreaded any association with Communism. They, too, were inclined to say: "Better Hitler than Stalin." Moreover, Benes was a man of peace. The Czechoslovak army was a formidable force, its well-equipped 34 divisions probably a match in themselves for the half-trained German army of 1938. Benes never intended to use it, except in the unlikely event of a general war. The Czechs were a small people. It had taken them nearly three hundred years to recover from the disaster of the White Mountain in 1620. Benes was determined that they should not suffer another such catastrophe. He was ready to play against

Hitler for high stakes; he would not risk the highest stake of all. In the last resort, he would bow his head to the storm and hope that the Czechs would survive it—as indeed they did.

Hitler and Benes both wished to increase the tension and to bring on a crisis. The British and the French, making the same calculation, had exactly the opposite aim: they wished to avert a crisis so as to avoid the terrible choice between war and humiliation. The British were the more urgent of the two. The French seemed the more exposed: they had the precise obligation of alliance with Czechoslovakia, whereas the British were uncommitted except as members of the moribund League of Nations. But the French could transfer their dilemma to the British. They could talk of resisting Hitler; and when the British refused to back them, it was the British who would take the blame. This had a curious result. Hitler, Benes, and even the French, could wait for the crisis to mature, confident that this would force a decision from the British. For this very reason, the British had to act. They were most remote from the Czechoslovak question, yet the most insistent on raising it. Their motives were of the highest. They wished to prevent a European war; they wished also to achieve a settlement more in accordance with the great principle of self-determination than that made in 1919. The outcome was the precise opposite of their intention. They imagined that there was a "solution" of the Sudeten German problem and that negotiations would produce it. In fact the problem was insoluble in terms of compromise, and every step in negotiations only made this clearer. By seeking to avert a crisis, the British brought it on. The Czechoslovak problem was not of British making; the Czech crisis of 1938 was.

The British were alert to the problem from the very moment of the *Anschluss*—long before Hitler had formulated his intentions. On 12 March, when the French ambassador called to discuss the Austrian question, Halifax replied by asking: "What would be the French conception of rendering assistance to Czechoslovakia?" The ambassador "had no short answer." Ten days later the British provided their own answer, or lack of it. In a memorandum for the French government, they stressed their commitments under Locarno. "Those commitments are, in their view, no mean contribution to the maintenance of peace in Europe, and, though they have no intention of withdrawing from them, they cannot see their way to add to them." There was "little hope" that military operations by France and the Soviet Union could prevent the occupation of Czechoslovakia by Germany; the British, even if they entered the war, could offer no more than the "economic pressure" of blockade. Hence the Czechoslovak government should be pushed into finding "such a solution of German minority questions as would be compatible with ensuring the integrity of the Czechoslovak State." Privately Halifax added other arguments. "Quite frankly, the moment is unfavourable, and our plans, both for offence and defence, are not sufficiently advanced." He said also to the French ambassador: "The French were disposed, perhaps, to rate more highly than ourselves the value of strong declarations." The British had already rejected one such declaration. On 17 March the Soviet government proposed a discussion, "in the League of Nations or outside of it," of practical measures "for the collective saving of peace." Halifax did not think that this idea "had any great value"; and the Russians were told that a conference, "designed less to secure the settlement of outstanding problems than to organise concerted action against aggression . . . would not necessarily have a favourable effect upon the prospects of European peace."

The French naturally disliked being prompted to make up their minds one way or the other. On 15 March the French Committee of National Defence discussed the question of aid to Czechoslovakia. Gamelin answered: the French could "tie down" some German troops; they could not break through the Siegfried line (which did not in fact exist at this time); hence the only effective way of attacking Germany was through Belgium, and, to secure permission for this, British diplomatic support was necessary. It was his usual equivocation. The politicians asked a military question; and Gamelin, in reply, talked diplomacy. Paul-Boncour, the foreign minister, tried to take this strong line so far as diplomacy was concerned. He told Phipps, the British ambassador, on 24 March that "a definite warning to Germany by the two countries [Great Britain and France] . . . would be the best means of avoiding war . . . Time was not on our side, for Germany . . . was getting stronger and stronger, until she would finally attain complete hegemony in Europe." The British did not reply to these remarks which they had often heard before. Nor did they need to. Paul-Boncour's days were numbered. On 10 April the government of Léon Blum, which had been in office less than a month, was itself overthrown. Daladier, the next prime minister, first thought of keeping Paul-Boncour; then took alarm at his talk of standing firm now, rather than fighting later in still more disastrous circumstances. Daladier telephoned to Paul-Boncour: "The policy you recommend is fine and worthy of France. But I do not believe that we are in a position to follow it. I am going to take Georges Bonnet." Daladier survived as prime minister until April 1940; Bonnet as foreign minister until September 1939. These two men were to lead France into the second World war.

It was an uneasy partnership. Daladier was a Radical of the old tradition, anxious to preserve the honour of France and convinced that a firm policy could alone stop Hitler. But he was at a loss how to do it. He had served in the trenches during the first World war, and shrank with horror from a new holocaust. On every occasion he spoke decisively against appeasement, and then acquiesced in it. Bonnet, on the other hand, was appeasement personified, ready to pay almost any price in order to keep Hitler quiet. He believed that the pillars of French power had collapsed; and his main aim was to put the blame for the consequences on others—the British, the Czechs, the Poles, the Russians, he did not mind on whom, so long as his record, and France's looked clean on paper. Never for one moment did either Daladier or Bonnet contemplate taking the lead in the hope that the British and others would follow. Rather they looked plaintively to London for some twist which would enable them to escape from their impossible situation.

In London, too, the partnership of Chamberlain and Halifax was by no means easy. Chamberlain had the strongest character of the four men who determined British and French policy. Timidity, or doubt of British strength, did not affect his calculations, though he had a natural dislike of war. He believed that Hitler could be won for peace; he believed also that Hitler had a good case so far as Czechoslovakia was concerned. Hence he was determined to act on these two beliefs, whatever the opposition at home or abroad. He is often accused of ignorance in foreign affairs. But his opinions were shared by those supposedly most competent to judge. Nevile Henderson, the ambassador at Berlin, was equally confident that Hitler could be won for peace; and he had been chosen for the post by Vansittart as the best available British diplomatist. Both Henderson at Berlin and Newton at Prague insisted that the Sudeten claims were well founded morally and that the Czechoslovak government were making no genuine attempt to meet them. Phipps at Paris stressed, and perhaps exaggerated, French weakness. Some members of the Foreign Office disliked Chamberlain's policy. But they were in much the same position as Daladier: though they disliked the policy, none of them could suggest an alternative. They regretted that Great Britain and France had not acted against the German reoccupation of the Rhineland; they thought that Hitler ought to be "hit on the head." But they had no idea how this operation could be performed. None of them placed any hope in the United States. None of them advocated alliance with Soviet Russia, Chilston the ambassador at Moscow least of all. He wrote, for instance, on 19 April: "The Red army, though no doubt equal to a defensive war within the frontiers of the Soviet Union, is not capable of carrying the war into the enemy's territory. . . . I personally consider it highly unlikely that the Soviet Government would declare war merely in order to fulfil their treaty obligations or even to forestall a blow to Soviet prestige or an indirect threat to Soviet security. . . . The Soviet Union must be counted out of European politics." These views were fully accepted by the Foreign Office. Chamberlain had to devise policy where before there was none.

It is difficult to say whether Halifax agreed with this policy, still more difficult to discover one of his own. He was fertile in negations. He was contemptuous of French statesmen, particularly of Bonnet; he seems to have been sceptical about Soviet Russia and the United States. He had no sympathy with the Czechs, and much impatience with Benes. Had he any greater faith in appeasement? Probably his visit to Berchtesgaden had given him a permanent distaste for Hitler; but Halifax passed much of his life among people whom he disliked. A Viceroy who could welcome Gandhi to his palace was not likely to be affected by personal feelings. The object of his policy, so far as he had one, was to buy time—though without any clear idea what use to make of it. His immediate object, like Bonnet's, was to keep his record clean. Unlike Bonnet, he succeeded. Halifax was steadily loyal to Chamberlain; this loyalty took the form of allowing Chamberlain to shoulder all responsibility, which he was eager to do. Yet now and then Halifax gave a tug in the opposite direction; and this tug sometimes had an effect at the decisive moment. Such were the four men who, between them, settled the destinies of Western civilisation. . . .

The conference at Munich was meant to mark the beginning of an epoch in European affairs. "Versailles"—the system of 1919—was not only dead, but buried. A new system, based on equality and mutual confidence between the four great European Powers, was to take its place. Chamberlain said: "I believe that it is peace for our time"; Hitler declared: "I have no more territorial demands to make in Europe." There were still great questions to be settled in international affairs. The Spanish civil war was not over. Germany had not recovered her colonies. More remotely, agreements would have to be reached over economic policy and over armaments, before stability was restored in Europe. None of these questions threatened to provoke a general war. The demonstration had been given that Germany could attain by peaceful negotiation the position in Europe to which her resources entitled her. The great hurdle had been successfully surmounted: the system, directed against Germany, had been dismantled by agreement, without a war. Yet, within six months, a new system was being constructed against Germany. Within a year, Great Britain, France, and Germany were at war. Was "Munich" a fraud from the start—for Germany merely a stage in the march towards world conquest, or, on the side of Great Britain and France, merely a device to buy time until their re-armament was more advanced? So it appeared in retrospect. When the policy of Munich failed, everyone announced that he had expected it to fail; and the participants not only accused the others of cheating, but boasted that they had been cheating themselves. In fact, no one was as clear-sighted as he later claimed to have been; and the four men of Munich were all in their different ways sincere, though each had reserves which he concealed from the others.

The French yielded most, and with least hope for the future. They surrendered the position of paramount European power which they had appeared to enjoy since 1919. But what they surrendered was artificial. They yielded to reality rather than to force. They had supposed all along that the advantages won in 1919 and subsequently—the restrictions on Germany and the alliances with East European states— were assets which they could supinely enjoy, not gains which they must fiercely defend. They did not lift a finger to assert the system of Versailles after the occupation of the Ruhr in 1923. They abandoned reparations; they acquiesced in the re-armament of Germany; they allowed the German re-occupation of the Rhineland; they did nothing to protect the independence of Austria. They kept up their alliances in Eastern Europe only from the belief that these would bring them aid if ever they were themselves attacked by Germany.

They abandoned their ally, Czechoslovakia, the moment she threatened to bring them risk instead of security. Munich was the logical culmination of French policy, not its reversal. The French recognised that they had lost their predominance in Eastern Europe, and knew that it could not be restored. This is far from saying that they feared for themselves. On the contrary, they accepted the British thesis, preached ever since Locarno, that they were in less danger of war if they withdrew behind the Rhine. They had preferred safety to grandeur—an ignoble policy perhaps, but not a dangerous one. Even in 1938, though they feared air bombardment, they did not fear defeat if war were thrust upon them. Gamelin was always emphatic that the democratic powers would win; and the politicians believed him. But what would be the point of war? This was the argument which had prevented French action since 1923, and which prevented it now. Germany, even if defeated, would still be there, great, powerful, determined on redress. War might stop the clock. It could not put it back; and afterwards events would move forward to the same end. The French were therefore willing to surrender everything except their own security, and they did not believe that they had surrendered this at Munich. They had a firm and, as it turned out a well-founded, faith that the Maginot line was impregnable—so much so that they regarded the Siegfried line, less correctly, as impregnable also. They assumed that a stalemate had been established in Western Europe. They could not impede the advance of German power in Eastern Europe; equally Germany could not invade France. The French were humiliated by Munich, not—as they supposed—endangered.

The British position was more complicated. Morality did not enter French calculations, or entered only to be discarded. The French recognised that it was their duty to assist Czechoslovakia; they rejected this duty as either too dangerous or too difficult. Léon Blum expressed French feeling best when he welcomed the agreement of Munich with a mixture of shame' and relief. With the British, on the other hand, morality counted for a great deal. The British statesmen used practical arguments: the danger from air attack; the backwardness of their re-armament; the impossibility, even if adequately armed, of helping Czechoslovakia. But these arguments were used to reinforce morality, not to silence it. British policy over Czechoslovakia originated in the belief that Germany had a moral right to the Sudeten German territory, on grounds of national principle; and it drew the further corollary that this victory for self-determination would provide a stabler, more permanent peace in Europe. The British government were not driven to acknowledge the dismemberment of Czechoslovakia solely from fear of war. They deliberately set out to impose this cession of territory on the Czechs before the threat of war raised its head. The settlement at Munich was a truimph for British policy, which had worked precisely to this end; not a triumph for British policy, which had no such clear intention. Nor was it merely a triumph for selfish or cynical British statesmen, indifferent to the fate of far-off peoples or calculating that Hitler might be launched into war against Soviet Russia. It was a triumph for all that was best and most enlightened in British life; a triumph for those who had preached equal justice between peoples; a triumph for those who had courageously denounced the harshness and short-sightedness of Versailles. Brailsford, the leading Socialist authority on foreign affairs, wrote in 1920 of the peace settlement: "The worst offence was the subjection of over three million Germans to Czech rule." This was the offence redressed at Munich. Idealists could claim that British policy had been tardy and hesitant. In 1938 it atoned for these failings. With skill and persistence, Chamberlain brought first the French, and then the Czechs, to follow the moral line.

There was a case against ceding Sudeten territory to Germany—the case that economic and geographic ties are more important than those of nationality. This had been the case against breaking up the Habsburg Monarchy; the Czechs who had taken the lead in breaking up the Monarchy could not use this argument, nor could their advocates in Western Europe. The dispute had to be transferred from the field of morality to that of practical considerations—to what is disapprovingly called *realpolitik*. The most outspoken opponents of Munich, such as Winston Churchill, asserted quite simply that Germany was becoming too powerful in Europe and that she must be stopped by the threat of a great coalition or, if necessary, by force of arms. Self-determination—the principle to which Czechoslovakia owed her existence—was dismissed as a sham. The only moral argument used was that the frontiers of existing states were sacred and that each state could behave as it liked within its own borders. This was the argument of legitimacy; the argument of Metternich and the Congress of Vienna. If accepted, it would have forbidden not only the break-up of the Habsburg Monarchy, but even the winning of independence by the British colonies in America. It was a strange argument for the British Left to use in 1938; and it sat uneasily upon them— hence the hesitations and ineffectiveness of their criticism. Duff Cooper, First Lord of the Admiralty, had no such doubts when he resigned in protest against the Munich settlement. As became an admiring biographer of Talleyrand, he was concerned with the Balance of Power and British honour, not with self-determination or the injustices of Versailles. For him, Czechoslovakia had no more been the real issue in 1938 than Belgium had been in 1914. This argument destroyed the moral validity of the British position in the first World war, but it had an appeal for the Conservative majority in the House of Commons. Chamberlain had to answer it in its own terms of power. He could not stress the unwillingness of the French to fight, which had been the really decisive weakness on the Western side. Therefore he had to make out that Great Britain herself was in no position to fight Germany.

Chamberlain was caught by his own argument. If Great Britain had been too weak to fight, then the government must speed rearmament; and this involved doubt in Hitler's good faith, whether avowed or not. In this way, Chamberlain did more than anyone else to destroy the case for his own policy. Moreover, one suspicion breeds another. It is doubtful whether Hitler ever took Chamberlain's sincerity seriously before Munich; it is certain that he did not do so a few days afterwards. What was meant as appeasement had turned into capitulation, on Chamberlain's own showing. Hitler drew the lesson that threats were his most potent weapon. The temptation to boast of Munich as a triumph of force was too great to be resisted. Hitler no longer expected to make gains by parading his grievances against Versailles; he expected to make them by playing on British and French fears. Thus he confirmed the suspicions of those who attacked Munich as a craven surrender. International morality was at a discount. Paradoxically, Benes was the true victor of Munich in the long run. For, while Czechoslovakia lost territory and later her independence also, Hitler lost the moral advantage which had hitherto made him irresistible. Munich became an emotive word, a symbol of shame, about which men can still not speak dispassionately. What was done at Munich mattered less than the way in which it was done; and what was said about it afterwards on both sides counted for still more.

Many historians, including for example Mowat, see Hitler's occupation of Prague as the act that destroyed the policy of appeasement; after this event, they maintain, British policy assumed a new course. CHRISTOPHER THORNE (b. 1934) cannot be counted in this group. In the following selection, he argues that appeasement did not really end until Britain declared war on Germany on September 3, 1939. Thorne is currently with the British Broadcasting Corporation as head of Further Education. He is editor of the series "The Making of the Twentieth Century"; the selection that follows is taken from a book written for the series.*

Christopher Thorne

Continuing Appeasement

The German occupation of Bohemia and Moravia spread alarm and confusion throughout Europe. Julius Streicher was already declaring at Nuremberg that the act "was only a beginning" and that "greater achievements would follow." "We have so many open doors in front of us," observed one of Goebbels's lieutenants to Coulondre on 18 March, "so many possibilities, that we don't know which way to turn."

In some fear bred an anxiety to please, and the Secretary-General of the Turkish Foreign Ministry assured the German chargé d'affaires in Ankara that his country would "co-operate actively" in making the Balkan area "more than ever an economic hinterland of Germany" and "a reliable source of supplies in time of political

crisis." Others waited to see where self-interest lay, and though a strong protest was despatched from Moscow, the German Embassy there observed that alternative lines of action were being kept open. The new Pope and his Cardinal Secretary of State, for their part, continued in private to manifest an "unmistakably forthcoming attitude" towards the Third Reich, for in the Vatican, as for long in the private temples of Halifax's Anglo-Catholicism and Lothian's Christian Science, no outright condemnation on spiritual grounds of a régime of manifest and unparalleled barbarity could be allowed to intrude upon political considerations.

It was in Poland and Rumania that the repercussions appeared greatest, however. The reduction of Slovakia to a state of vas-

---

*From Christopher Thorne, *The Approach of War, 1938–1939* (London: Macmillan & Co. Ltd., 1967), pp. 113–114, 118–120, 128–131, 197–202. Reprinted by permission of Macmillan & Co. Ltd. and St. Martin's Press, Inc. Footnotes omitted.

salage was a serious blow to Warsaw, and the treaty of protection which provided for a zone of German military presence at once increased current tension and the potential threat from the south. For Bucharest, too, the possibility of German attack came nearer, and the hostile presence of Hungary in Ruthenia complicated strategic and minority problems as well as serving a vital railway link with Poland. . . .

As tension between Poland and Germany increased, so did the pressure on the British Government to commit themselves openly. On the 28th Churchill, Eden and thirty-two others—nearly all Conservatives—tabled a motion in the Commons calling for the formation of a genuine National Government with full emergency powers, and neither Chamberlain's hint that moves were being planned which went "a good deal further than consultation," nor a countermotion by the latter's supporters, removed the widespread disquiet. Though the official Soviet reaction was becoming increasingly cold in the face of rebuffs, Maisky, the Ambassador in London, was assuring Sir Alexander Cadogan on the 29th that a British offer of military aid to Poland and Rumania "might have far-reaching results (and) would increase enormously the confidence of other countries." Perhaps the decisive conversation of that day, however, was the one Cadogan, Halifax and Chamberlain had with Mr. Ian Colvin, the Berlin correspondent of the *News Chronicle,* for the latter had come hot-foot from Germany bearing somewhat premature evidence and the warnings of General Beck's circle to the effect that Hitler was determined to attack Poland and that the Polish Foreign Minister might be in German pay. Something of the atmosphere in Berlin from which he had come may be gauged by a suggestion from the British military attaché which was also forwarded on the 29th, urging

that London should welcome an early war as the only means of avoiding "certain eventual elimination."

More than ever was Poland seen, in Halifax's phrase, as "the key to the whole situation." In the words of a Foreign Office memorandum of the 29th:

The absorption of Czecho-Slovakia has clearly revealed Germany's intentions . . . and there is every reason to suppose that the treatment applied [there] will be extended to other countries, notably Rumania and Poland. . . . It is [Germany's] purpose gradually to neutralise these countries, deprive them of their armies and incorporate them in the German economic system. When this has been done, the way will have been prepared for an attack on the West. . . .

Poland is no longer in a position to sit comfortably on the fence between the Soviet Union and Germany. . . . Circumstances would seem to dictate closer association with Russia, but there is much anti-Soviet feeling in Conservative and Catholic circles, and the Poles have not forgotten the Soviet invasion of 1921. . . . Poland has reached the parting of the ways.

On the 30th, therefore, a fresh proposal was put to Warsaw and Bucharest in the name of the British and French Governments: if they were ready to defend their independence, the West would assist them, though in Poland's case a promise to aid Rumania and a reciprocal guarantee of Britain and France were required. Even this was held to be too slow in the face of fresh alarms, however; on the evening of the 30th Kennard conveyed to Beck Chamberlain's enquiry as to whether he would accept an interim and unilateral guarantee of his country pending negotiations. In the time taken to smoke a cigarette, as he liked to say later, Beck agreed. Though Greenwood, Alexander and Dalton for the Labour Party attempted to persuade Chamberlain that no announcement should be made until Russia had been brought in, the decision was made. In the Commons on the 31st the Prime Minister inaugurated a fundamental change, on the surface at least, of British foreign policy: a wide and binding commitment would be undertaken in Eastern Europe. If Poland's independence were "clearly threatened" during the period of consultations, and she resisted, Britain and France would "feel themselves bound at once to lend her all support in their power." At Newcastle on the same day, Eden was able to declare happily that it was "unadulterated nonsense" to suggest that there was dissension in Government ranks over foreign policy.

Beck visited London from the 4th to the 6th April and made the most of the favourable position in which he had been placed. In the face of Chamberlain's suggestions concerning Poland's need for military supplies from Russia he maintained his view that any closer association with Moscow would provoke war; nor would he go beyond a promise of discussions with Rumania to provide for their mutual security. Reassuringly, however, Beck also informed his listeners that no written German demands had been presented to Poland, airily remarking that he "did not propose to trouble His Majesty's Government with the various phases through which the Danzig question might pass." It was finally agreed that a permanent and reciprocal agreement would be drawn up in which France should join. War by the West on behalf of other European countries might be included as an act which would incur Polish obligations; in the light of Germany's past methods of subversion, a case of indirect aggression was also to be allowed for. Meanwhile a communiqué was issued which announced the new, mutual basis of the forthcoming pact, and extended the interim guarantee. It seemed at last everyone knew where they stood. . . .

If the Polish partner in the new guarantees was, in some quarters, not wholehearted, the same was true of the other two. Having rushed in to avert apparent disaster, both the British and French Governments were left to contemplate their handiwork with some uneasiness. The Franco-Polish alliance of 1921 already called for rapid mutual aid against aggression, but there were many in France who had come to feel that a dangerously rigid commitment was involved and who coupled a desire for flexibility with the assurance that Poland would be bound to fight anyhow if France were to be attacked. Gamelin and Weygand for the army were joined by Noël and Bonnet in this matter. Few staff talks had taken place between the allies, and good feeling was not increased by the behaviour of Warsaw during the Munich crisis or the increased anti-Semitism which followed. That autumn Noël, though warning against the danger of throwing Beck towards Berlin, advised that the 1921 treaty should be revised, and Bonnet's eager agreement was known in London. But though the Foreign Minister thought he could see "sufficient loopholes" in the treaty to shelter France from the risk of war, Poland had not proved receptive to any ideas of change by the time the March crisis arrived.

Nor did fresh ties do much to increase the enthusiasm or determination of France, for the swift British guarantee all too clearly relied upon French troops for its effectiveness; there were those in office who would privately have echoed Marcel Déat's forthcoming question: "pourquoi mourir pour Dantzig?" The drafting of a new military agreement and political protocol with Poland in May was the occasion of some confusion and suspicion at the time and much specious pleading afterwards, and French promises of relieving assaults in the West meant little. General

Ironside saw the military plans of both countries that summer: "The French have lied to the Poles in saying that they are going to attack," he wrote. "There is no idea of it."

Though public determination over Poland was greater in Britain than in France, there, too, there were second thoughts in high places. The pressure of altered circumstances had to struggle with echoes of Austen Chamberlain's aside in 1925, that "for the Polish Corridor no British Government ever will or ever can risk the bones of a British grenadier." As recently as September 1937 Eden had apparently told Burckhardt that his country was disinterested in Danzig, and Halifax had declared to the same listener in the following summer that "Danzig and the Corridor were an absurdity . . . probably the most foolish provision of the Treaty of Versailles." Berlin had been informed on both occasions, and even in the 1939 *volte-face* could find some elements of comfort. "No sir," Chamberlain replied to a questioner in the Commons on 30 March who asked if war materials were to be withheld from Germany, and neither National Service nor a Ministry of Supply was announced as a concomitant of the guarantee. The weeks that followed did not produce ratification of the new agreement, but did witness Poland's depression and alarm at the failure of her mission in London to obtain economic aid adequate to offset the strain of having to remain semi-mobilised. For all its sound reasoning, the Treasury fed the Nazi propaganda machine with jeers, while Ironside returned from a special mission to Poland to find that in military circles, too, there was little interest in the new ally.

More ominous still for the opponents of appeasement was the reaction to the news of the guarantee in some quarters of the British press. On the evening of 31 March Reuters suggested that to guarantee Polish independence did not mean that concessions over Danzig and the Corridor were out of the question. "Independence" was not the same as "integrity" echoed *The Times* the next day, adding: "The new obligation does not bind Great Britain to defend every inch of the present frontiers of Poland." With Munich in mind it was extremely sinister, as Churchill was quick to point out, and doubly so for those few who knew that Dawson had been seen outside Chamberlain's room at the House of Commons on the evening of the 31st. Yet the views expressed were not long without support. On 3 April, for instance, *The Times* published a letter from Arthur Bryant hailing the "wisdom" of what it had written.

In fact, though the motive of Chamberlain and his closer associates in undertaking a guarantee of Poland seemed plain enough on the surface—Hitler must be stopped at all costs—the matter was more complex, as Halifax's earlier musings to Kennedy suggest. There was the pressure of public rage and the need to provide a positive answer to the anti-Munich scorn which so worried Henderson; there was the urge, in a world gone mad, to re-state in forceful terms the moral basis of British foreign policy; and there was the bewildering and urgent impetus of the events, pleas and rumours themselves. Was there also, one wonders, the unconscious need to save oneself from another sell-out? Did that joyless band sign the pledge, as it were, in part to erect a barrier between themselves and the tempting memories of past intoxications?

At the time the guarantee was criticised mainly on the grounds of its leaving the decision of peace or war for Britain in the hands of another country. In fact, given Hitler's general intentions it was the timing rather than the likelihood of British involvement in war which was affected, and in the event Warsaw behaved with extraordinary coolness and responsibility under pressure. Far more serious was the effect of the pledge to Poland, together with that to Rumania which followed, on the Soviet Union. Without Soviet participation, Western assistance in Eastern Europe could scarcely amount to much in practice. Yet Stalin was now protected from German attack by a belt of guaranteed intervening territory; not having had to commit himself beforehand, he could therefore watch the development of events and name his own terms, or at least sell himself to the highest bidder. Conversely, the new situation made a Soviet understanding all the more attractive to Germany. "Après avoir poussé Staline vers Hitler à Munich," wrote Coulondre later, "c'est maintenant Hitler que l'on pousse vers Staline."

The guarantee of Rumania came about in muddled fashion considering the original alarm over that rich prize, and the aim of bringing Poland into it was never achieved. When it was suggested to Chamberlain that public sentiment and military circles in Poland were so much more anti-German than Beck that the latter could be pushed harder and more openly in this matter, the Prime Minister merely confessed: "I don't know much about conditions in Poland." It was an apt comment on a great deal of his foreign policy. . . .

Poland was invaded at dawn on Friday 1 September. The SS had already created incidents on the border to provide one last, transparent excuse, the SA in Danzig were ready, and the *Schleswig-Holstein* opened up from the harbour with her big guns. At 5.40 a.m. Berlin radio broadcast the text of the Fuehrer's proclamation to his army in which bloodthirsty persecutions and frontier violations on the part of Poland were blamed for the war—though German diplo-mats were instructed to avoid the word "war," and to describe events as "engagements brought about by Polish attacks." Hitler also got off a private explanation to Mussolini in which he showed why he did not "want to expose [the latter] to the danger of assuming the role of mediator," though this did not prevent an Italian declaration of neutrality later in the day.

At 10 a.m. Hitler drove through silent streets to address the Reichstag and assured his audience that if victory were not forthcoming he would not survive the outcome. Goering took Dahlerus to see him on his return. With staring eyes, the Fuehrer screamed and gesticulated as he proclaimed his unshakeable determination to smash his enemies. Here, then, was "Germany's destiny." His breath was foul.

In London the Foreign Office knew from Kennard by 8.30 that Cracow and other cities were being bombed and that the German Army had crossed the frontier. Count Raczynski arrived at 10.30 with similar information, expecting a swift implementation of the Anglo-Polish treaty and aid from the air if possible. Halifax was sympathetic rather than decisive, but at least he did not conceal his doubts when the German chargé d'affaires explained that it was only a case of shooting back at the aggressive Poles. Nor did a series of now-fatuous telephone calls from Dahlerus in Berlin receive much sympathy during the day when they offered a similar interpretation, and at 2 p.m. it was known that Beck was breaking off all relations with Berlin. Even Henderson at last saw hope only in an "inflexible determination on our part to resist force by force."

The action expected of the West was not forthcoming, however. Bonnet was still clutching at the idea of an Italian-sponsored conference, and as well as sending a fulsome reply on the subject to Ciano had the temerity to sound Beck through Noël.

"We are in the thick of war as the result of unprovoked aggression," Beck replied. "The question before us is not that of a conference but the common action which should be taken by the Allies to resist." And though British forces were mobilised and a War Cabinet was being formed which included Churchill, Chamberlain had nothing final to announce to the Commons that evening, however forthrightly he denounced Hitler and Nazism. He could say, however, that Henderson had been instructed to convey a warning to Berlin:

Unless the German Government are prepared to give His Majesty's Government satisfactory assurances that [they] have suspended all aggressive action against Poland and are prepared promptly to withdraw their forces from Polish territory, His Majesty's Government ... will without hesitation fulfil their obligations to Poland.

The French Cabinet also issued a firm statement during the evening, and Coulondre followed Henderson to present a similar communication to Ribbentrop at 9 p.m. But when the British and French Ministers at the Vatican suggested that the Pope, too, should make known his grief that Hitler had plunged the world into war less than 24 hours after His Holiness's appeal for peace, the Cardinal Secretary of State refused. The grounds were to become familiar: it would "involve specific intervention in international politics." Poland's own staunch Catholicism was not decisive.

The anguish of Poland and of those concerned for Britain's honour continued throughout the following day. Delay stemmed from Paris above all. Bonnet persisted with the idea of a conference and the French Army begged for more time to prepare for battle, while there was some confusion in London as to whether or not the assent of the Chamber would have to be awaited before Daladier could declare war. "We shall be grateful for anything you can do to infuse courage and determination into M. Bonnet," telegraphed Halifax to Phipps during the morning, but he soon learned that a 48-hour limit was still being proposed for any ultimatum that might be presented at Berlin.

Moreover the hope of obtaining a conference still had some hours before it died altogether. To Hitler's annoyance and "yielding to French pressure," Mussolini had enquired again through Attolico at 10 a.m. whether such a move would be acceptable if the armies could stop "where they are now." In turn Ribbentrop had played for time by asking for confirmation that the West's declarations of the previous evening were not ultimata, in which case Hitler would reply "in a day or two." A series of frantic visits and telephone calls between Rome, London and Paris then confirmed that no ultimata had been delivered, though Halifax made it clear to Ciano and to a dissident Bonnet that Britain must demand a prior withdrawal of German troops. Meanwhile, of course, those troops moved deeper into Poland, and fresh appeals for help in warding off the overwhelming strength of the *Luftwaffe* were received through Kennard.

The Cabinet met in London at 4.30 p.m., and at Hore-Belisha's urging it was unanimously agreed that an ultimatum should be presented to Germany, expiring at midnight. But the decision reached neither Berlin nor the British public. Cadogan did attempt to convince Bonnet by telephone of the need to draw the line at midnight, but the latter held out for a delay of two more days and coolly denied that the Polish Ambassador in Paris had asked for any assistance. In Halifax's words, the position was "very embarrassing to His Majesty's Government," and he confirmed to Ciano that there could be no conference without a German withdrawal. Despite better news from Paris, however,

Prime Minister and Foreign Secretary were still prepared to betray their Cabinet, and to the widespread amazement and disgust of Members, it was of the continued possibility of a conference that Chamberlain spoke when he rose in the Commons at 7.44 p.m. If German troops would withdraw, he said, the Government "would be willing to regard the position as being the same as it was before the German forces crossed the Polish frontier," and Halifax sent the text to Henderson for him to pass on to Dahlerus and Goering. Greenwood "spoke for England" in the Commons, and hard words were used on the telephone to Corbin by some of his friends in London.

But the time for wriggling was almost over. At 8.50 p.m. Ribbentrop informed Attolico that there would be no withdrawal of German forces, and at 9.30 Loraine reported that Mussolini was abandoning his efforts. The violence of the Commons' reaction was further brought home to Chamberlain and Halifax when a Cabinet deputation waited upon them at Downing Street with the determination to tolerate no further delay. "Right gentlemen, this means war"; as the Prime Minister acquiesced a histrionic crash of thunder sounded outside. At Corbin's suggestion a direct telephone call from Chamberlain to Daladier then by-passed Bonnet at last, and though a deadline was still not agreed, its early settlement came a stage nearer. After Raczynski had again called to voice his country's suspicions and appeals, Halifax insisted to Bonnet at 10.30 that the British ultimatum would have to expire by noon, even if France had to delay another 24 hours. He received the reluctant assurance that Paris, too, would act during the 3rd. At 12.25 a.m. Henderson was instructed to seek an interview with Ribbentrop at 9

that morning; Coulondre was to follow him three hours later.

Some approached the point of no return with reluctant steps. At 10 p.m. Dr. Hesse had arrived from the German Embassy to see Sir Horace Wilson, bringing an invitation from Ribbentrop to a secret meeting with Hitler "to discuss the whole position, heart to heart." Wilson refused and reiterated his Government's position, but according to the German report he still assured Hesse that if there were a withdrawal London "would be prepared to let bygones be bygones." Bonnet, too, went on trying, and had Ciano wakened to see "if we could not at least obtain a symbolic withdrawal of German forces." Ciano threw the message in the waste-paper basket and went back to bed.

Henderson delivered the British ultimatum at the German Foreign Office at 9 a.m. It gave Hitler until 11 a.m., British Summer Time, to announce his withdrawal from Poland. Ribbentrop would not deign to receive the Ambassador and Schmidt, who was to stand in his place and had overslept, only just arrived in time by slipping in at a side door as Henderson went in at the front. The interpreter took the document over to where Hitler and Ribbentrop waited in the Chancellery. They read, and there was silence; then, with a savage look at Ribbentrop, Hitler asked: "What now?" Outside the room Goering muttered: "If we lose this war, then God have mercy on us." Goebbels stood alone in a corner; he looked downcast and absorbed with his thoughts. Between them, these men, their movement, and the nation which had spawned and followed them had brought war to an unhealthy Europe. The timing and circumstances had been to a certain extent fortuitous. The responsibility was not.

Professor of modern European history at the University of Wisconsin, Milwaukee, ROLAND N. STROMBERG (b. 1916) writes about the attitude of the United States toward the Central European crisis. Erosion of the position of Britain and France had momentous consequences for the security of the United States, but the Americans, as during the Ethiopian affair, maintained a colossal disinterest in the affairs of Europe. Just as appeasement was popular with the average Briton and Frenchman, so isolation was with the American public. Like Feis, Stromberg finds much to criticize in this attitude, especially when manifest by American leadership.*

Roland N. Stromberg

The United States and Collective Security

"Quarantining the Aggressors"

On October 5, 1937, the President made an effort to lay a basis for such a policy. The "quarantine speech" has become famous, though it appears to be somewhat misunderstood in most accounts. It is often assumed to reflect a full-blown collective-security outlook which Roosevelt allegedly believed in but which, proving too much for an "isolationist" public, was sadly abortive. When the President hinted at a "quarantine" and spoke of "putting an end to acts of international aggression" by "positive endeavors to preserve peace," was he not, however guarded his language, suggesting the policy of joining with other nations in the application of sanctions against

the aggressors? Many of his critics then, and his admirers later, took him to mean that. But it is by no means certain that he did.

It may have been more nearly "collective neutrality" or simply a unilateral American embargo against Japan that Roosevelt meant. The next day, Senator Pittman, often close to Roosevelt on foreign policy (the President was just returning from a trip through Pittman's West), gave out that "Japan's invasion of China can be stopped within thirty days without firing a shot"—by an American economic embargo. Cabinet member Harold L. Ickes claims credit in his diary for the quarantine metaphor; he does not explain what he meant, but speaks of nations "quar-

*From Roland N. Stromberg, *Collective Security and American Foreign Policy* (New York: Frederick A. Praeger, Inc., 1963), pp. 117–126. Footnotes omitted.

antining *themselves* against," rather than imposing a quarantine on, a "diseased" nation. The speech itself was cryptic enough, and the remarks of the President in the ensuing press conference seemed to mean that the new policy was conceived as something other than sanctions ("a terrible word to use") and as consistent with neutrality and nonentanglement. ("It might be a stronger neutrality. . . . There are lots of methods in the world that have never been tried yet. . . . By no means is it necessary that that way be contrary to the exercise of neutrality.") A careful recent inquiry by Miss Dorthy Borg seems to conclude that Roosevelt and his advisers had in mind cooperation among the neutrals involving economic pressures but standing apart from the League and avoiding any "commitments." (He had had similar ideas in 1935.) The word "quarantine" is, after all, a milder word than "ostracism," and we know from first-hand sources that Roosevelt was aware of this. League sanctions were almost certainly *not* the idea of Roosevelt at this time.

Nevertheless, what Roosevelt and his friends did have in mind bore the brand of collective security in that it contemplated striking down the aggressor, by the painless, short-of-war method of economic boycotts and embargoes. In a letter of October 16, Roosevelt, referring to his speech, wrote of "quarantine" policy as the alternative to war: "I am inclined to think that this is more Christian, as well as more practical, than that the world should go to war with them." At this time also, Henry L. Stimson, in a letter to *The New York Times,* called for an arms embargo on Japan. (A boycott of Japanese goods was welcomed by labor organizations, evidently for economic reasons.) Henry Morgenthau, the excitable Secretary of the Treasury, who now began to agitate for bold policies in all directions, consulted with

Roosevelt about a plan to seize Japanese assets in this country as a measure of "quarantine." "We don't call them economic sanctions; we call them quarantines," he quotes Roosevelt as saying. These vaguely conceived measures were somewhat impromptu (Mr. Morgenthau once startled John Simon considerably with a transatlantic telephone call, which accomplished nothing) and were never meant to lead to war. They were based on that persistent belief that somehow there was a magic method, involving economic boycotts, that would "stop the aggressors in their tracks" without war. The quarantine idea fizzled out because it had never had any precision and turned out to be faulty on the merest analysis. Such actions as seizure of Japanese assets would have relatively little effect, and a major economic boycott or embargo would mean war, from which everyone shrank. But the word was almost an *idée fixe* with FDR.

Whatever the President had in mind, it became lost in the confusion that followed. There was an unmistakable national reaction against the speech in so far as it was taken to mean an abandonment of neutrality and noncommitment. Secretary Hull was very upset, the more so because the speech bore the marks of Sumner Welles's hand. (Shortly before this, Roosevelt had appointed Welles as Undersecretary of State against Hull's wishes, thus starting a feud that contributed its bit to hampering American foreign policy for a number of years.) The chief diplomatic consequence of the October 5 pronouncement was the Brussels Conference, which turned out to be one of the strangest in history. The other powers looked for American leadership but found it was not there. Mutual recriminations resulted from the feeling in Europe that the United States, having talked big on October 5, had ignominiously shirked responsibility and from the feeling here that the United States had been tricked into an impossible situation. Very clearly, "the temper of the country was definitely against any form whatsoever of pressure against Japan." A conference that fails is worse than no conference. In this case, "the Brussels Conference was worse than a fiasco, it was a disaster. It completely discredited the concept of collective action, and it contributed to the ruin of such chance as existed in 1937 of restoring peace between Japan and China." Japan, feeling that the Conference proposed to sit in judgment on her, refused to attend while China was encouraged by the same false hopes that had buoyed up the King of Ethiopia. The Brussels Conference denied that it had any intention of condemning Japan or seeking sanctions; it only wished a compromise settlement. How this was to be brought about by a formal meeting in Belgium of many powers, which Japan did not even attend, was not entirely clear. President Roosevelt thought (says Hull) that the Brussels Conference should be prolonged, bringing "all possible moral pressure" to bear on Japan and "repeatedly calling upon Japan to come into the conference"—apparently a sort of perpetual establishment for the public reproach of that country. But, in the event, the powers slunk away from Brussels leaving international comity, as well as international morality, very much in the lurch.

Undeterred by the Brussels disaster, Roosevelt and Welles (against the opposition of Hull) pursued, from October until January, the vague scheme of a grandiose international conference to promote world peace, which, fortunately perhaps for world peace, never came off. The conference was premised on no commitment or political involvement by the United States. This unpromising feature, which implied a repetition of the Brussels failure, coupled

with the unyielding nature of the American position in the Far East was responsible for Prime Minister Neville Chamberlain's doubts about the wisdom of such a conference—for which Churchill later took him to task. The United States was in the position of pushing policies that might well lead to war, while abjuring all responsibility for such a war. (For some vigorous comments controverting Churchill's view that Chamberlain's rebuff of this American overture was a disastrous mistake, see the memoirs of Lord Halifax and Viscount Templewood.)

Confronted with the need for a foreign policy after years of withdrawal, the American instinct was to hold huge ceremonial conclaves at which moral creeds would be drawn up. A great deal of groping and fumbling was in evidence. One could just perceive amid the shadows the shape of the old Wilsonian ideal of collective security—an ideal not very precisely defined, but one of the few unmistakable landmarks in the history of American internationalism. Early in 1938, a poll conducted by the *Nation* showed a surprising five-to-one majority in favor of some sort of cooperative or collective policy as against isolation. Though the poll was probably loaded in its language and confined heavily to a particular group, its findings nevertheless appear significant.

The Impact of Munich

Europe in 1938 and 1939 was hardly free at any time from the threat of general war—until war came in September, 1939. The year 1938 began with the *Anschluss* of Austria and continued with the agonizing crisis culminating in the Munich Conference of September 29–30, whereupon a fearful world relaxed briefly, knowing that more would come, as it soon did. The year 1938 saw Hitler add not merely Austria and the Sudetenland to his conquests but also the German army, which yielded up its honor and its independence in the Fritsch affair and thus removed the last possible check on Nazi fanaticism in Germany. It also brought, in November, an upsweep in the anti-Semitic outrages that produced so strong a reaction against Germany in this country that the German Ambassador lost any hope he still held for the German cause in the United States. The American Ambassador was recalled to Washington from Berlin.

From early in 1938, the pattern was reasonably clear: the erosion of Europe by a steadily increasing German power that would mean, in time, either a disastrous European war or the ultimate reduction of both France and Great Britain to second-rate powers—with momentous consequences for the United States. A State Department memorandum by George Messersmith on February 18, 1938, declared that "it is difficult to see how the disintegrating movement in Southeastern Europe can be stopped. . . . This can mean only the gradual disintegration of the British Empire . . . which I believe we in this country cannot look upon with unconcern." (It was a line of thought that had already occurred to Henry Morgenthau, the belligerent Treasury Secretary: "You going to sit here and wait until you wake up here in the morning and find them [the Japanese] in the Philippines, then Hawaii, and then in Panama? Where would you call a halt?" It had much more reality in Europe than in the Pacific in 1937–38.) The steep and slippery slope that led through Munich and down to war could not now be blocked up by enough power to check the Nazi *enragés*. Italy was shaken by the German capture of Austria, but Mussolini was now too committed to Hitler and too estranged from the democracies to be won back though Neville Chamberlain made a gesture in this direction. (The Span-

ish Civil War completed what Ethiopia began, and the friendship of Hitler seemed to Mussolini more promising than that of the democracies while Hitler's strength was too formidable to defy with safety.) To ally with Soviet Russia still seemed to be a casting out of one devil by another, and any such policy came up against the fact that the countries of Eastern Europe wanted no Russian troops in their countries on any sort of mission, "friendly" or otherwise. (The sequel was to prove their fears all too justified.) The Poles, destined to be Germany's next victim, eagerly joined in the German despoiling of Czechoslovakia.

Thus, an organization of powers to meet and turn back the challenge of Hitler failed to materialize. While collective security under the League of Nations had ceased to be a possibility, a gathering together of states against the overly mighty power of Germany, on the principle of the balance, might have been and was expected. But in practice, it was not yet attainable. Bullitt reported that Premier Chautemps of France was speculating that "Central and Eastern Europe would slip into the hands of Germany without war; that the overwhelming power of Germany would then bring together all the other states of Europe just as the states of Europe had been united to oppose Napoleon. The end of the phase of German domination might well come after years of conflict between Germany and the Russian colossus supported by the other states of Europe." (Chautemps has declared in a letter to the *Washington Post,* that his Government, on the eve of leaving office, was prepared to oppose the Nazi occupation of Austria but received no backing from Rome or London.) In April, at a moment of decision for France, Premier Daladier chose Georges Bonnet over J. Paul-Boncour and voted for the gamble of appeasing Hitler in preference to the gamble of waging war against him with Russia as an ally. It was a choice between evils, but it did not then seem an unreasonable one. Daladier, who certainly did not admire Hitlerism, found his spirits even more depressed by the alternative: "The Cossacks will rule Europe."

The great German diplomatic victory at Munich, when the Czech state was dismembered without the striking of a blow, owed much to the simple fact that it was impossible to defend Czechoslovakia directly, because of the lack of a common frontier. Poland and Rumania refused the Soviet Union permission to send troops across their territory and in any war at this time, would have been on the side of Germany. France and Britain could have attacked Germany from the West, thus starting a general war, but they could not prevent Germany from overrunning Czechoslovakia. That the Western powers abjectly gave in to Hitler "just to avoid a war" (as an American diplomat put it) has been criticized as cowardly, but the responsibility of beginning a war was a large one. The conflict that would ensue would hardly be "just a war" but, as the British note to Germany of August 28, 1939, remarked, "a calamity without parallel in history." The only victor in such a war was likely to be Russia. The German cause, justified on grounds of national self-determination, seemed plausible enough to create pressure for a last experiment in drawing Germany into the European system. (There was some British and neutral sympathy for Sudeten "self-determination.") It would be a war, too, that as the London *Times* editor ("an impenitent supporter of Munich" as he later wrote) reflected, "at that time and on that issue would have bewildered and antagonized all the British Dominions and found even this country deeply divided." Critics of the Munich settlement are often grossly unfair in not dealing with the alter-

natives and pointing out the circumstances.

Yet the remorseless fact of its failure to stop the disintegration of Europe before Germany was all too evident. In the face of all this, the United States remained rigidly aloof. It continued to declare its entire disinterest in European political questions. An invitation to mediate in the Spanish conflict was declined in 1938. The British resigned themselves in May to "go ahead independently on their war plans without looking for any support or help from America." The American chargé in Vienna received a rebuke from Washington for having said that he thought the United States hoped Austria would resist threats to her independence. In 1938, Europeans were suggesting that Congress might repeal the arms embargo as a gesture of encouragement, but this was not recommended to Congress until March, 1939. The summer-long Czech crisis elicited no American reaction until war loomed up as a possibility in late September, whereupon, on September 26 and 27, President Roosevelt sent messages expressing a general hope of peaceful settlement. The United States officially refrained from passing any judgment on the Munich settlement itself. But Roosevelt sent to Neville Chamberlain what he described as his briefest cablegram: "Good Man!" Bonnet, the French Foreign Minister, has recounted bitterly that from the United States he could count on "not a man, not a sou." While President Roosevelt issued appeals for a compromise peace, he privately threatened France with the application of the arms embargo under the Neutrality Act if war should begin.

If Roosevelt thought Chamberlain a "good man" for avoiding war, and had urged compromise on him, he also felt a sense of distress and mulled over with Morgenthau what might be done against

Germany if she did invade Czechoslovakia. Again, a boycott was suggested, and the predilection for this sort of weapon appeared in Roosevelt's remark that if there was war, the French ought to stay on the defensive behind the Maginot line and "bring the Germans to their senses" by organizing an embargo. (He had talked about this before.) If nothing was done, it was perhaps from fear of "untoward domestic effects." Certainly, Secretary Hull was still adamant against any foreign meddling.

American opinion was not so languid as this policy of more or less masterly inactivity might indicate. Munich stirred the country. A commentator observed that "save Czechoslovakia" meetings were held in many American cities though someone else was expected to do the saving. Americans of the most isolationist hue, such as Senator Borah, were subsequently moved to denounce the Munich pact as "cruel, cowardly, treacherous" on the part of Britain and France; they would never have fought for Czechoslovakia themselves, but they expected others to do so. From the account of Cabinet discussions in the Ickes diary, one can trace a similar pattern: scorn for the "Judas Iscariot" role of Chamberlain, then, when war loomed, a moment of sobriety ("Who is in a position to pass judgment on England and France? What would the United States have done if we had had to face the terrible issue that confronted those two countries?"), followed by a return afterwards to the feeling that the solution had been "totally disgraceful" and that "the President may want to dissociate himself" from it. (Roosevelt had sent pleas for a settlement without war, thus playing some small part in bringing about the Munich agreement, which he had clearly favored.) It was unanimously agreed by the Cabinet that this country could not go to war, *nor* send delegates to a conference, which would be "mixing into a foreign affairs that did not concern us." But later, there was Ickes' contemptuous reference to "spines of spaghetti."

In January, President Roosevelt accompanied a request for rearmament with one of his more famous phrases: a reference to "methods short of war but stronger than mere words" to handicap the aggressors and aid the "victims of aggression." What these actions might be was not immediately clear: perhaps a trade embargo, perhaps amendment of the Neutrality Act to permit the sale of arms. Neither action was proposed for the moment though there was an appeal for the cessation of airplane sales to Japan. A small loan to China had been arranged in December. There was continuation of what *The New York Times* on January 15, 1938, referred to as the "elaborate fraud" of failing to invoke the Neutrality Act in the Far Eastern war, thus making it possible for China to buy arms. These gestures did not amount to very much and did not relieve the British from severe pressure and the necessity of some "appeasement" of Japan in the summer of 1939. A considerable movement, backed by students, intellectuals, and former Secretary of State Stimson, to repeal the arms embargo in the Spanish Civil War so as to permit the legal government to buy arms failed, a repeal resolution in the House of Representatives being badly beaten. In his January rearmament message, the President strongly implied that the United States would not participate in European wars. In this speech, the President declared that the "God-fearing democracies of the world which observe the sanctity of treaties and good faith in their dealings with other nations" were under attack from "international lawlessness" and "acts of aggression" but suggested that this aggression might be stopped by "methods short of war," as we have noted, and discussed the problem of national defense in a way that suggested the United States should prepare only to meet an attack on this hemisphere.

And yet men were beginning to acquire a sense of urgency and a feeling that, as Roosevelt said, "the world is marching too fast." With Europe seemingly in retreat before Germany, and Asia before Japan, there developed the significant theory of a great plot by the "aggressors," a plot now rapidly moving toward its denouement. "The events of the past weeks have brought home to all the increasing effectiveness of the forces of aggression," Morgenthau wrote to Roosevelt, October 17, 1938. "Since 1931 we have seen, succeeding each other with briefer and briefer intervals between, the fall of Manchuria and the invasion of China, the conquest of Ethiopia, fomented unrest in Latin America and in the Near East, armed intervention in Spain, the annexation of Austria, and the dismemberment of Czechoslovakia—all in seven short years."

A turning point came in March. Here, as in Britain, Hitler's destruction of what remained of the Czech state was construed by the public as clear confirmation of his intention to dominate Europe and be bound by no promises, which may have been a considerable oversimplification. Roosevelt indicated that he would now press for repeal or revision of the neutrality law. Since November, the step had been urged by a number of the peace organizations, which were switching from a neutral-

ist program, as well as by the beleaguered European democracies. The debate that followed revealed substantial support for amending the law so that war goods might be sold to Britain and France. "The one way to prevent war in Europe within the next few months is to convince Hitler that he can't win a war." Plain indications that the United States was moving toward their side might stiffen the anti-German forces of Europe and would give the German dictator pause if anything could. But half the nation was still convinced that, if war came in Europe, the United States should stay out of it. They could imagine no worse tragedy for civilization than to be dragged into the storm of hatred and violence about to break out in Europe. Though the above quotation is from a letter he received, the mail of Senator Borah ran ten to one in the other direction. Though newspaper editorials ran heavily in favor of repeal, public opinion was about 50–50, and it was one of the proudest boasts of President Roosevelt's liberal supporters that they could successfully defy the "lords of the press." By the closest possible vote in the Foreign Relations Committee, the arms embargo was retained despite Roosevelt's appeal. (Changes in the neutrality law would not have had any influence on Hitler, it seems clear, at this stage.) Only after the outbreak of war was it finally removed (in November), permitting the shipment of arms on a cash-and-carry basis.

Although neither the Soviet Union nor the United States was party to the Munich agreement, the USSR was more immediately affected by the results. Stalin had seemed willing to come to the aid of the Czechs, and as a member of the League of Nations and one of the most ardent propagandists for the principles of collective security, Russia showed herself an obvious ally in any policy to check Hitlerian power. Was the failure to sign an alliance with the Soviets one of the great lost opportunities of the time? What might have been changed? GEORGE F. KENNAN (b. 1904) believes that Russia was not really a fit partner for the West in resisting dictatorship. A former ambassador to Moscow and a member of Princeton's Institute for Advanced Studies, Kennan is the author of numerous scholarly works, one of which, *Russia Leaves the War* (1956), won a Pulitzer prize for history.*

George F. Kennan

Russia and the Czech Crisis

Russia's brief participation in the Spanish civil war represented the last bizarre phase of Moscow's effort to strengthen the antifascist cause in western Europe. Like the other attempts, it foundered—partly on the timidity and vacillation of the French and British, whose behavior was indeed not such as to encourage any successful collaboration in resistance to Hitler, but partly, too, on Stalin's extreme fear of any extensive intimacy with the liberal and socialist world of the West—of any intimacy which could expose his own apparatus of power to Western influence and give sustenance to the opposition currents against him at home.

In this series of events, certain deeper realities seem to emerge. From the beginning of 1934—from the time when Stalin first became seriously aware of the dangers of Hitlerism—the great question was whether there was a real possibility of an effective coalition embracing both Russia and the major powers of western Europe, for the purpose of frustrating Hitler's aggressive ambitions and preventing the catastrophe of a second world war. Many Western liberals thought then that there was such a possibility, and many have continued to believe down to this day that there was. They blame primarily the French and British governments for the fact that this dream was never realized. They charge that these governments, by their timid, vacillating policies of appeasement, left the Soviet government no choice

*From *Russia and the West under Lenin and Stalin* by George F. Kennan, by permission of Atlantic-Little, Brown and Co. Copyright © 1960, 1961 by James K. Hotchkiss, Trustee. Pp. 312–313, 315–317, 320–330. Footnotes omitted.

but to go its own way. Certainly, the French and British governments were vulnerable to such criticism. And the role of our government, too, which kept aloof from the whole affair, was not particularly glorious.

But actually this is not all of the answer. The fact is that Stalin's Russia was never a fit partner for the West in the cause of resistance to fascism. Russia herself was, throughout these years, the scene of the most nightmarish, Orwellian orgies of modern totalitarianism. These were not provoked by Hitler's rise. They originated, as we saw, in 1932, at a time when Stalin did not yet have any proper understanding of the Nazi danger. This internal weakness of the Soviet regime (for what else but the most extreme weakness can it be when a man sees himself unable to govern except by methods such as these?)—this weakness lay in Stalin's own character. It was this that caused him to fear an intimacy with Hitler's opponents no less than he feared the military enmity of Hitler himself. To the moral cause of an antifascist coalition, the Soviet government of 1934 to 1937 could have added little but hesitant, halfway measures, and a nauseating hypocrisy.

Anyone who looks deeply at the history of these years cannot, I think, avoid the conclusion that Russia was never available, in the sense that Western liberals thought she was, as a possible partner of the West in the combatting of Nazism. Her purposes were not the purposes of Western democracy. Her possibilities were not the possibilities open to democratic states. The damage that had been done with the triumph of Bolshevism in Russia went deeper than people in the West supposed. By the mid-Thirties the Western democracies, whether they realized it or not, were on their own. There was no salvation for them from the East. In those initial years of Hitler's power, they would have done well to

place greater reliance on their own beliefs and their own strength. At that time, this strength, if resolutely mobilized, would still have been enough. Two years later, it would not be. Hitler's rearmament of Germany was moving too fast. Two years later they would be unable to defeat Hitler without accepting the aid of Russia; and for that aid there would then be a price—a bitter price—the full bitterness of which we of this generation are now being compelled to taste. . . .

Stalin was by 1937 deeply disillusioned with the prospects for inducing the French and British to put up any effective opposition to Hitler. Hitler's next moves, it was clear, would be towards the east, and it was not to be expected that the Western powers would do anything serious to oppose him. Plainly, this posed for Stalin the alternative of attempting to resist the German advance alone, by force of arms, or of coming to some sort of accommodation with Hitler. The weight of evidence suggests that it was the second course which most appealed to Stalin, and on which he began, in 1937, to stake his expectations and his policies.

The purges were at this moment just getting into high gear. Had Stalin at this time envisaged military resistance as the preferred course, then the first thing he should have done would be to halt the purges, to launch out on a policy of national unity (as indeed he later did when the war was really on), and to begin at once to build up both the strength and the morale of the Red army. If the prospect was resistance, the continuation of the purges made no sense.

If, on the other hand, Stalin was going to seek his safety in a deal with Hitler, then it was best that he should first settle his scores with his Party rivals—that he should get all these people out of the way who might make trouble for him in the implementation of such a policy, who might introduce irrelevant ideological arguments, who might attempt to mobilize against him—as he thought they were already secretly trying to do in Spain—the aroused liberal idealism of the Western world. In contemplating a deal with Hitler, Stalin must surely have had in mind the precedent of the Brest-Litovsk Treaty, by which Lenin had traded space for time and had kept the Germans at arms' length in 1918. He must have remembered that Lenin, on that occasion, had been faced with most bitter opposition on the part of certain Party comrades—opposition so bitter, in fact, that it had brought him to the verge of resignation from his position as leading secretary of the Party. All this could happen again.

If, then, it was a deal with Hitler towards which Stalin was steering his course, the purges made some sense, though even then only to a very abnormal mind. And it was along this line that Stalin's policy proceeded. Throughout 1937 and the first months of 1938 the purges were at their high point. Not only did Stalin decimate the ranking civilian echelons of the bureaucracy but he proceeded in midsummer, 1937, to slaughter off the major military leaders as well, and to follow this up with purges that destroyed or removed a very high percentage of the senior officers' corps of the armed services generally. There is no evidence to suggest that these purged officers were the least competent ones militarily, or that, even if they had been, *these* violent means would have been the best way to achieve their elimination. There are other ways of doing things. This reckless attack on the armed services was not the work of a man intending to improve military efficiency or of one preparing a serious effort of military resistance. It was the work of a pathologically suspicious and fearful person, who saw himself being pressed into a situation where he would probably have to make cynical and shabby compromises with a terrible adversary, and who feared that certain of his political and military associates, if left alive, would attempt to profit from his embarrassment.

The year 1937 was a year of watchful waiting in Soviet foreign policy. Very delicately, I think, behind the scenes, Stalin was already beginning to detach himself from any one-sided commitment to the policy of collective security against Hitler. For example, the Soviet ambassador in Berlin, Jacob Suritz, who was a Jew and therefore scarcely suitable as a possible vehicle for new political contacts with the anti-Semitic Nazis, was cautiously replaced by a non-Jew. But Stalin was too wise a bird to force the pace; and the Nazis, for their part, continued to exhibit nothing but the wildest and most flamboyant hostility to Russian Communism.

Litvinov was permitted, therefore, to continue to plug publicly the collective security line. It was, after all, an anchor to windward. He was also permitted to continue to prod the reluctant French and British into putting up greater resistance to the German and Italian intervention in Spain. So long as the Germans remained engaged there, Stalin felt that he had some respite and could take time to complete the purges. But even here, time was running out. Stalin knew very well, from the beginning of 1937, that the Spanish Republic would be defeated in the end. We may be sure that he watched with the most anxious intensity for any slackening off of the German activity in Spain, because he knew full well that this would probably be the signal for the dreaded switch of German policy towards the East. . . .

In the days of the Weimar Republic, the French and British had sternly forbidden the so-called *Anschluss*—the union of Austria and Germany. As late as 1932, when a friendly gesture to Chancellor Brüning might have helped him to avert the Nazi take-over, they had sternly reproved his foreign minister, Dr. Julius Curtius, for merely suggesting an economic union between Germany and Austria as a means of alleviating the economic crisis. Now, when Hitler seized Austria in a spirit of complete defiance, they remained inactive. This was partly the result, no doubt, of their dislike for the conservative, semi-fascist, but still moderate government of Schuschnigg. Like Stalin, the Western statesmen of that day found it hard to distinguish between traditional conservatives and Nazis. This was again a hang-over from World War I, when people in London and Paris had felt that their main enemies were the conservatives of Germany and Austria. For this reason Czechoslovakia, not Austria, was their darling. Czechoslovakia was a new republic, established by sincere protagonists of political democracy, created by process of liberation from the Austro-Hungarian monarchy. All this seemed virtuous and commendable. But over the little rump-state of Austria there still hovered, for Western eyes, something of the stigma of the old Hapsburg court: too much charm, too much skepticism and despair, too little righteousness, too great a tolerance of human weakness. For these same reasons, perhaps, Western liberals have subsequently tended to pass over Austria's downfall and to identify the demise of Czechoslovakia, six months later, as the great turning point in European affairs generally, and in Soviet policy in particular.

I cannot quite see it this way. To Stalin's sensitive and suspicious mind Austria's fall must have represented, I think, a development of crucial significance. He must have drawn from it, right then and there, practically all the conclusions he

was later believed to have drawn from the fall of Czechoslovakia.

It was, at any rate, immediately after the seizure of Austria, in March 1938, that the signs began to multiply of a readiness on the Soviet side for a rapprochement with Berlin. Repeated warnings were given—the first of them in a statement made by Litvinov by way of reaction to Austria's fall—that time was running out on the Western powers if they still expected to have Russia's help against Hitler.

Stalin's desire to avoid trouble with Hitler was unquestionably greatly heightened in midsummer, 1938, by the outbreak of serious hostilities between the Russians and the Japanese in the area of the junction of the Soviet, Korean, and Manchurian borders. There was no official declaration of war, but there was some severe fighting. Stalin was at all times keenly aware of the danger of becoming simultaneously embroiled with the Germans and the Japanese, and the fact that he was involved in hostilities with one of these parties must have increased his determination to keep himself at peace with the other. Hitler, too, in mid-1938, with the delicate task of cracking the Czechoslovak nut looming immediately before him, appears finally to have felt the need for doing what he could to keep the Russians quiet through the coming crisis. For these reasons, both sides were inclined to a relaxation of the tension between them; and the signs of this were clearly apparent as the summer advanced.

Throughout that summer of 1938, the Nazi buildup against Czechoslovakia proceeded apace; and in September there occurred the celebrated Munich crisis which rocked Europe to its foundations. With the details of this crisis—Chamberlain's meeting with Hitler at Bad Godesberg, his later dramatic flight to Munich, his concession that Hitler should have the Sudeten areas of Czechoslovakia, the Czech capitulation, the fall and flight of the Czech government, the occupation by the Germans of a large part of Bohemia and Moravia, and the reduction of what was left of the Czechoslovak Republic to the condition of a defenseless dependency of Germany—with all this, we are familiar. European history knows no more tragic day than that of Munich. I remember it well; for I was in Prague at the time, and I shall never forget the sight of the people weeping in the streets as the news of what had occurred came in over the loud-speakers.

The Munich agreement was a tragically misconceived and desperate act of appeasement at the cost of the Czechoslovak state, performed by Chamberlain and the French premier, Daladier, in the vain hope that it would satisfy Hitler's stormy ambition, and thus secure for Europe a peaceful future. We know today that it was unnecessary—unnecessary because the Czech defenses were very strong, and had the Czechs decided to fight they could have put up considerable resistance; even more unnecessary because the German generals, conscious of Germany's relative weakness at that moment, were actually prepared to attempt the removal of Hitler then and there, had he persisted in driving things to the point of war. It was the fact that the Western powers and the Czechoslovak government did yield at the last moment, and that Hitler once again achieved a bloodless triumph, which deprived the generals of any excuse for such a move. One sees again, as so often in the record of history, that it sometimes pays to stand up manfully to one's problems, even when no certain victory is in sight.

The great issue at stake in the Munich crisis was, of course, the validity of Czechoslovakia's treaties of alliance with France and with Soviet Russia. The Soviet treaty with Czechoslovakia provided that Russia was obliged to come to Czechoslovakia's assistance *only if France did the same.* As the crisis developed just before Munich, the Soviet government reiterated, with impeccable correctness, its readiness to meet its treaty obligations to Czechoslovakia, if France would do likewise. This confirmed many people in the West in the belief that only Russia had remained true to her engagements at that crucial moment—that Russia had been prepared to assume the full burden of a war with Hitler over the issue of Czechoslovakia, had the Western powers only played their part.

This was substantially accurate in the juridical sense; but things were not exactly this way in practice. You must remember a basic geographic reality which underlay the entire chapter of Soviet participation in the policy of collective security, and particularly the pacts with the French and the Czechs. This was the fact that whereas the Western powers had, in effect, a common border with Germany, the Soviet Union did not; it was separated from Germany and from Czechoslovakia by two countries, Poland and Rumania, both of which feared any movement of Russian troops onto their territory as much as they feared a similar movement of the troops of Hitler, and neither of which was at any time willing to say that it would permit Soviet troops to cross its territory in the implementation of Russia's obligations to Czechoslovakia or to France. This meant that no military planning for a passage of Russian troops across these countries was possible; and in the event of a war with Germany in which all three countries—France, Czechoslovakia, and Russia—might have been involved, the Western powers and Czechoslovakia could expect to become immediately engaged, whereas any Russian action would still have to await clarification of the Soviet right of passage across these intervening countries. In the reluctance of the Polish and Rumanian governments to permit transit of Soviet troops, the Soviet government had a ready-made excuse for delay in meeting its obligations of mutual assistance. This impediment was apparent at the time of Munich: the Rumanian government, in particular, was heavily pressed by the Czechs and the Western powers to declare its readiness to permit Soviet troops to pass; but I cannot find that it ever clearly did so. In any case, I myself had it from no less an authority than the German military attaché in Prague, whose task it had been to study this problem for the German High Command, that the physical characteristics of the Rumanian railroad network were such that, even had the Rumanians permitted the passage, it would have taken the Soviet command approximately three months to move a division into Slovakia over this primitive and indirect route. The implications of this state of affairs are obvious. The Russian expression of readiness to assist Czechoslovakia if France did likewise was a gesture that cost Moscow very little. It is fair to say that had the Czechs decided to resist, there was, for various reasons, a good chance that they might have been saved. It is hardly fair to say that they would have been saved by the troops of the Soviet Union.

After Munich, events took a rapid and dramatic course. Hitler, instead of being directed onto the paths of peace, was irritated and disturbed by the reaction to Munich in the West, particularly by the signs of a growing realization on the part of the Western governments that it was high time they rearmed. He had no intention whatsoever of foregoing the remainder of his program: the demands on Poland, Memel, and Danzig. Yet the sharp reaction to Munich in the West implied the danger that London and Paris might not be prepared to take any more of this lying down. The beginnings of the French and British rearmament effort meant that time was running out on him. This presented him with a difficult problem of policy.

For some weeks at the outset of 1939 Hitler appears to have toyed with the possibility of inducing the Poles to agree to the peaceful incorporation of Danzig into the Reich, and to the cutting of the Polish Corridor by a new German corridor across it. But the Poles, in a series of conversations conducted in January 1939, resisted these approaches. Furious at this recalcitrance, which cut off his easiest and most favorable prospects, Hitler made his first major mistake. He proceeded, in March 1939, to occupy all of what was left of Czechoslovakia, except the easternmost province of Ruthenia, which he tossed contemptuously to the Hungarians. He had delayed this move, which was bound to frighten the Poles, so long as there was a chance that Poland would give him what he wanted by peaceful agreement. Since the Poles proved obdurate, he petulantly went ahead to extinguish what was left of the Czechoslovak state.

By this move, Hitler placed himself on Poland's southern flank, and improved, of course, his position for further pressure against the Poles. But this represented a flagrant violation of the assurances he had given to the British at Munich; and it forced people in London and Paris to realize that even the ultimate act of appeasement involved in the Munich settlement had been a failure—that Hitler could not safely be permitted to gain any more bloodless victories. The British reacted by summoning the Polish Foreign Minister Josef Beck, to London for negotiations, and by proclaiming a British guarantee of the integrity of the territory of Poland. Together with the French, they also entered into negotiations with the Soviet government to see whether a real and effective alliance against Hitler could not at last be brought into being. These negotiations, which began in the middle of April 1939, were pursued in Moscow throughout the summer.

All this put Hitler in a difficult box. As things now stood, he could not gain his objectives without an attack on Poland. He was obliged to recognize that he could not attack Poland, in the face of the British guarantee, without risk of involving himself in a war with France and Britain. For a time, he thought of attacking England and France first, letting Poland go until later. But even this he could not risk if there was any possibility that France and England might be joined by Russia. Russia had, therefore, to be neutralized. It had to be neutralized whatever he did, whether he attacked Poland first or England and France. This meant that the Soviet negotiations with the French and British in Moscow had somehow to be spiked. If they could be spiked, perhaps this would not only keep Russia out of the conflict but England and France would then not dare to fight at all. How could this be done? Only by a deal with Stalin.

Hitler viewed only with deepest distaste and suspicion the prospect of negotiating with the Russians. While he personally admired Stalin, he was sincere in his loathing for Russian Communism. For some weeks, from mid-May to early July, while permitting lower-level German representatives to take soundings of various sorts with their opposite Soviet numbers, Hitler wrestled with this problem. For a time he appears to have toyed, as an alternative, with the idea of contenting himself for the moment with a bloodless seizure of Danzig alone.

Stalin, meanwhile, sensing the approach of the final crisis, convinced that Hitler was going to strike somewhere, and determined to purchase his own safety, played his cards with consummate skill. To the Germans he made absolutely clear his willingness to discuss a deal. On March 10, 1939, even before the German occupation of Bohemia and Moravia, he had said, in a celebrated speech to the Eighteenth Party Congress in Moscow, that Russia did not propose to pull anybody else's chestnuts out of the fire for them. This was another way of saying that Russia was not going to fight Britain's or France's battles—that she would look after herself in her own way. A clearer hint to the Germans could scarcely have been devised. The Germans indicated that they understood and were interested. Six weeks later, Stalin removed Litvinov as foreign minister and turned the job over to Molotov. This was the first time since 1918 that the Foreign Affairs Ministry had been given to a member of the Politbureau. The change demonstrated that Stalin was preparing for major moves of foreign policy. At the same time, he continued to draw out the negotiations with the French and British, in order to have a second string to his bow and as a means of frightening the Germans into agreement.

For some reason—perhaps because he had become convinced that the Russians were serious in their desire for a deal, perhaps because the Poles had made it evident that they would regard even a bloodless seizure of Danzig as a *casus belli*—but certainly in any case, with the knowledge that the season was advancing and military decisions could no longer be postponed, Hitler, in early July, stopped his hesitation and made up his mind to attack

Poland. Secret orders were at once issued to the armed forces to be prepared to launch the attack at the end of August. The all-clear signal was given, for the first time, for intensive, far-reaching negotiations with the Soviet government.

From now on, it was high politics, in the most dramatic and sinister sense of the term. On July 26, in the private dining room of a Berlin restaurant, Russian and German representatives got down to brass tacks. It was hinted to the Russians that Germany would be prepared to pay for Soviet neutrality, in the event of a German-Polish war, by turning over to the Soviet Union considerable areas of eastern Europe. Armed with this secret knowledge, Stalin and Molotov increased the pressure on the unsuspecting British and French negotiators in Moscow. In veiled terms the question was put to the French and British: would *they*, in the event of a war, be prepared to place large sections of eastern Europe at the mercy of Russia? Would *they*, for example, consent to regard Moscow as the guarantor of the three Baltic States, and entitled to do what it wanted there? And would *they* compel the Poles and Rumanians to accept Soviet troops on their territory in the event of an action against Germany?

You can see what was going on. Stalin, with both sides competing for his favor, was trying to find out who was the highest bidder. Of the two bidders, only one, the Germans, knew that the other side was bidding; the other bidder seems to have had no knowledge that any other bid was being made. Faced with these demands, the French and British temporized. They wanted Russian help against Germany, but they did not feel that they could buy it at the price of the sacrifice of their Polish allies or of the Baltic States. The Germans, of course, had no such inhibitions. Hitler,

calculating out of his own infinite cynicism and opportunism, figured that he could always handle the Russians later; if he could be sure of getting his half of Poland now, and getting it without great danger of a world war, let the Russians, for the moment, have the rest, and certain other parts of eastern Europe in the bargain.

Seeing that the Russians were inclining in this direction, and with his own military deadline for the attack on Poland crowding in on him, Hitler decided to force the issue. On August 15 the Soviet government was informed that the Germans were prepared to send their foreign minister, Ribbentrop, to Moscow in the near future, "to lay the foundations for a definite improvement in German-Soviet relations." This meant that the Germans were willing to do business on the basis discussed in the secret talks. The next day another message arrived asking that the date of Ribbentrop's arrival be advanced to August 12, only two days hence, on the grounds that

. . . in view of the present situation, and of the possibility of the occurrence any day of serious incidents . . . , a basic and rapid clarification of German-Russian relations and the mutual adjustment of the present questions are desirable.

This meant that the German attack on Poland was only a matter of days.

The moment of decision for Stalin had now arrived. The Japanese had again been acting up. Major hostilities involving, in fact, several divisions—tanks, artillery, aircraft, the entire paraphernalia of war— were just then in progress on the Mongolian frontier. The British and French negotiators, still in Moscow, suspected nothing. If Stalin turned down the German offer, he would of course have to come to some agreement with the British and French; he could not leave himself in a position of complete isolation in the face of the German attack on Poland. But he could then expect no mercy at the hands of Hitler; and if the British and French failed to engage Hitler's force in the West, Russia would be confronted at last by that war for which she was so ill-prepared: a war on two fronts, against both Germany and Japan. He would have to accept combat, furthermore, along the existing western Soviet frontiers, uncomfortably near to both the great cities of Leningrad and Moscow. If, on the other hand, he accepted Hitler's offer, he could not only remain aloof initially from the impending German-Polish conflict, with the possibility that Hitler might even become involved with the French and British, but he would be permitted, in the bargain, to take over a large area of eastern Europe. He could use this as a buffer zone in case Hitler attacked him at a later date. Meanwhile, the acquisition of it would be a great boon to his prestige.

To Stalin a bird in the hand was worth two in the bush. He chose, as he had perhaps secretly known all along that he would choose if he had the opportunity, for Hitler. The answer was given to send Ribbentrop along.

The Germans were mad with elation over the Soviet answer. They interpreted the negotiations which the French and British had been conducting so openly all summer with the Soviet government to mean that Britain and France, unless assured of Russian help, would never dare to oppose a German attack on Poland. Soviet acceptance of Ribbentrop's visit excluded even the possibility of the British and French going to war. Hitler it seemed had played, this time, for the highest stakes and had won. The last of his great objectives was about to be achieved; and it would be achieved, like the others, without

bringing about the world war which the pessimists had always warned would be the result of his adventures.

You know the rest. On August 23, Ribbentrop flew to Moscow for twenty-four hours of hectic negotiation. That night, the German-Soviet Nonaggression Pact was signed. Its publication burst on the unsuspecting world like a bombshell, throwing consternation into the Western chanceries, bewilderment into the ranks of the Western liberal friends of the Soviet Union, and utter chaos into the foreign Communist parties which for six years, at Moscow's direction, had been following the most violent possible anti-Nazi line and denouncing anyone who as much as said a civil word in Hitler's direction.

Both sides, in signing this pact, were aware that it sealed the fate of Poland, that war—a German-Polish war, that is—would be only a matter of days. One week later, the Germans attacked. Contrary to the expectations entertained in Berlin when Ribbentrop signed the Pact, the British and French did declare war. With this series of events, World War II had begun.

It had begun, let us note, with a situation similar to that of the period of Brest-Litovsk: namely, with the British and French facing a strong German enemy in the west, with Russia on the side-lines, and with a government in Moscow wishing for the warring powers nothing better than mutual exhaustion. "A plague on both your houses" was the sentiment with which Moscow had seen the old war out, in 1918; "a plague on both your houses" was the sentiment with which Moscow, in its innermost thoughts, saw the new one in, in 1939.

For a time, in the mid-Thirties, many people in the West had thought that it might be possible to have Soviet Russia as a voluntary partner in the effort to contain

Hitler. Events had proved them wrong. A whole series of factors—Stalin's personal nature, his domestic-political predicament, the concern of his regime for the safety of Russia's Far Eastern frontiers, the inhibitions of the Poles and Rumanians, and the indecisive, timid policies of the Western powers themselves in their response to the Nazi danger—all these things had operated to keep Russia aloof from the war in its initial stages, and to leave the French and British face to face with a fanatical German opponent far stronger than themselves.

Member of the Académie des Sciences Morales et Politiques of the Institut de France, historian MAURICE BAUMONT (b. 1892) has had a career as diplomat, international civil servant, and professor, the latter at the Sorbonne and the University of Geneva (Institut Universitaire de Hautes Études Internationales). He was also the French editor-in-chief for publication of the German Foreign Office archives. His writings include *L'Essor Industriel et l'Imperialisme Colonial* (3rd ed., 1965), *Les Gloires et Tragédies de la Troisième République* (1956), and *La Faillite de la Paix* (1960), which is acknowledged to be among the best general histories on the period 1919–1939. In the following selection, he discusses the controversy in France over appeasement. Although written several years after World War II, this article contains the essential lines of dispute which remain today.*

Maurice Baumont

French Critics and Apologists Debate Munich

After nine years, Munich is still much debated in France. The intense emotions aroused at the time have not yet been calmed, as the number of French apologias and criticisms now being published indicates. With the documents which have recently been made available elsewhere, in particular the intensely interesting German documents, they enable us to form a more precise idea of the motives of those who called the fateful conference in September 1938.

Georges Bonnet, Minister of Foreign Affairs from April 1936 to October 1939, has published his testimony in Switzerland.[1]

Living in retirement in that country, he appeals to history to alter the judgment of so many of his contemporaries about his diplomacy. Léon Noël, former Minister at Prague and Ambassador at Warsaw from 1935 to 1939, in a well-documented study,[2] characterizes Bonnet's policy as "the uncertain policy of a timid man." General Gamelin, himself greatly criticized, goes much further in his memoirs[3] and denounces Bonnet's "ill-omened action." He writes: "M. Georges Bonnet saw in everything only his personal interest of the

[1] Georges Bonnet, "Défense de la paix. De Washington au Quai d'Orsay." Geneva: Editions du Cheval ailé, 1946, 390 p.

[2] Léon Noël, "L'agression allemande contre la Pologne." Paris: Flammarion, 1946, 510 p.

[3] General Gamelin, "Servir. I — Les armées françaises de 1940. II — Le prologue du drame, (1930-août 1939)." Paris: Plon, 1946, 380 p. and 480 p.

*Maurice Baumont, "French Critics and Apologists Debate Munich." Reprinted by special permission from *Foreign Affairs,* July, 1947, pp. 685–690. Copyright 1947 by the Council on Foreign Relations, Inc., New York.

moment. . . . One could never have confidence in his words." Although Bonnet did not actually accompany his chief, Premier Daladier, to Munich, he appears in France as the incarnation of the Munich policy. His book, though it claims complete objectivity, is in fact clever special pleading. The author excels in talking beside the point, and his selection of documents is very careful.

A number of Bonnet's colleagues in the government have also provided evidence about Munich. Edouard Daladier himself, in a speech before the Constituent Assembly on July 18, 1946, replied to some of those who had vehemently accused him. Another impassioned Munich apologist, Anatole de Monzie, former Minister of Public Works, who died at the beginning of 1947, made the mistake, during the German occupation, of publishing a kind of journal of the prewar period.[4] For a long time de Monzie had seemed called to a great political destiny. A man of fascinating intelligence, he was likened by Poincaré to Talleyrand, "with the same limp and the same genius for accomplishment." But he died under sharp fire. Among the diplomats directly involved in the Munich affair, François-Poncet, Ambassador at Berlin from 1931 to 1938, has provided some brilliant souvenirs of Hitlerian Germany.[5] Paul Reynaud, an ardent opponent of the Munich policy, has announced that he is going to publish his memoirs.

Just after Munich particular attention was paid to the various *volte-face* that were supposed to have occurred, and to discovering where and why the chief actors had changed their positions and aims. Perhaps the course of events was less complicated than many political reporters imagined.

Since the recent publication in England of Keith Feiling's biography of Neville Chamberlain, containing excerpts from his diary and letters, we know exactly what circumstances and reasoning led the British Prime Minister successively to Berchtesgaden, to Godesberg and to Munich. There is no doubt that it was he who took the principal initiative. To this extent it must be recognized that Georges Bonnet and François-Poncet are perfectly justified in asserting that France only followed England.

Analyzing the conference that brought the French and British Ministers together in London on April 28 and 29, 1938, Bonnet states: "The British Government asserted its solidarity with us solely to the degree to which Franco-British joint action would permit of reaching an amicable arrangement, and of averting war. It rejected any new engagement with Czechoslovakia; it offered only its good offices, its mediation, its arbitration!" And he adds that this English position was to "remain the same up to Munich, and would be recalled to us repeatedly through diplomatic channels."

At the end of 1938 and in 1939 it was usually believed (and, indeed, a French historian, J. Tchernoff,[6] holds the position still) that "Chamberlain thought he saw war coming in the threats that were exploding, whereas it was only a bluff." Learned works in 1939 asserted that "the German army was incapable of maintaining a European war," and thoughtful people wrote that the military power of Germany was not a substantial fact. In the light of pres-

[4] Anatole de Monzie, "Ci-devant." Paris: Flammarion, 1941, 292 p.
[5] André François-Poncet, "Souvenirs d'une ambassade à Berlin." Paris: Flammarion, 510 p.

[6] J. Tchernoff, "Les démagogies contre les démocraties. Préliminaires et causes de la deuxième grande guerre." Paris: Pichon et Durand-Auzias, 1947, 440 p.

ent knowledge it seems impossible to believe any longer that Hitler at Munich was only cashing in on an immense bluff.

In September 1938 the situation was no longer what it had been in March 1936 at the time of the German military reoccupation of the Rhineland. One could not now, as then, hope reasonably that Germany would back down. It was only a question of deciding whether the western Powers would have more or less to lose in postponing the date of the conflict.

The fact that Hitler's military chiefs were for the most part hostile to the undertaking does not in the least permit the belief that he himself was not ready, as he proved he was in 1939, to throw himself into war against anybody and everybody. Certainly the German military leaders did not conceal their fears from the Führer. General Beck, Chief of Staff at the time, told him that a policy of force would result in the formation of a coalition capable of conquering Germany for a second time. From that moment Beck began considering the organization of a conspiracy; he wanted to proceed with the arrest of Hitler, accusing him before the German people of provoking a disastrous war. This was the conspiracy that eventually failed in July 1944, and for which Beck, Field Marshal von Witzleben and many others paid with their lives. To the extent that a conspiracy might have succeeded in 1938, the voyage of Chamberlain may be said to have saved the Führer. Schacht likewise has claimed that as early as 1938 he began helping to organize the plot against Hitler, and that he had gained the participation of Generals von Brauchitsch and Halder (something Beck was never able to secure). To the extent that this may be true, Schacht's plans, too, were upset by the Munich agreement. Social Democrats like Hilferding and Breitscheid have also maintained that Munich assured the consolidation of Hitlerism. According to their statements, made in exile, the remnants of their party were then in touch with the German military, who were hostile on professional grounds to what they knew was an infinitely bold adventure.

Without casting doubt upon the sincerity of Beck or of these Socialists, nor even perhaps on that of Schacht, one may wonder if a conspiracy which waited until July 1944 to break out, and then failed, could have succeeded in 1938 or could even have been put seriously in train, Munich or no Munich. Hitler's tyranny already knew and brooked no counterweight in Germany; no will counted against his.

Besides, in contrast with the prudence of the German military, there was no lack of frenzied agitators in Germany to whom Munich seemed a wasted opportunity to annihilate Czechoslovakia totally. Ciano shows Himmler "in despair because an agreement had been concluded and the war seemed to have been averted." Noël, in January 1939, notes that the German leaders "regretted not having attacked and destroyed Czechoslovakia." The Führer himself had desired "the march on Prague" to "settle the Czechoslovak question." That question he was determined to settle, with or without a European war. He coolly accepted the risk of it. Afterwards he bitterly regretted having "compromised" to the extent of accepting "the partial solution" which Chamberlain had presented to him. At the beginning of October, the Munich agreement scarcely signed, he asked Keitel what military force would be needed to "be able to crush the rest of Czechoslovakia instantly." The ideal solution, of course, would be to "break" the Czechoslovak state by a localized war. But he was prepared for anything.

How did the military situation stand in 1938 in the event of a European war?

Georges Bonnet has no doubt that Czechoslovakia would have been conquered immediately. The events of the spring of 1940 would simply have occurred at a still more terrifying rhythm. France would have been "defeated and occupied"; Great Britain would then perhaps have succumbed. Here is perhaps the strongest argument put forward by the partisans of Munich. They point out that England in 1938 was nearly totally devoid of aviation, but that thanks to the delay afforded by Munich she was able to develop at least enough protection to avert invasion in the summer of 1940. Likewise, by 1940 she had been able to complete the construction of certain large warships.

On the other hand, it is not established, as Bonnet insists, that Germany's military superiority in 1938 would have been any more crushing than it proved to be in 1940. Germany turned the year of respite to at least as much advantage as did her adversaries; Hitler's preparation for total war was total. Unfortunately, the same was not true of France.

Bonnet stresses the lamentable state of French military forces in 1938. The German artillery was greatly superior, notably in antiaircraft defense and in speed of planes. The British, alarmed at the weakness of the French air force, often reverted to this subject in their talks with French ministers. The British themselves had an army of only 230,000 men, including reserves and rear services. In September 1938 they could have sent only 30,000 men and 120 planes to the aid of France. General Gamelin does not doubt that if the French had accepted battle England would have been led in self-defense to help them. But he writes: "She could have brought us only insignificant assistance on land at first. In the air, she was then only at the beginning of her effort."

Nevertheless, experts claim that in 1938 the German troops would have been unable to strike as violent a blow as the one that annihilated the French armies in the spring of 1940. By then Germany's equipment of motorized and armored divisions, as well as her manufacture of airplanes, had far surpassed her 1938 levels. Furthermore, in 1938 she had the resources and army of Czechoslovakia against her; in 1939 those resources were at her disposal.

Bonnet holds that it would have been necessary to wait until 1941–1942 in order for the Allies to realize their armaments programs. In spite of this apparent wisdom, the opinion may be held that in August 1939 Mussolini was, as he thought, "right" as "always," in wishing to delay the conflict for three years. He set forth various reasons: the German fleet would be stronger; Spain, once she had recovered from the exhaustion of the civil war, could actively support the Axis; Roosevelt would no longer be President of the United States (in peacetime, a second re-election seemed impossible) and matador of the democracies in the political arena. Indeed, there seems little reason to believe that the military superiority of Germany over her adversaries would have diminished. But, as François-Poncet writes, one cannot reconstruct history after the event, "for there is no sure way of knowing what would have happened if that which happened had not happened."

Poland played an important role throughout the Munich crisis. At Warsaw, even the most francophile elements deplored Czech obstinacy in the matter of Teschen and blamed Beneš; while the Czech Ambassador at Paris, M. Osusky, professed to be favorable to an arrangement. The fact is that Poland was, as stated by Gamelin, "on the side of our enemies."

The men of Munich stress the resistance which the Polish army would have opposed to any Soviet military move. The critics of Munich assert either that Poland would have been unable to hold her own against the Red Armies or that a military alliance with Germany would have been too unpopular to become a reality, and that the patriotism of the Polish nation would have forced the Government to place itself at the side of France.

In a recent work, Adam Rosé, Polish Minister for Commerce in several Beck ministries, notes the existence of certain documents indicating that his government would have been ready to "march against Germany, if the western democracies had decided to defend Czechoslovakia, arms in hand."[7] Daladier did not ignore this hope. Gamelin, it is true, raises the question: "Once committed, how would Poland be able to turn about?" And he points out that "if she attacked Czechoslovakia . . . she would be our enemy, and we would only need to let Russia take action against her."

When Gamelin saw the Russian Military Attaché on September 28, several hours before the decision for Munich was reached, he gave him a communication for Marshal Voroshilov. This stated the hope that, since France was acting to keep Poland on her side, "the Soviet armies will not take the offensive against Poland without previous notification to us." The wish, formulated with such supreme discretion by the French generalissimo, shows to what a pass French relations with Colonel Beck had come. In fact, Beck was

then suggesting in Berlin that there should be joint German, Polish and Hungarian economic pressure against Prague, and that a study should be made for a simultaneous advance of the troops of those nations into Czechoslovakia.

Russia was ready to carry out her obligations toward Czechoslovakia. She thought that in the case of German aggression France would mobilize and that England would follow. The Germans, not only those in command at Berlin but also the diplomats at Moscow, had no doubt that Russia wished for war; and they greatly rejoiced at the disappointment which Munich provoked in the Kremlin. Czech opinion was that Russia alone had acted as a faithful ally; but one section of the Agrarian Party, according to a remark which remained famous at Prague, "preferred to be invaded by Hitler than defended by Voroshilov." An eminent historian, Camille Bloch, studying the role played by Soviet Russia, reaches the conclusion that in the Czechoslovak crisis she was in spite of herself reduced to impotence.[8]

General Gamelin is of the opinion that in September 1938 "from the military point of view everything depended upon Russia." He writes: "If Russia were ready to commit herself fully, as the Russian military attaché told me . . . the situation would be saved. So much the worse for Poland! . . . The air force alone of the U.S.S.R. could compensate for our weakness in that respect." In his opinion, Soviet support would have been effective.

If the attitude of the Soviet Union in 1938 was irreproachable, there is no lack of skeptics to observe that geography deprived it of great importance. For Russian troops could not cross Poland or Rumania, and Moscow had to turn to the

[7]Adam Rosé, "La politique polonaise entre les deux guerres." Neuchâtel: la Baconnière, 1945, 202 p.

[8]*Bulletin de la Société française d'histoire moderne*, Communication de mars 1947.

French to try to obtain that right. Poland gave a frankly hostile reply. The Rumanian response, although likewise negative, was at least friendly. From it one might deduce that Rumania would close her eyes, at any rate to the violation of her skies even if not of her territory. At the time of Munich, more than 200 Soviet airplanes actually landed in Czechoslovakia, having flown over Rumania. King Carol had given Gamelin and Paul-Boncour to understand that Russian troops could pass also. However, the Rumanian Minister of Foreign Affairs, Commène, pointed out that no direct railroad communication existed between Russia and Czechoslovakia across Rumanian territory; while the roads were few and bad and in wet weather unusable.

The moral as well as the military aspect of Munich must be considered. Here it must be admitted that in delivering up a small country to a powerful neighbor the western Powers played a far from noble role.

Bonnet provokes a smile when he evokes "the inflexible will" of the British Prime Minister which "nothing could divert from the purpose to which it had been set." If the will of Chamberlain was "inflexible," how describe that of Hitler? The people towards whom Chamberlain was "inflexible" indeed were the Czechoslovaks, in the certainty, as he wrote to the Archbishop of Canterbury, that one day they "will see that what we did was to save them for a happier future."

Following Chamberlain's example, Bonnet was, according to Noël, "firmly determined not to have recourse to war . . . and gave the impression to the German leaders that their country . . . would henceforth have, in fact, a free hand in the east."

One instance will summarize the moral aspect of the conduct of the western Powers. In London the policy of appeasement followed by Chamberlain and his personal collaborator, Sir Horace Wilson, encountered the opposition of the Foreign Office and, above all, Sir Robert Vansittart. Following Camille Bloch's statements, mentioned above, Pierre Comert, who was Director of the Press Service at the Quai d'Orsay in 1938, has brought forward some information of real interest in this connection. On the afternoon of September 26 a communiqué of the British Foreign Office announced that "if in spite of all efforts of the British Prime Minister, a German attack is made in Czechoslovakia, the immediate result must be that France will be bound to come to her assistance and Great Britain and Russia will stand by France." This communiqué, which was obviously of exceptional importance, probably originated with Vansittart, who desired to give effective encouragement to French opinion in a decisive moment. It had the approval of Lord Halifax, Secretary of State for Foreign Affairs.

To thwart this action, which de Monzie rashly described as a *coup de Farnac* (a stab in the back), the associates of the French Minister for Foreign Affairs persistently spread the rumor that the communiqué was not genuine. Warned of this by Comert, the French Ambassador in London hastened to send a telegram to Paris underscoring the importance and authenticity of the communiqué. When Bonnet received this message, he forbade its distribution to the department sections in the Foreign Ministry. Simultaneously, Comert had begged his colleague in the British Foreign Office to confirm the communiqué to the representative of the Havas Agency at London. This was done; but Bonnet directed Havas to ignore the telegram and forbade its issuance to the press. Thus French opinion either remained in ignorance of the British communiqué or supposed that it was not genuine.

In his book Bonnet gives a résumé of the communiqué which is both brief and inexact. He adds that according to the British Ambassador in Paris, Sir Eric Phipps, the declaration did not emanate from the Secretary of State and "did not modify in any way the fundamental position of the British Government. ... The French Government was not expected to see in it more than a final attempt to impress Hitler and to force him to settle the Sudeten question in a peaceful manner." Bonnet adds, with more justification: " 'The authorized declaration' had scarcely been given to the press when Mr. Neville Chamberlain addressed a new appeal for conciliation over the radio." And the next day the British Government issued a note asserting that "nothing can save Czechoslovakia."

Tchernoff's summing up of Munich is severe: "fundamentally an act of cowardice."

The following article by D. C. WATT, senior lecturer in
International History at the London School of Economics,
is as helpful in bibliography as it is for its important
insights into historical interpretation. In this selection Watt
indicates also areas where additional research on the
subject of appeasement is essential. He shows that
although much has already been written, final conclusions
may still be premature.*

D. C. Watt

The Rise of a Revisionist School

In 1961, in a review of Professor Arthur
Furnia's somewhat perverse study of the
Diplomacy of Appeasement, Professor W. N.
Medlicott wrote[1] "Appeasement should
now be added to imperialism on the list of
words no scholar uses." This is a counsel of
perfection—or desperation. The word has
now passed irretrievably into historical
usage to cover the period of European politics immediately preceding the outbreak of
the second world war. It has taken to itself
the status of a myth—loaded with implica-
tion, undertones, and overtones. It is ex-
pounded in countless lectures and tuto-
rials, embodied in examination questions
and is now in the last stages of fossilisation,
that of incorporation into textbooks for secondary schools.

At the International Conference of Historians held at Rome in 1956, five years
before Professor Medlicott's lapse into ex-
asperation, the late Professor Mario Toscano of Italy remarked, that, by contrast
with the controversies which had raged
over the origins of the first world war,
there reigned general agreement among
historians of all nations as to the origins of
and responsibilities for the outbreak of the
second world war. His views were challenged only by the Soviet delegation,[2] then
as today still very much governed by the

[1] In *International Affairs,* 1961, pp. 84–85.
[2] A. D. Nikonov (ed.), *The Origin of World War II and
the Pre-war European Political Crisis of 1939* (Moscow,
1955. Reports of the Soviet delegates to the X International Congress of Historical Science in Rome.)

*D. C. Watt, "Appeasement, the Rise of a Revisionist School?" *The Political Quarterly,* April-June
1965, pp. 191–201, 207–213. Some footnotes omitted.

Stalinist version of the 1930s. (It is interesting to observe that deStalinisation, though rampant among Soviet military memoir writers and historians, has not even touched their diplomatic equivalents.) Apart from a certain amount of scattered sniping, Professor Toscano's views remained largely unchallenged for another four years. Since 1960, however, this is no longer the case. There is still a residual conviction that the origins of the second world war are uniquely different from those of the first—that the second was deliberately "unchained,"[3] while the first was largely a matter of miscalculation. But recent work in Britain and the United States has thrown a great deal of doubt upon much of the basis for the views hitherto accepted by the vast majority of historians. Since the appearance of Mr. A. J. P. Taylor's *Origins of the Second World War* in 1961, these views have been directly challenged. The controversy which followed, in the pages of *Encounter*,[4] in *The Times Literary Supplement*,[5] and even, in one of the least effective confrontations ever staged, on B.B.C. television, is fresh in everyone's memory. The orthodox view, though recently repeated by two young Oxford historians, Martin Gilbert and Richard Gott,[6] is now definitely on trial; and those reviews of this last book which sprang from academic pens rather than from the self-appointed historical pundits of the press, showed even among those who had voiced similar views in the past a distinct dissatisfaction and disenchantment with their restatement. The runaway success of Mr. William Shirer's *Rise and Fall of the Third Reich* shows that this disenchantment has yet to spread

[3] Walther Hofer, *Die Entfesselung des zweiten Weltkrieges* (1954).

[4] *Encounter*, July 1961, September 1961.

[5] *Times Literary Supplement*, April 21, May 12, May 26, June 2, June 9, 1961.

[6] *The Appeasers* (1963).

to the lay reading public in Britain and the United States. But within the academic world one can say with some confidence that the once orthodox view is no longer so easily accepted.

The Orthodox View

What one may for our purposes today call the orthodox view of the events of the 1930s can in fact be divided into two theses, each of which presupposes the accuracy of the other. One of these covers the policy followed by Hitler after his achievement of power in January 1933. According to this thesis, Hitler came to power with certain set long-term aims, and his actions betray a considered and premeditated drive to achieve German hegemony in Europe. He first outlined his aims in *Mein Kampf*, although he had begun to formulate them earlier; and *Mein Kampf* has been called a "blueprint for aggression," which, if read properly and taken seriously by western statesmen on his achievement of power, would have alerted them in time to the reality of the challenge they faced. On his achievement of power he first took steps to break Germany free of the trammels of inter-war internationalism, taking Germany out of the League of Nations and the Disarmament Conference, meanwhile speeding German rearmament in secret. Thereafter he secured his rear by the German-Polish non-aggression pact of January 1934, and after a bad miscalculation over the abortive putsch in Vienna in July 1934, turned towards the west, wooing Britain while challenging France. In March 1935 he threw off the restrictions on German armament imposed at Versailles. The following year he took advantage of the Italo-Abyssinian crisis to reoccupy the Rhineland, and began the construction of the West-Wall which would enable him to turn eastwards. The same year he secured the support of Japan in the anti-comintern pact and Italy in the Axis, taking advantage of the outbreak of civil war in Spain to prevent any reconciliation between Mussolini and the West, to tie Mussolini more firmly to him, to experiment with new military techniques and to distract the western Powers from central Europe. The same year he speeded up German rearmament still more in the Four-Year Plan. On November 5, 1937, he outlined his plans for achieving a German empire in Eastern Europe in a long address to his military commanders and to selected Ministers, his remarks being recorded in what has been called the Hossbach protocol. In 1938 he was forced to act quickly to prevent Austria voting itself out of his reach. Thereafter he turned his attention immediately towards Czechoslovakia. Baulked of a nice short war by British and French pusillanimity, he swallowed Czechoslovakia in two bites, the Sudetenland after Munich and Bohemia and Moravia quickly followed by Memel in March 1939. The next month he turned against Poland, of which he finally swallowed the western half in September 1939, after having done a deal with the Soviet Union. British and Polish obstinacy meant, however, that he had to fight for this, not only with Poland but also Britain and France. Thus the second world war sprang from his basic drive for world dominion by military aggression.

He did not survive the war, as we know. Those who were present at the vital conference of November 5, 1937, and at subsequent conferences in May and August 1939 were justly prosecuted as accessories before the fact on a charge of conspiracy to commit aggressive war—"war premeditated" in the English title of the Swiss-German historian Dr. Walther Hofer's study of the events of August 1939.[7]

The parallel thesis depicts an England upset by Hitler's initial actions but determined after the summer of 1934 on taking the nationalist steam out of the grievances believed to inspire Hitler's policy by a policy of concessions. This policy is usually taken as having had its origin in the Anglo-French meeting of February 1935 and the Simon-Eden visit to Berlin which followed. French objections to German rearmament voiced at Stresa were set at naught in June 1935, by the conclusion of the Anglo-German Naval Agreement. The reoccupation of the Rhineland was dismissed as a mere invasion of Germany's own back-yard. What was important was the offer with which Hitler accompanied it to negotiate a substitute for Locarno and to re-enter the League. A blind eye was turned towards German and Italian intervention in Spain because of dislike of the Spanish Republican Government and through fear of jeopardising the chances of a rapprochement in Central Europe. Chamberlain's accession to the Prime Ministership in May 1937 brought to the top a man determined, from a mixture of ignorance of foreign affairs, pacifism, and overweening self-confidence, on an intensification of the policy of appeasement. He took the first step with the dispatch of Lord Halifax to Germany in November 1937, following this in January 1938 by the rejection of an American offer of mediation, the removal to a position of honorific powerlessness of his principal opponent in the Foreign Office, Sir Robert Vansittart, and the forced resignation of Eden. He refused to involve England in a guarantee of the *status quo* in Central Europe and did his best to achieve a settlement of the Sudeten issue by the dispatch of a mediator, Runciman, to Czechoslovakia, and when that failed he went himself to Germany. The outcome was Munich, and the Anglo-German declaration, which he regarded as a

---

[7] Walther Hofer, *War Premeditated* (1955).

personal pledge of Hitler's word to himself and therefore to be taken differently from the various pledges Hitler had made, and broken, in the past. Only on the occupation of Prague did he realise how he had been deceived. Even then his Ministers continued, via various nondiplomatic channels, to seek an agreement with Germany. Only public outcry in the Commons forced him finally into war after Poland had been attacked.

These two theses were advanced and defended by nearly all of Britain's leading historians to be interested in the history of the recent past. The second is dependent upon the first. Criticism of the failure of British statesmen to see that Hitler was single-mindedly determined on German hegemony and German empire in Eastern Europe, falls to the ground once the latter is questioned. Contrariwise, if one attacks Chamberlain's will to peace as insincere, as the notorious Dr. Hoggan has done in Germany, one frees Hitler and Germany from the accusation of aggressive war. If one only argues that Hitler blundered into war with Britain in 1939, one is still left with the need to construct an entirely different picture of the conceptions which underlay British policy, and one is left to wonder uneasily whether past condemnations of Sir Nevile Henderson's view of Hitler's motives and consequent recommendations on policy should not now be revised. There is more to it than that. Past criticism of British policy has depicted the war of 1939 as an "evitable" war,[8] which could have been avoided if Hitler had been "stopped" earlier. Three moments are usually selected when such action would have been effective; that of an alleged Polish offer to invade Germany in April 1933[8a]; that of the reoccupation of the Rhineland when it is alleged—without

any documentary evidence—that French counter-action would have been followed by a new evacuation of the demilitarised zone;[8b] and thirdly, the month of September 1938. The objection that positive action of the sort advocated would simply have involved the outbreak of a European war earlier than 1939, was to be met by the argument that Hitler had twice climbed down when threatened—once in July 1934 over Austria, and once in the "weekend crisis" of May 1938. When these views became untenable two other arguments were substituted. The cruder of these is that the balance of power was much more tilted against Germany[9] before 1939. The subtler is that such action would have encouraged the conservative opposition to Hitler to remove him from power. (No one asked why this did not take place when he *was* made to climb down.) Neither of these arguments has carried enough weight to rout their critics, even though such critics, apart from Professor Feiling, tended to come more from former members of Chamberlain's administration[10] than from the historical profession. Academic discussion has tended to dwell, particularly in its discussion of British policy, on certain well worn stereotypes. Chamberlain is depicted as a Birmingham

---

[8] Sir Lewis Namier, *Europe in Decay* (1950).

[8a] On this see Z. Gasiorowski, "Did Pilsudski attempt to initiate a preventive war in 1934," *Journal of Modern History* (1955); Hans Roos, "Pilsudski's Präventivkriegspläne von 1933," 3, *Vierteljahresheft für Zeitgeschichte*, 1955; Boris Celovski, "Pilsudski's Präventivkrieg gegen des Nationalsozialistische Deutschland," 14, *Welt als Geschichte* (1954).

[8b] This story, current immediately after the occupation, is based on a misunderstanding of the actual German military orders which envisaged a fighting retreat to the Rhine for those few troops which had actually crossed it. See D. C. Watt, "German Plans for the Reoccupation of the Rhineland: A Note," *Journal of Contemporary History*, vol. I, No. 4.

[9] See, for example, Sir Charles Webster, "Munich Reconsidered," 37, *International Affairs*, No. 2, April 1961.

[10] K. Feiling, *The Life of Neville Chamberlain* (1946).

business man, ignorant of foreign affairs, and easily gulled by Hitler. The back-stage influence of the Treasury, particularly of Sir Horace Wilson, is adduced to explain why his views were not more enlightened by Foreign Office information. *The Times,* the Cliveden set, and in some versions anti-Communism and the desire to set Nazi Germany against the Soviet Union,[10a] are also brought into the picture.

Its Origins and Proponents

What has so far escaped comment is that these views of British and German policies, despite their impressive historical documentation, both originated long before that documentation became available, taking on nearly their present form even before the outbreak of war in 1939. Those who gave them such currency in the late 1940s and early 1950s, were nearly all themselves involved in the controversies of the 1930s and belong to one or other of the two groupings who opposed appeasement, the right-wing patriotic-chauvinist Germanophobe realists of the Churchill–Amery–Sir Lewis Namier school, or the liberal internationalist and left-wing Popular Frontists who saw the events of the 1930s as a European civil war between populist democracy and oligarchic totalitarianism. The political right as here defined included, of course, the right-wing social patriots of the Labour Party, such as Dalton, Bevin, and Josiah Wedgwood. The political left as here defined included all brands of collectivist, from liberal advocates of collective security to socialist and communist collectivists in a rather different sense. The most important element in the second category for their influence on the formulation of the views here discussed was the bulk of the corps of international press and radio

foreign correspondents, especially those from Britain, the United States and, to a lesser extent, France. If the British press at home was mostly pro-appeasement, the foreign correspondents, men such as Douglas Reed of *The Times,*[11] G. E. R. Gedye[12] and M. W. Fodor[13] of the *Manchester Guardian,* with Claud Cockburn and his newssheet *The Week,*[14] were the reverse. In academic terms, this group was supported by figures like R. W. Seton Watson,[15] and Miss Elizabeth Wiskemann,[16] A. L. Rowse,[17] and after 1936, Arnold Toynbee, and, in literary terms, by the publications of the Left Book Club and the Friends of Europe. Their views were to be popularised, publicised, and censured in the Gollancz wartime series, *Guilty Men, Tory M.P., Your M.P., Brendan and Beverley,* in which, behind various Roman pseudonyms, journalists trained in the Beaverbrook press, like Michael Foot and Frank Owen, were to put their talents and training to very un-Expressly ends.

Their views were adopted lock, stock, and barrel by the historians who wrote after 1945, drawing on the flood of captured Nazi documents and justificatory memoirs. Now the patriotic anti-German school greatly outnumbered the ideologically anti-Nazi. The lead was taken by Sir Lewis Namier,[18] Sir Llewellyn Woodward,[19] and Sir John Wheeler-Bennet.[20]

---

[11] *Vanity Fair* (1938); *Disgrace Abounding* (1939).

[12] *Fallen Bastions* (1939).

[13] *South of Hitler* (1938).

[14] *In Time of Trouble* (1956); *I Claud* (1968); Patricia Cockburn, *The Years of the Week,* (1969).

[15] *Britain and the Dictators* (1938); *Munich and the Dictators* (1939); *From Munich to Danzig* (1939).

[16] *Czechs and Germans* (1938); *Undeclared War* (1939).

[17] *The End of an Epoch* (1947).

[18] *Diplomatic Prelude* (1948); *Europe in Decay* (1950); *In the Nazi Era* (1952).

[19] An editor of the 3rd Series of *Documents on British Foreign Policy.*

[20] *Munich, Prologue to Tragedy* (1948); *The Nemesis of Power* (1953).

[10a] C. Martin Gilbert, *Britain and Germany between the wars* (1964); Claud Cockburn, *I Claud,* (1968).

They were seconded by Mr. Alan Bullock,[21] Sir Charles Webster,[22] Professor Mansergh,[23] Professor Laffan for Chatham House,[24] Professor Trevor-Roper,[25] Mr. Hinsley,[26] Mr. Joll,[25] Professor T. F. D. Williams,[27] and Professor Mowat.[28] The anti-Nazi left were represented by Miss Wiskemann[29] and Mr. Taylor,[30] Mr. A. L. Rowse,[31] and Professor Geoffrey Barraclough;[30] their views were taken up in the younger generation by Mr. Gilbert and Mr. Gott, and at some stages in his career by Professor W. V. Wallace of the New University of Ulster.[32] On the far left, Mr. Andrew Rothstein,[33] made himself the mouthpiece of the Soviet viewpoint.[34] So far as I can trace the only critical voices raised then were those of Professor Max Beloff in 1950–1951 in the *Fortnightly*[35] and

in *Foreign Affairs*,[36] who called this school "revisionist," Mr. Michael Vyvyan of Cambridge in various reviews in the now defunct *Cambridge Journal*, and the author of this paper.[37]

Sir Winston Churchill's Statements

These massive statements of a view everyone was by then predisposed to accept were buttressed by the magnificent, though highly tendentious, sweep of Churchill's first volume of War Memoirs. They thus had not only the authority and scholarship of Britain's leading historians but bore also the magisterial stamp of the man who was at once historian and politician, a successful Thucydides, the Cassandra of the 1930s, and the Carnot of the 1940s. These statements appeared almost entirely in the years from 1946–1954. Their evidential basis was, beside the Nuremberg documents, the two series of British and German diplomatic documents, one of which began at varying dates in 1936–1937, and the other in 1938. In the six years which followed Sir Lewis Namier's return to the politics of the eighteenth century, research and publication on the history of the 1930s in Britain seemed to have ceased. Practically nothing of any consequence was published by any British historian of any standing. The field was left to the historians of the Continent—to the younger generation of historians writing in German and clustered at various removes around the Munich *Institut für Zeitgeschichte*, men like Max Braubach, Hans Roos, Ulrich Eichstadt, Werner Conze, Boris Celovsky, Paul Kluke, to name only a few; to the small group of French historians and political scientists led by J. B. Duroselle and Henri Michel, publishing in the government-sub-

---

[21] *Hitler, a Study in Tyranny* (1952).

[22] Webster, *op. cit.*

[23] *Survey of Commonwealth Affairs, Problems of External Policy, 1931–1939* (1962).

[24] *Survey of International Affairs, 1938*, Vol. II; *The Crisis over Czechoslovakia* (1951).

[25] In numerous reviews and in the introductions to various works of Hitleriana.

[26] *Hitler's Strategy* (1951).

[27] "Negotiations leading to the Anglo-Polish Alliance" (1956) 10 *Irish Historical Studies*.

[28] *Britain between the Wars* (1955).

[29] *The Rome-Berlin Axis* (1949).

[30] Mainly in reviews.

[31] *All Souls and Appeasement* (1961).

[32] "New documents on the History of Munich," *International Affairs*, October 1959; "Roosevelt and British Appeasement, 1938," *Bulletin of the British Association of American Studies*, New Series, No. 5, December 1962; "The Foreign Policy of President Benes in the Approach to Munich," xxxix *Slavonic and East European Review*, December 1960. "The Making of the May Crisis of 1938," XII *Slavonic and East European Review*, No. 97, June 1963; see also D. C. Watt, "The May Crisis of 1938: A Rejoinder to Mr. Wallace" and W. V. Wallace, "A Reply to Mr. Watt," XLIV, *Slavonic and East European Review*, No. 103, July 1966.

[33] *The Munich Conspiracy* (1958).

[34] Now repeated in M. Maiski's third volume, and apparently accepted by its reviewer in *The Times Literary Supplement*.

[35] "Professor Namier and the Prelude to War," *Fortnightly*, April 1950.

[36] "Historians in a Revolutionary Age," 29 *Foreign Affairs*, No. 2, January 1951.

[37] D. C. Watt, "Sir Lewis Namier and Contemporary European History," *Cambridge Journal*, 1954.

sidised *Revue d'Histoire de la deuxième Guerre Mondiale;* and to the indefatigable Professor Toscano in Italy. American historians were tending to turn their attention towards domestic German history, and to Weimarian foreign policy, especially to the much worked over field of German-Soviet relations. Non-academic British historians, such as Mr. Gerald Reitlinger, were also turning towards the study of the machinery of the Nazi state. The interested younger British historians were at this period the merest handful, limited in number by the almost total absence of any teaching posts in the field outside the University of Oxford, their research confined to occasional articles for which it was then, as now, difficult to find a publisher in Britain.

The New Criticism

Since 1960, this position has begun to undergo profound modifications. Both aspects of the accepted thesis have come under critical attack. It is perhaps premature to hail the appearance of a new revisionist school as such. The critics disagree profoundly among themselves, and have yet to produce a really defensible alternative version. But the hitherto accepted view no longer reigns unquestioned, and it is difficult to see how it can be sustained much longer.

The first attack on the orthodox version of Hitler's policy came not from an historian but an economist, the American scholar, Burton Klein's study of *Germany's Economic Preparedness for War.* There is much that was unsatisfactory about this book, particularly in its failure to examine the process by which Germany did prepare for war, the policy debates, and the policy decisions. But it disproved entirely the idea of a massive German rearmament effort, and of a planned mobilisation of Germany's resources for war. Goering's famous

slogan, "Guns before Butter," took on the aspect of a pious hope rather than a totalitarian injunction. The attack on the military aspects of the orthodox version came much later, from the young British historian E. M. Robertson in his study of *Hitler's Pre-war Policy and Military Planning.* Again this was a book to which exception could be, and was, taken, particularly in its account of the interaction of military and diplomatic considerations in the earlier years of Hitler's rule. But it was by no means the mixture as before. Both works suffered inevitably from their reliance on that part of the official version, the major part, which their own researches had not led them to question. The orthodox view is so well constructed that it can only be replaced by a totally new synthesis based on a wide review of all the evidence. The attempt to do this could come only from much more senior men than these. It came in fact already before the publication of Mr. Robertson's work, with Mr. A. J. P. Taylor's *Origins of the Second World War* (1961). It was followed by a work much slighter in size but the product of the same prolonged study of the diplomatic and economic evidence, Professor W. N. Medlicott's Historical Association pamphlet, *The Coming of War in 1939* (1963). He enlarged on these views subsequently in his *Contemporary Britain* (1967) and *British Foreign Policy Since 1919* (1968). Of the two, Professor Medlicott had most to say in amendment of the orthodox version of British and French policy; while the novelty of Mr. Taylor's work lay in the attack he launched on the orthodox version of Hitler's policy. Both, however, agreed in focusing on the question of the degree to which the image of German policy held by the statesmen of the Western democracies accorded with reality. Although they disagreed considerably as to the nature of that image and that reality, neither accepted the versions of either which had hitherto obtained. Of the two it would not be unjust to say that Professor Medlicott's inherent conservatism led him to accept and expound the principles of British policy, while Mr. Taylor's radical instincts drove him to seek to understand it as a preliminary to criticising it. Professor Medlicott is inclined to think of it as inevitable, Mr. Taylor as the product of accident and misconception.

What Hitler Said—And Did

The main point of attack on the orthodox version of Hitler's foreign policy turns on the failure of Hitler's actions to accord with his statements. In *Mein Kampf* and many of his later speeches, Hitler formulated the idea of a German colonial empire to be carved out of European Russia. He hardly mentions Czechoslovakia or Poland in the book which is supposed to be "a blueprint of aggression." He criticises both Imperial and Weimarian Germany for not seeing that Germany's natural allies were Britain and Italy, her natural enemy France. In the Hossbach speech he announced his intention of taking over Czechoslovakia and Austria before 1942 only in the event of civil war in France or an Anglo-Franco-Italian war in the Mediterranean. In the draft orders for an attack on Czechoslovakia he commented that the attack should fall *"Blitzartig schnell"* without forewarning or elaborate propaganda preparation. Yet instead of allying himself with Britain against Russia, he found himself at war with Britain with benevolent Russian support. And he finally involved himself in a two-front war, with the Soviet Union, gratuitously involving the United States into the bargain in December 1941, a policy very close to that which in *Mein Kampf* he had so bitterly criticised Imperial Germany from following.

Germany's Unpreparedness for War

This attack can be broken down into two parts: Hitler's failure to prepare Germany thoroughly for the war in which he found himself involved in 1939; and the failure of his military actions to accord with the strategy he had laid down. The first, examined in Dr. Klein's study of German rearmament, on which Mr. Taylor has drawn heavily, led Dr. Klein to hypothesise that Hitler never intended to become involved in a major and long-drawn-out European war, since he thought he could obtain his objective by a series of short localised diplomatic-military conflicts. The second led Mr. Robertson to the implicit conclusion that from 1937 onwards Hitler's long-term objectives were changed and submerged in a series of improvisations which eventually in August 1939 escaped his control and involved him in the European war he had not expected for another two to three years.

The first edition of Mr. Taylor's work antedated that of Dr. Robertson by two years, and went a great deal further than Dr. Robertson did in assaulting the basis of the orthodox view. Mr. Taylor, in fact, chose to assault the validity of the Hossbach record as such, representing this mainly on the authority of Admiral Raeder's testimony at Nuremberg, repeated in his memoirs, as a manoeuvre in domestic affairs, aimed to isolate Dr. Schacht from the other conservatives, and to prod General Fritsch, Chief of the Army Staff, into demanding a larger arms programme. He went on to say that none of the participants gave it another thought until the document was produced at Nuremberg as evidence of the conspiracy to make war. There is a good deal more in support of his thesis than his critics have hitherto admitted, even though his deductions from the speech remain a little difficult to accept. . . .

The Need for More Evidence

What seems clear is that the evidence available must be re-examined with an open mind, and a detailed attention to German economic and military planning on the lines developed by Dr. Klein and Dr. Robertson. But if there is need for more research into the German side of the orthodox thesis there is far more need to investigate its British and French aspects. The orthodox thesis is infinitely weaker here than on its German side. Partly this is due to the lacunae in the evidence. The publication of the third series of British documents begins at least eleven months too late to cover adequately the development of Chamberlain's policy towards Germany, and its coverage of British policy towards Italy does not really begin until after Munich. The vital field of Anglo-American relations is given the scantiest coverage, and the intervention of Far Eastern considerations and anxieties masked by their treatment in two separate volumes which appeared much later than those dealing with Germany. We are better served by the memoirs, although Lord Vansittart died when his memoirs[38] had only attained the events of the year 1936; Sir Horace Wilson has kept his silence as have Lord Runciman, Sir Thomas Inskip, and Sir Kingsley Wood. Lord Halifax has not preserved his silence but he might just as well have done,[39] while Sir John Simon deliberately limited his memoirs to the scope of what was already known.[40] On the French side we are still less well served, although it is to be hoped that the series of documents now launched[41] will appear faster than their British counterparts. One may also express the hope that whoever is appointed

to succeed the late Professor Toscano will turn his talents to filling in the earlier volumes of the eighth series of Italian documents, and that the rich treasures of the Japanese,[42] Portuguese,[43] and Hungarian documentary publications[44] will not be left to the bare handful of students linguistically equipped to exploit them. The nature of these publications has tended to confirm the tendency of British historians to think in compartments, so that—apart from Professor Medlicott and Mr. Taylor—there is no major discussion of British foreign policy in the 1930s which faces the problems, as the Chamberlain administration had to, as part of a concurrent though rarely concerted attack on Britain's position in Europe, in the Mediterranean and Middle East, and in East Asia and the Pacific.

British Resources and Motives

It is in the failure to co-ordinate the evidence on British policy towards the three aggressor nations, that the orthodox view of British policy is most open to attack, and in the degree to which its assertions about the motives of British policy have never been tested by historical research. Those who have defended the policy of the Chamberlain government, particularly Professor Feiling and the late Lord Templewood,[45] have emphasised the disparity between Britain's will-power and her military and economic strength on the one hand and the threat of three aggressor states simultaneously on the rampage on the other. These arguments have the ring

---

[38]*The Mist Procession* (1958). [39]*Fulness of Days* (1957).
[40]Viscount Simon, *Retrospect* (1954).
[41]*Documents Diplomatiques Françaises, 1932–1939*, 2⁰ Serie (1936–1939), Tome I.

[42]The Japanese Foreign Office archives are all available on microfilm in the United States. Photostat copies of the archives of the Japanese Embassy in Rome are in the Foreign Office Library in London.
[43]*Dez Anos de politica externa, 1936–1947*, Part I, Vols. I and II. *O rearmamento do Exercito no quadro politica de Aliança Luso-Britanica, 1936–1939.*
[44]Historical Institute of the Academy of Sciences, Budapest, Vols. I and IV.
[45]Viscount Templewood, *Nine Troubled Years* (1954).

of truth to men who live in the last stages of the contraction of British world power as we do today. Yet in the writings of the orthodox school animadversions to Britain's economic and financial weakness are briefly dismissed with a reference on only half-understood Keynesian lines to the unemployed resources of manpower available; those to Britain's military weakness are met with the bare comparison of military strengths referred to earlier, and those to the divisions of British opinion and the lack of will-power to the tasks of political leadership in a democracy. There may be a genuine answer to these objections. Lord Ismay, who as Hankey's successor as Secretary of the Committee of Imperial Defence can speak with inside knowledge, has supported the idea that war was feasible in 1938.[46] The three Chiefs of Staff flatly contradicted him. We still await a really telling examination of these arguments. And as for the state of British opinion it is a somewhat shaming comment on the adequacies of British scholarship that there is still no adequate study of the attitude of British opinion to the dictators and to appeasement. For twenty-five years now there has been assertion and counter-assertion without any resort to the normal investigative methods of historical scholarship. Professor Epstein of Wisconsin has recently shown us that this could be done for the Suez crisis of 1956. All we have apart from a handful of articles are five books— Professor Bassett's monumental study of British opinion and the Manchurian crisis;[47] Dr. Watkins' study of British opinion and the Spanish Civil War, suggestive rather than conclusive;[48] a general study of the attitude of the Labour Party to collec-

tive security and Europe over the whole interwar period;[49] Dr. Brigitte Granzow's outstanding study of the attitude of the quality press to the rise of Nazism, published early in 1964;[50] and a frequently tendentious collection of writings published recently by Mr. Martin Gilbert.[51] One should also note the article on "Middle Opinion in the 1930s" by Dr. Arthur Marwick, in a recent number of the *English Historical Review*.[52] We lack any study of the Peace Ballot; of the League of Nations Union which organised it; of the Quaker influence in the Liberal and Labour Parties; of Popular Frontism; of the Friends of Europe; even of the Conservative anti-appeasers. The field is virgin. Equally in the field of armaments and strategy we still await Professor Gibbs' volume of official history—we have no study of British armament apart from that in the official history.

Nor is that the sum total of the weakness of the orthodox school. The circumstances of its origin of which I spoke earlier led it to pay too much attention to the personalities and character defects of the principal actors in the story, Sir Lewis Namier and Sir Charles Webster combining to assure us that their real fault was that they were intellectual mediocrities, timid men, "lacking guts" in Sir Charles Webster's own phrase. No attention has been paid to the breakdown of both Parliamentary and Cabinet Government in the 1930s—the power of the senior civil servants whose length in office in two significant cases, those of Lord Hankey and Sir Warren Fisher, antedated the entry into Cabinet

---

[46] *The Memoirs of Lord Ismay* (1960), p. 92.

[47] R. L. Bassett, *Democracy and Foreign Policy* (1951), and *Collective Security Problems, 1920–1939* (Geneva, 1950).

[48] *Britain Divided* (1963).

[49] W. R. Tucker, *The Attitude of the British Labour Party towards European Affairs* (Geneva, 1950).

[50] *A Mirror of Nazism* (1964).

[51] *Britain and Germany between the Wars* (1964).

[52] Arthur Marwick, "Middle opinion in the Thirties," lxxix, *English Historical Review*, No. 311, April 1964. See also his *Clifford Allen, Open Conspirator* (1964).

Office of any Minister holding office in the 1930s until Mr. Churchill's return to office in 1939. No one has examined the curious conception of the Chief Advisers, Sir Frederick Leith Ross, Sir Horace Wilson, Lord Vansittart himself—posts for which there is no warrant in British procedure and which derogate from the status of the Cabinet. No one should be Chief Diplomatic, Chief Economic, Chief Industrial adviser to the Government except the appropriate Cabinet Ministers. More than that there was a significant loss of faith in democratic processes, a conviction that dictatorship and collectivism must be more efficient, a conviction shared by such politically diverse persons as Stanley Baldwin and Beatrice Webb. The parliamentary opposition of the Labour Party was weak, and strikes the casual observer as divided, unrealistic, and irresponsible on matters of foreign policy throughout much of the 1930s. It has still to be adequately investigated. There is no adequate study as yet, either of the principal advocates of appeasement of Germany, nor of their principal opponents either on the Conservative or the Labour benches. The by-election results of the early thirties have been weighed but not examined, the Peace Ballot of 1935 evoked by both sides without attention being paid to anything except its actual text. No one has attempted to evaluate the element which has done more to divert the debate on appeasement into false trails, the contradiction between the language in which the policy of appeasement was defended by ministerial spokesmen and their supporters in Parliament and in the country and the language and considerations they held and weighed among themselves.

The evidence recently published in Mr. John Blum's extracts from the diaries of the American Secretary to the Treasury,[53]

the Avon memoirs, and the memoirs of the Canadian High Commissioner in London in the 1930s, Viscount Massey,[54] make it virtually impossible to maintain the picture of a pro-German Chamberlain, gulled by Hitler and ignorant of foreign affairs. His policy appears more and more to have been contingent on estimates of Hitler's aims and reliability which he was very far from taking for granted, a policy aimed at the avoidance of war but not at the avoidance of a confrontation, a policy explicable in the fashionable jargon of today as one of "containment," "co-existence," "negotiation from strength." He was not opposed to the use of power but only concerned, as must be any democratic head of government, with doing his best to avoid the hazard of a general war.

Such an investigation may well show an immediate recognition by all in British Government circles of the danger from Hitler's Germany, together with an overplaying of their hand by the alarmists, and a fruitless attempt to buy off Japan in 1934 and Italy in 1935. The investigation may well confirm also the fears of Britain's Conservative leaders of the unrealism of current British opinion, and the existence of a degree of military weakness in 1935–36 which paralysed Britain's military planners, giving them years of sick apprehension as their daily companion. It may reveal three services so unable to agree on a common strategy that one was imposed on all three of them by the Treasury, obsessed not with Britain's economic strength at home, but with the state of her gold and dollar balances, her foreign investments, and her earning power abroad. It may reveal a Commonwealth divided on everything else but its dislike of Versailles and its wish for non-involvement in European affairs. It may reveal a policy of appease-

[53] John W. Blum, *From the Morgenthau Diaries* (Boston, 1959), Vol. I, pp. 458–467.

[54] Vincent Massey, *What's Past is Prologue* (1964).

ment of Germany embarked on with no particularly high hopes of its success but with the aim of avoiding trouble until Britain was rearmed and in a position to tame Hitler by showing him he could not get away with unilateral action any more. On the diplomatic side it may see the Anglo-German Naval Agreement as a misconception, the disaster of the Hoare-Laval proposals as a product of a divided Cabinet and Foreign Service; the failure to react to the reoccupation of the Rhineland as a direct consequence of British military weakness; the so-called farce of the Non-Intervention Committee as one of Lord Avon's most brilliant diplomatic devices for the avoidance of a European war; his resignation as the product of a personal quarrel rather than one on policy. It may see Munich as a shameful but inevitable consequence of an attempt to have isolationism but call it collective security. It may find the events of March 1939 following not a change in the aim of British policy only an intensification of effort along the lines already laid down, an attempt to stop Hitler analogous with the action of the driver in the American game of "Chicken" who dismantles the steering wheel and throws it out of the window.

There is one further point to which Mr. Taylor has called attention, the role and personality of Lord Halifax, his degree of commitment to and public identification with Mr. Chamberlain's foreign policy and the relations between himself and the Prime Minister. We have little or no information on the course of Cabinet discussions between the resignations of Lord Avon and Mr. Duff Cooper in 1938 and the return to office of Mr. Churchill in 1939. The fact that in 1940 the Labour Party leadership were prepared to accept Lord Halifax as Premier of a coalition government suggests that much of the parliamentary controversy over Mr. Chamber-

lain's policy was aroused by his personality and not by the policy itself, since only an expert in Byzantine theology could distinguish between the policies advocated by the two men.

The Need for Revision

This essay has argued that there is a need for a serious revision of the orthodox view. So far such historical work as there has been has only examined the course of British policy towards Germany. Little or no work has been done on Anglo-Italian or Anglo-Japanese relations. Much about British policy between October 1938 and March 1939 remains obscure. There is room for much controversy over the negotiations with the Soviet Union in the summer of 1939; on which Professor Medlicott has daringly suggested that British policy was conditioned by a failure to share the confidence of their political opponents in Soviet military strength, while Mr. Taylor has depicted a reluctant Government driven by parliamentary pressure into a policy ideological antipathy prevented them from taking seriously. There is room, too, for a general study of Anglo-Soviet relations in the 1930s if only to prove or disprove the continued Soviet thesis that Britain's main aim was to turn Nazi aggression eastwards. Even on Poland in August 1939, much remains unclear. Was the British Government preparing for another Munich as Mr. Taylor and others maintain, or had it, *pace* Professor Medlicott, largely abandoned the role of mediator for that of guarantor of Poland at least getting fair play?

This essay has sought to show that there are grounds for the profoundest dissatisfaction with the present state of British historiography of the 1930s, and that there are the beginnings of a school, or rather of two schools, of revisionists. Their main difficulty has been to know what to preserve and what to revise of the orthodox version, what must be discarded and what can stand up to criticism in the light of the new evidence. Mr. Taylor is vulnerable to criticism on many points, particularly in his handling of the military and financial considerations underlying British policy. Professor Medlicott is equally open to charges of neglecting the public debate on appeasement and accepting perhaps too readily the estimate of its inflexibility advanced by its Conservative apologists. Both are, however, concerned to understand the processes by which British and German policy were formulated, the different kinds of advice and pressure fed into the policy machine, and the manner in which the principal actors saw their roles. This is a welcome change from the gruff dismissal of all concerned as pusillanimous, stupid, ill-informed, and weak-charactered which used to pass as historical criticism amidst the plaudits of the press a decade and a half ago.

Suggestions for Additional Reading

The student of twentieth-century history has the problem of too much rather than too little material. All bibliographies that cover a subject as many-faceted as appeasement are therefore of necessity selective. Most of the principal powers—Great Britain, the United States, France, and Italy—have published or are publishing their major documents. Archives of the Third Reich were published by the three Western allies. The Soviet Union has published almost nothing of its own material.

Two of the best general histories of the period are Maurice Baumont, *La Faillite de la Paix, 1918–1939*, vols. I and II (Paris, 1960–1961) and Pierre Renouvin, *Histoire des Rélations Internationales, VII* and *VII* (Paris, 1957, 1958). For general histories in English, see C. E. Black and E. C. Helmreich, *Twentieth Century Europe* (New York, 1966) and H. Stuart Hughes, *Contemporary Europe* (Englewood Cliffs, N.J., 1961). For invaluable surveys, see: *The Annual Register* and the Royal Institute's *Survey of International Affairs* edited by Arnold Toynbee. One might also use profitably the official *History of the 'Times,'* (London, 1952).

There is an enormous literature on the policy of Great Britain. Some good introductions are the masterfully comprehensive *Britain Between the Wars, 1918–1940* (Chicago, 1955) by Charles Loch Mowat and the more recent *Contemporary England* (New York, 1967) by W. N. Medlicott. Among the studies on foreign policy one can recommend R. W. Seton-Watson, *Britain and the Dictators* (London, 1938); E. H. Carr, *Britain: A Study of Foreign Policy from the Treaty of Versailles to the Outbreak of War* (London, 1939); and the excellent studies of Lewis Namier: *Diplomatic Prelude 1938–1939* (London, 1947) and *Europe in Decay, 1936–1940* (London, 1950). Arnold Wolfer, *Britain and France Between the Wars,* (New Haven, Conn., 1940) is also good. For material by Winston Churchill, see his *The Second World War, The Gathering Storm* (London, 1948) and the following volumes of his collected speeches:

Step by Step, 1936–1939 (London, 1939), *While England Slept* (London, 1938), and *Arms and the Covenant* (London, 1938).

On the failure of collective security there is the general history of the League of Nations written by former Deputy Secretary-General F. P. Walters, *The History of the League of Nations,* (London, 1952). Specialized studies concerning the Ethiopian crisis are: André Mandelstam, *Le Conflit Italo-Ethiopien devant la Société des Nations* (Paris, 1937); P. Vaucher et P. H. Sirieux, *L'Opinion Britannique, La Société des Nations et la Guerre Italo-Ethiopienne* (Paris, 1936); Royal Institute of International Affairs, *International Sanctions* (London, 1938); Raffaele Guariglia, *Ricordi 1922–1946* (Naples, 1950); Jean Schwoeble, *L'Angleterre et la Securité Collective;* and George Baer, *The Coming of the Italian-Ethiopian War* (Cambridge, Mass., 1967).

On the Spanish crisis, see the general histories by Pierre Broué and E. Timimé, *La Révolution et la Guerre d'Espagne* (Paris, 1961) and Hugh Thomas, *The Spanish Civil War* (London, 1961). Monographs include Patricia van der Esch, *Prelude to War* (The Hague, 1951); D. A. Puzzo, *Spain and the Great Powers, 1936–1941* (London, 1962); W. Laird Kleine-Ahlbrandt, *The Policy of Simmering: A Study of British Policy during the Spanish Civil War, 1936–1939* (The Hague, 1962); and K. W. Watkins, *Britain Divided: The Effect of the War on British Public Opinion* (London, 1963).

Most works on appeasement center on the Munich crisis. A good overall study is John Wheeler-Bennett, *Munich—Prologue to Tragedy* (London, 1948). A provocative revisionist account is Laurence Thompson, *The Greatest Treason* (New York, 1968). Boris Celovsky, *Das Münchener Abkommen von 1938* (Stuttgart, 1958) is equally good. Andrew Rothstein has presented the Soviet thesis in *The Munich Conspiracy* (London, 1958). Other works include: Keith Eubank, *Munich* (Norman, Okla., 1963); Arthur H. Furnia's polemical *The Diplomacy of Appease-*

ment (Washington, 1960); W. M. Jordan, *Great Britain, France and the German Problem, 1918–1939* (London, 1943); W. H. Chamberlain, *Appeasement, Road to War* (New York, 1962); Donald N. Lammers, *Explaining Munich: The Search for Motive in British Policy* (Stanford, Calif., 1966); W. R. Rock, *Appeasement on Trial: British Foreign Policy and Its Critics* (Hamden, Conn., 1966); Henri Noguères, *Munich* (London, 1965); and Helmut Ronneforth, *Die Sudetenkrise in der Internationalen Politik* (Munich, 1961). See also a book of readings well-edited by Francis L. Lowenheim, *Peace or Appeasement? Hitler, Chamberlain and the Munich Crisis* (Boston, 1965) with its good bibliography of articles.

On the background, character, and psychology of appeasement, John Connell (John Henry Robertson), *The Office: A Study in British Foreign Policy and Its Makers, 1919–1951* (London, 1958); A. L. Rowse, *Appeasement: All Souls and Appeasement* (London, 1961); Martin Gilbert and Richard Gott, *The Appeasers* (London, 1963); Martin Gilbert, *The Roots of Appeasement* (London, 1966); Margaret George, *The Warped Vision: British Foreign Policy, 1933–1939* (Pittsburg, 1965); Pertinax (André Geraud), *The Gravediggers* (New York, 1943); and the bitter Cato, *Guilty Men* (London, 1940). Also, there is J. F. Kennedy, *Why England Slept* (New York, 1940); the superb social history by R. Graves and A. Hodge, *The Long Weekend* (London, 1941); and Reginald Pound, *The Lost Generation of 1914* (New York, 1965).

More than those of any other nation, the British have produced a wealth of memoirs; Chamberlain seems to be an exception. From men who held government posts, see: The Earl of Avon (Anthony Eden), *Facing the Dictators* (New York, 1962); Alfred Duff Cooper, *Old Men Forget* (London, 1954); Robert Vansittart, *The Mist Procession* (London, 1958); Rubreagh Minney, ed., *The Personal Papers of Hore-Belisha* (London, 1960), all of which tend to be critical of the government's policy. Defenders of appeasement are: Viscount Templewood (Sir Samuel Hoare), *Nine Troubled Years* (London, 1954); Viscount Simon, *Retrospect* (London, 1952); Lord Halifax, *Fullness of Days* (London, 1957); Viscount Maugham, *The Truth about the Munich Crisis* (London, 1944); and *At the End of the Day* (London, 1954). Works by persons outside the center of power, but still important figures, are Leopold Amery, *My Political Life, III* (London, 1955); Viscount Rothermere, *Warnings and Predictions* (London, 1939); Thomas

Jones, *A Diary with Letters, 1931–1950* (London, 1954); and Harold Nicolson, *Diaries and Letters, 1935–1939;* (New York, 1966). Accounts by the Opposition include Clement Attlee, *As It Happened* (London, 1954); Hugh Dalton, *Call Back Yesterday* (London, 1933); Herbert Morrison, *Autobiography* (London, 1960); Fenner Brockway, *Inside the Left* (London, 1942); Lord Citrine, *Men and Work* (London, 1964); the Duchess of Atholl, *Working Partnership* (London, 1958); and the reminiscenses of M. A. Hamilton, *Remembering My Good Friends* (London, 1944).

Among the military and diplomatic memoirs are: Lord Ismay, *Memoirs* (London, 1960); Lord Strang, *Home and Abroad* (London, 1956); Sir John Slessor, *The Central Blue* (New York, 1957); Lord Chatfield, *It Might Happen Again* (London, 1947); Major-General Sir Edward Spears, *Assignment to Catastrophe* (New York, 1954); Arthur C. Major-General Temperley, *The Whispering Gallery of Europe* (London, 1938); and R. McLeod and D. Kelley, eds., *The Ironside Diaries, 1937–1940* (London, 1961). Also, Sir Nevile Henderson, *Failure of a Mission* (London, 1940) and *Water Under the Bridges* (London, 1945); Sir Walford Selby, *Diplomatic Twilight* (London, 1943); Sir Robert Hodgson, *Spain Resurgent* (London, 1953); Sir Ivone Kirkpatrick, *The Inner Circle* (London, 1959); and Maurice Peterson, *Both Sides of the Curtain* (London, 1950). The postwar British Broadcasting System's interviews with prominent pre-World War II personalities are published in *The Listener* (London, 1948).

Biographies generally give sympathetic treatment to their subjects. This is especially true of two on Chamberlain: Keith Feiling, *The Life of Neville Chamberlain* (London, 1947), the "official" biography which quotes from the Prime Minister's correspondence; and the more recent *Neville Chamberlain* (London, 1961) by Iain Macleod. Studies of other appeasers are: Earl of Birkenhead, *Halifax* (London, 1965); Stuart Hodgson, *Lord Halifax* (London, 1941); Alan Campbell-Johnson, *Viscount Halifax: A Biography* (New York, 1941); G. M. Young, *Stanley Baldwin* (London, 1952); John Bowle, *Viscount Samuel* (London, 1957); Sir James Butler, *Lord Lothian* (New York, 1960); Evelyn Wrench, *Geoffrey Dawson and Our Times* (London, 1955). On Anthony Eden there are: Lewis Broad, *Anthony Eden: The Chronicle of a Career* (New York, 1955); Alan Campbell-Johnson, *Sir Anthony Eden* (London, 1955); and the critical account by Randolph Churchill, *The Rise and Fall of Sir Anthony Eden* (London, 1959). Biographies of British as well as Continental diplomats can be found in the valuable work of Gordon Craig and Felix Gilbert, eds., *The Diplomats* (Princeton, N.J., 1953).

Not as numerous as the studies concerning Britain, those on France leave much to be done, particularly in the field of foreign affairs. For the better general treatments, see the relevant volumes in Jacques Chastenet, *Histoire de la Troisième République* (Paris, 1964), also Denis Brogan, *France Under the Republic,* (London, 1940). More specialized studies are: W. M. Jordan, *Great Britain, France and the German Problem, 1918–1939* (London, 1943); H. Beuve-Méry, *Vers la Plus Grande Allemagne* (Paris, 1939); P. Lazareff, *Deadline: The Behind the Scenes Story of the Last Decade in France* (New York, 1940); Daniel Halévy, *1938, Une Année d'Histoire* (Paris, 1938); E. R. Cameron, *Prologue to Appeasement* (London, 1942); André Tardieu, *L'Année de Munich* (Paris, 1939); and Alexander Werth's astute observations, *France and Munich: Before and After the Surrender* (London, 1939), *The Destiny of France* (London, 1937), and *The Twilight of France, 1934–1940* (London, 1942). Concerning rearmament there are Robert Jacomet, *L'Armement de la France, 1938–1939* (Paris, 1945) and J. Minart, *Le Drame du Désarmement Français* (Paris, 1959). Although the French government has only begun the publication of its documents, there is some material in Pierre Mazé and Roger Genebrier, *Les Grandes Journées du Proces de Riom* (Paris, 1945) and *Les Evénéments Survenue en France de 1933–1945* (Paris, 1947-1951).

Although less prolific than the British in writing memoirs, the French have nonetheless produced some important works. Among those by former ministers: Joseph Paul-Boncour, *Recollections of the Third Republic* (Paris, 1946); Pierre-Étienne Flandin, *Politique Française, 1919–1940* (Paris, 1947); Pierre Cot, *The Triumph of Treason* (New York, 1944); Georges Bonnet, *De Washington au Quai D'Orsay* (Geneva, 1946) and *Fin d'une Europe* (Paris, 1948); Paul Reynaud, *In the Thick of the Fight* (New York, 1955); Edouard Herriot, *Episodes* (Paris, 1950); and Léon Blum, *L'Histoire Jugera* (Paris, 1945).

Diplomatic memoirs include the indispensable books of André François-Poncet, *French Ambassador in Berlin, 1931–1938* (New York, 1949) and *Au Palais Farnese* (Paris, 1961); and Robert Coulondre, *De Staline à Hitler; Souvenirs de Deux Ambassades* (Paris, 1950), Also of interest is

Jules F, Blondel, *Au Fil de la Carrière* (Paris, 1960). Among military memoirs are: Général Maurice Gamelin, *Servir: Le Prologue du Drame, 1930–1939* (Paris, 1946); Charles De Gaulle, *War Memoirs* (New York, 1955); and General Chauvineau, *Une Invasion est-elle encore possible?* (Paris, 1939).

The United States was not directly involved with the policy of appeasement, but mention of a few of the better American books is essential to supplement the European picture. For example, James MacGregor Burns, *Roosevelt: the Lion and the Fox* (New York, 1956); Thomas A. Bailey, *A Diplomatic History of the American People* (New York, 1940); W. H. Shepardson, *The United States in World Affairs* (New York, 1939); Charles A. Beard, *American Foreign Policy in the Making, 1932–1940* (New Haven, Conn., 1946); William Leuchtenburg, *Franklin D. Roosevelt and the New Deal, 1932–1940* (New York, 1963); and William Langer and Everett Gleason, *The Challenge to Isolation, 1937–40* (New York, 1952).

Of the policy of the dictatorships, the amount of material on Germany is thunderous, and since only a brief sampling can be set forth the student would do well to see the very excellent bibliography provided in Robert Waite *Hitler and Nazi Germany,* which is published in the same European Problem Studies series as the present volume. In addition to German Foreign Policy documents there are the publications that resulted from the Nuremburg War Crimes Trials: *Nazi Conspiracy and Aggression* (Washington, 1946) and *The Trial of the Major War Criminals before the International Military Tribunal* (Washington, 1947–1949). Of further utility are *The Speeches of Adolf Hitler,* I and II (New York, 1942), edited by Norman H. Baynes. Among the better general histories on the Nazi period are William L. Shirer's comprehensive *The Rise and Fall of the Third Reich* (New York, 1961) and Hannah Vogt, *The Burden of Guilt: A Short History of Germany, 1914–1945* (New York, 1964). Important essays on the period are to be found in a book edited by Maurice Baumont et al., *The Third Reich* (New York, 1955). The best biography of Hitler is by Alan Bullock, *Hitler: A Study in Tyranny* (New York, 1962), which contains a lucid description of the foreign policy of the late 1930s. Of further help in analyzing the character of the dictator is James McRandle, *The Track of the Wolf* (Evanston, Ill. 1965).

More specialized treatment can be found in Paul Seabury, *The Wilhelmstrasse: A Study of German Diplomats under the Nazi Regime* (Berkeley,

Calif., 1954); Radomir Luza, *The Transfer of the Sudeten Germans: A Study of Czech-German Relations, 1933–1962* (n.p., 1964); the two monographs by Elizabeth Wiskemann, *Czechs and Germans* (London, 1938) and *The Rome-Berlin Axis* (London, 1949); Gordon Brook-Sheperd, *The Anschluss* (New York, 1963); Gustav Hilger and Alfred Meyer, *The Incompatible Allies, German-Soviet Relations, 1918–1939* (New York, 1944); Bernd-Jurgen Windt, *München 1938: England Zwischen Hitler und Preussen* (Frankfurt, 1965); and several books on the role of the military on policy: Telford Taylor, *Sword and Swastika* (New York, 1950); John Wheeler-Bennett, *The Nemesis of Power: The German Army in Politics, 1918–1945;* and E. M. Robertson, *Hitler's Pre-war Policy and Military Plans, 1933–1939* (London, 1959).

Memoirs by former Nazis are few; those that do exist usually are either whitewashes or reveal little. See those by Ernst von Weizsaker, Joachim von Ribbentrop, Paul Schmidt, Fritz von Papen, and Herbert von Dirksen.

On Italy, a good survey is Denis Mack Smith, *Italy* (Ann Arbor, Mich., 1959) and the excellent biography of *Mussolini* by Sir Ivone Kirkpatrick (London, 1964). Italian foreign policy is discussed in many of the books already mentioned in this bibliography, but some additional works may be added: The apologetic *Italian Foreign Policy under Mussolini* (New York, 1956) by Luigi Villari; Ernest Work, *Ethiopia, a Pawn in European Diplomacy* (New Concord, Ohio, 1935); Ludwig Schaefer, ed., *The Ethiopian Crisis, Touchstone of Appeasement?* (Boston, 1961); F. William Deakin, *The Brutal Friendship* (New York, 1962); Mario Toscano, *Le Origini del Patto d'Acciaio* (Florence, 1956); M. Macartney and P. Cremona, *Italy's Foreign and Colonial Policy, 1914–1937* (New York, 1938); E. Monroe, *The Mediterranean in Politics* (London, 1938); G. T. Garrett, *Mussolini's Roman Empire* (London, 1938) and *Gibraltar and the Mediterranean* (London, 1939); and Gordon East, *Mediterranean Problems* (London, 1940). Among the memoirs, the diaries of the Fascist foreign minister are most valuable; Galeazzo Ciano, *Hidden Diary 1937–1938* (New York, 1953) and *The Ciano Diaries, 1939–1943* (New York, 1945); and *Ciano's Diplomatic Papers* (London, 1948), edited by Malcolm Muggeridge. Also of value are Elizabeth Cerruti, *Je Les Ai Bien Connus* (Paris, 1950); Pietro Nenni, *La Guerre d'Espagne* (Paris, 1959) and *Vingt Ans de Fascisme, de Rome à Vichy* (Paris, 1960); M. Magistrati, *L'Italia a Berlino, 1937–1939* (Milan, 1956); Pompeo Aloisi, *Journal, 1932–1936* (Paris, 1957); Emilio De Bono, *La Conquista dell'Impero, la Preparazione et le Prima Operazione* (Rome, 1937).

Material on the remaining topics is scant and of mixed value. On the Soviet Union, with the exception of the Treaty series edited by Leonard Shapiro and the collection of documents published by the Royal Institute of International Affairs under the editorship of Jane Degras, some three volumes, there is virtually nothing. Soviet statesmen do not write memoirs, or if they do, the memoirs are not published: an exception is Ivan Maisky, *Who Helped Hitler?* (London, 1964). A few of the better books on Soviet foreign policy might be mentioned. Max Beloff, *The Foreign Policy of the Soviet Union, 1929–1941* (London, 1946, 1949) and F. Borkenau et al., *World Communism: A History of the Communist International* (London, 1939). Of further interest, see: David T. Cattell, *Soviet Diplomacy and the Spanish Civil War* (Berkeley, Calif., 1957); V. M. Molotov, *Soviet Foreign Relations* (London, 1940); M. M. Laserson, ed., *The Development of Soviet Foreign Policy in Europe, 1917–1942; A Selection of Documents* (London, 1943); J. T. Murphy, *Russia on the March: A Study of Soviet Foreign Policy* (New York, 1941); and the work of George F. Kennan.

Although works by Czechs are not numerous, some should be mentioned. Among those available in English, see especially: E. Beneš, *Eduard Beneš in His Own Words* (London, 1945) and *From Munich to New War and Victory* (New York, 1954); Herbert Ripka, *Munich, Before and After* (London, 1939); and Koloman Gajan and Robert Kvacek, *Germany and Czechoslovakia, 1918–1939* (Prague, 1965). Articles on various aspects of the East European crisis have appeared from time to time in the *Journal of Central European Affairs*, the *Slavonic and East European Review*, and *Foreign Affairs*.

Finally, a mixed bag of personal accounts: *Austrian Requiem* (New York, 1946) by the Austrian chancellor Kurt von Schuschnigg; Joseph Beck, *Final Report 1926–39* (London, 1957); J. Czenbek, *Journal 1933–1939* (Paris, 1952); Gr. Gafenco, *Derniers Jours d'Europe* (Paris, 1946); and B. Dahlerus, *The Last Attempt* (London, 1948); also, R Serrano Suner, *Entre les Pyrénées et Gibraltar* (Geneva, 1947); Julio Alvarez del Vayo, *Freedom's Battle* (New York, 1940) and *The Last Optimist* (New York, 1950); Louis Fisher, *Men and Politics* (New York, 1946); and G. Ward Price, *I Know These Dictators* (London, 1937).